AIR OFFICER COMMANDING

John T. LaSaine, Jr.

AIR OFFICER COMMANDING

HUGH DOWDING Architect of the Battle of Britain

ForeEdge

ForeEdge
An imprint of University Press of New England
www.upne.com

Manufactured in the United States of America
Designed by Mindy Basinger Hill
Typeset in Garamond Premier Pro

Library of Congress Cataloging-in-Publication Data

Names: LaSaine, John T., Jr., author.

Title: Air Officer Commanding : Hugh Dowding, Architect of the Battle of Britain / John T. LaSaine, Jr.

Description: Lebanon, NH : ForeEdge, 2018. | Includes bibliographical references and index.

Identifiers: LCCN 2017047929 (print) | LCCN 2018006821 (ebook) | ISBN 9781611689389 (epub, mobi, & pdf) | ISBN 9781611689372 (cloth)

Subjects: LCSH: Dowding, Hugh Caswall Tremenheere Dowding, Baron, 1882–1970. | Marshals—Great Britain—Biography. | World War, 1939–1945—Biography. | World War, 1939–1945—Aerial operations, British. | Great Britain. Royal Air Force—Biography. | Britain, Battle of, Great Britain, 1940.

Classification: LCC DA89.6.D6 (ebook) | LCC DA89.6.D6 L37 2018 (print) | DDC 358.40092 [B]— dc23

LC record available at https://lccn.loc.gov/2017047929.

5 4 3 2 1

For Karl

CONTENTS

PREFACE

The literature relating to the life and career of Hugh Dowding is robust. Two informative, authorized biographies were published in the subject's lifetime; monographs on specific aspects of his career subsequently added depth of research; innumerable books and articles on the history of the Royal Air Force and its leadership, the Battle of Britain, and many other cognate topics, place Dowding in various historical contexts. Documentary evidence is now available in print, and is becoming available electronically. An authoritative, scholarly biography synthesizing the primary source materials was published less than a decade ago. Although gaps remain (some of which, notably regarding Dowding's personal life, may never be filled in), the excellence of the Dowding scholarship obliges an author to explain the need for, or at least the purpose of, a new offering. My goal is to bring together insights obtained from the specialist, academic literature in ways that foster an appreciation, beyond the academy, of Dowding's complexity as a historical figure.

It was as an insatiable consumer of narrative histories of the Second World War that I first encountered the figure of Hugh Dowding. The Dowding of those narratives helped to define my conception of a "great commander"; indeed, he was the only airman in my personal pantheon of immortals. As I read more deeply, I learned that Dowding had been a controversial as well as an emblematic figure, both during and after his service career, at least among some airpower professionals and academic historians. As I read more broadly, I began to view Dowding from a variety of additional angles: as an exemplar of the first generation of world airpower leaders; as a leading innovator in the global, military-technological revolution across the era of the world wars; as a key participant in British civil-military relations during the crucial decade of the 1930s; as an icon in the historical mythology of "Their Finest Hour"; and finally, as a prophet of twentieth-century spiritualism.

This study is intended to present a balanced consideration of successive phases of Dowding's career: his early professional development in the years before the First World War; his professional growth and achievement during the 1914–18 war; his ascent to leadership in the RAF between 1919 and 1930; his years of extraordinary accomplishment as planner, organizer, and decision maker during the fateful 1930s; his performance as a high commander in the first year of the Second World War; and finally, his intellectual and spiritual odyssey during the last three decades of his life.

Hugh Dowding's career as soldier and airman illustrates the impact of a dynamic environment on military leadership: how crosscurrents of economic, political, social, technological, and cultural change shape and reshape the armed services as instruments of national policy. It also illuminates specific examples of military leaders grappling with rapid technological and organizational change, wartime expansion and postwar contraction. Finally, the Dowding story reflects the challenges met and overcome by the last cohort of military leaders to create an entirely new armed service; organizing, training, equipping, and operating it in a new dimension, a new domain of warfare.

In the seventy-five years since the 1940 Battle of Britain air campaign, research scholars have added much depth and complexity to our knowledge of Dowding and his accomplishments, as well as his personal and professional shortcomings. Yet as the Second World War has slowly begun to fade from living memory, the popular narrative of the war has simplified, and the Dowding narrative has simplified correspondingly, even as his place in the mythology of the war has seemed ever more secure: "the Victor of the Battle of Britain," "the Leader of the Few," or even, "the One." The following version of the Dowding narrative is offered as an attempt to help sustain contact between academic perspectives and popular perceptions.

ACKNOWLEDGMENTS AND DISCLAIMER

This book is a work of independent scholarship. The author is solely responsible for all statements of fact and expressions of opinion, which do not represent official statements by Air University, the United States Air Force, or any other agency of the US government. As author, however, I gratefully acknowledge successive commandants and deans of education at the USAF Air Command and Staff College who encouraged the pursuit of individual research and publication agendas by members of the ACSC faculty.

I am grateful to Stephen P. Hull, editor at the University Press of New England, for his open-minded consideration of this project, as well as the trust with which he allowed me time to complete it.

My thanks are due to the staff of the Air University Library, officially known as the Muir S. Fairchild Research Information Center, for the knowledge, energy, and courtesy with which they support the research of students and faculty alike. The entire AUL/MSFRIC staff is unfailingly helpful, but I must particularly acknowledge the many personal kindnesses of Donna Billingsley, Barbara Jiles, Mark Moore, Michael Rojas, and Josephine Turner.

As with the Air University Library staff, my professional and personal debts to faculty and staff members of the Air Command and Staff College are so numerous that it is painful to realize I cannot name them all. I can only hope that they will grant me the further kindness of accepting this acknowledgment.

Comments on the work in progress by Michael Kraig, Richard Muller, Thomas Ira Savoie, Thomas Whigham, and the late Karl Westhauser saved me from many errors and infelicities. My office mates during 2016–18, Richard Milburn and Tenaya Humphrey, not only patiently permitted me to think aloud, but also generously responded with much good advice as well as kindly encouragement. Jason Trew generously provided me with some of the fruits of his studies in history and myth; Wesley Hutto gave timely and much-needed assistance in my struggles with information technology. While all these colleagues and friends greatly contributed to any merit the work may possess, I must reemphasize that responsibility for its shortcomings is mine alone.

In a special category is Paul J. Springer, without whose intervention at a critical point, this book might never have been published.

John T. LaSaine, Jr. | September 2017

1
THE MAKING OF A SOLDIER
1882–1914

Hugh Caswall Tremenheere Dowding was born at Moffat, Dumfriesshire, Scotland, in 1882. The eldest of four children, son of a schoolmaster transplanted from Wiltshire, England, he descended from long lines of teachers and clergymen, variegated but apparently not greatly enriched by the occasional banker, and distinguished by an admiral (a paternal uncle) as well as a major general (his maternal grandfather). Young Hugh's formative environment was the gilded late afternoon of Victorian Britain. Five years old at the time of the Queen-Empress's Golden Jubilee, he experienced the hoopla surrounding Her Majesty's Diamond Jubilee in 1897 as a teenaged schoolboy. The intervening decade, Hugh's adolescent years, marked in many ways "the high tide and the turn" of British imperial power. The confident, indeed reflexive, midcentury identification of British preeminence with the natural order of things was already, at least in the eyes of the discerning, beginning to fray around the edges.[1]

As a youth, Hugh absorbed strict principles of conduct and duty: "truth, charity, diligence, and reverence" were exemplified as well as preached by his parents and grandparents, whose lives and outlook embodied the dominant social and cultural attitudes of the early and mid-Victorian generations. Theirs was a universe of hierarchies: the Christian religion was, inherently, the one true religion; European civilization was as self-evidently the greatest of world civilizations as the British Empire was the greatest of the European empires. At home, the classes and the masses alike were bound to elaborately intertwined economic, political, and social hierarchies culminating in the monarch; authority was tempered by responsibility, and deference upward was legitimated by obligation downward. For the midcentury generations, this Victorian worldview never lost its massive intellectual and emotional integrity. As Hugh's diplomatic contemporary Robert Vansittart put it, the education of their generation "lay entirely within the closing period of Victorian optimism." For them, the strain of reconciling inherited ideals with changing realities—economic, scientific and technological, military and political, social, intellectual and cultural—was to grow decade by decade throughout their lives.[2]

Imitating the custom of the British aristocracy, at thirteen Hugh left home and his father's preparatory school for one of Britain's historic and elite public schools—in his case, St. Mary College of Winchester. Like many such youths, Hugh was miserable at the time, but like many public-school graduates, later looked back on the experience with some satisfaction. Averse to the classical studies that dominated both public school and university curricula, he enrolled in Winchester's "army class." Escaping the conjugation of Greek verbs, Hugh thereby also ruled out following his father's footsteps to Oxford and, almost inadvertently, set himself on a path to a military career. Such "modern" military majors at schools like Winchester reflected the beginnings of a grudging, slow, and painful adaptation by Britain's ruling elite to the changing technological and organizational environment of public service, including the accelerating professionalization of military officership.[3]

In 1899, Hugh moved on from Winchester to the Royal Military Academy, Woolwich. Known affectionately as "The Shop," RMA Woolwich provided general and technical education to officer cadets seeking commissions in the artillery, engineer, and signals branches of the British army, or service in the army of Britain's Indian Empire. Sometimes regarded as more intellectually demanding but less socially prestigious than the better-known Royal Military College at Sandhurst, whose graduates were mostly commissioned in the infantry and the cavalry, Woolwich cadets in the middle decades of the nineteenth century had included such celebrities as Queen Victoria's son Prince Arthur (later Field Marshal the Duke of Connaught) and the Prince Imperial (son of Napoleon III, Emperor of the French), as well as such future British army luminaries as Charles Gordon (later a major-general, world-renowned as "Chinese" Gordon) and Herbert (later Field Marshal Lord) Kitchener.[4]

As Dowding and his Woolwich classmates were beginning their studies, the long-smoldering conflict between the British and the Boer Republics of South Africa exploded into full-scale war. The South African campaigns of 1899–1902—unexpectedly protracted, costly, and largely inglorious for the British—provoked upheaval in Britain's military policy and ferment within the British army itself. A minor instance of upheaval was the curtailment of the RMA course from two years to one, to help meet the sudden increase in demand for trained officers. Consequently, in 1900 Dowding was commissioned a subaltern (second lieutenant) of garrison artillery in the Royal Regiment of Artillery (the "Gunners") and assigned to a battery at the fortress of Gibraltar. Cadet Dowding had aspired to join the Royal Engineers (the "Sappers") but, distracted from study by his first taste of adult independence, had slipped too far down in academic standing to qualify. This early disappointment seems to have impressed upon Dowding the importance of hard work in his new profession.[5]

Sharing an experience common among newly commissioned military officers through the ages, at Gibraltar Dowding initially found himself inadequately prepared for his actual duties. As with most young officers, experience soon provided useful knowledge and skills the service had failed to impart through formal, professional education and training. Dowding developed a habit of volunteering to serve as range officer, carrying out the "arrangements" for firing practice and field exercises, as well as observing hits and estimating the distances of misses. These were unusually responsible duties for a subaltern; senior officers considered it desirable for their young lieutenants to gain experience by acting as assistant range officers under a captain. It was also an unpopular duty among Dowding's fellow subalterns, involving not only extra work, but also the high probability that blame for any mishaps would fall on the junior officer involved. Young Dowding, however, apparently relished the extra work and responsibility.[6]

For all his budding professionalism, Dowding did not enjoy his first station of assignment. With some six thousand men crammed onto "the Rock," garrison life seemed to him unduly to resemble prison life. The town of Gibraltar he found a disagreeable combination of suburban banality and subtropical squalor, too English to be pleasantly exotic, and too alien for comfort. Dowding quickly seized upon the means of physical and mental escape adopted by generations of British officers and gentlemen: the horse. During the next few years, he purchased, rented, or borrowed a succession of mounts, devoting considerable time and money to fox hunting, polo, and even racing as an amateur jockey. Dowding's liking for equestrian pursuits, which developed over the years into a broader taste for outdoor sports, may have led at least one of his regimental superiors to misjudge him as a stereotypical, gentleman-amateur type of officer.[7]

A year after Dowding's arrival at Gibraltar, his battery relocated, first to Ceylon for less than a year, then to Hong Kong. Dowding welcomed the wider social opportunities, and relished still more the increased scope for his rapidly diversifying sporting activities that these two important colonies offered a young officer. There was time for a two-month, sightseeing vacation in Japan with a friend from the Royal Engineers. Although he enjoyed such fringe benefits of peacetime soldiering in the colonies, and despite promotion from subaltern to (first) lieutenant, Royal Artillery, Dowding began to feel an absence of interesting professional challenges. He decided to seek a transfer from the garrison artillery to the mountain artillery, in hopes of more active service. Overcoming the objections of his colonel, ominously known as "Bloody Bill," in 1904 Dowding secured transfer to a mountain artillery battery stationed at Rawalpindi in the Punjab (since 1947 a province of Pakistan).[8]

Dowding's transfer to the mountain artillery marked the beginning of some six years of service close to the fabled northwest frontier of Britain's Indian Empire. He almost had his thirst for active operations satisfied at once, as his new battery had been alerted for an expedition to Tibet, but to his disappointment he was—understandably—displaced in favor of an officer with mountain-artillery experience. Continuing his practice of volunteering to serve as a range officer, this time in the demanding environment of the Himalayan foothills, Dowding soon secured experience of his own. At the head of range parties made up of "native" gunners and drivers, he found himself matching wits with local tribesmen of fearsome reputation, if not active hostility. Mastering the gunner's art under harsh conditions, Dowding displayed a degree of professional prowess that would have won him considerable distinction in wartime. On one occasion, he improvised a tactical crossing of the Ganges River at flood stage; on another, he moved troops and equipment safely along a mountain path in perilous, landslide conditions.[9]

The highlight of this stage of Dowding's career was a field exercise during which, with a two-gun section, he surprised and theoretically annihilated a detachment from the legendary Gurkha Rifle Regiment commanded by another young subaltern with a promising future, Cyril Newall. The subsequent rivalry between the two men in the Royal Air Force, as well as their respective roles in the Battle of Britain, renders the story of their first meeting an irresistible anecdote, but the memory of that day's maneuvers against the Gurkhas remained with Dowding for a different reason. Dowding's artillery section had been detailed to support an infantry unit newly arrived in theater, a battalion from another of the British army's elite rifle regiments. The British riflemen were unfamiliar with the mountainous terrain, and it showed in their performance against the Gurkhas. Dowding never forgot the way professional soldiers from a highly regarded unit quickly fell apart under pressure in an operational environment for which their training and experience had not prepared them.

Eager for professional advancement, Dowding naturally sought to take the next logical step in career progression for a British army officer of his generation: attendance at the Staff College, Camberley. Unfortunately, his commanding officer, a gunner of the old school who apparently disapproved either of Dowding, or of the staff college, or perhaps both, flatly refused to provide the required commander's recommendation. Not to be denied,

Dowding arranged a transfer to a native battery commanded by an acquaintance who was willing to oblige. Native batteries were led by a mixture of British and Indian officers; the enlisted ranks of No. 32 Battery, which Dowding joined at Dehra Dun in the far north of India, were filled by Sikhs and Punjabi Muslims—in segregated sections. Dowding in later life recalled his years with No. 32 Battery as some of his happiest, and the post at Dehra Dun as "the best station at which he ever served."[10]

Dowding's satisfactions at Dehra Dun were personal as well as professional. He sought out sporting activities of all kinds, especially first-rate polo. He continued to indulge his taste for sightseeing, traveling with a fellow officer through the historic Malakand Pass to Kashmir, where they explored the great limestone caves known as the Kashmiri Smuts. Tolerant of solitude, impatient with the tedium of social life in garrison (what a much later era would term "mandatory fun"), Dowding was by no means entirely unsociable. Sometimes, indeed, his social life was memorable. On one occasion he wrote home describing an encounter with a lady who acted as a medium for communication with the spirit world. Although the description was facetious, almost derisory, the letter constitutes early evidence of Dowding being influenced by the fascination with spiritualism that was to become a peculiar characteristic of his generation of Britons.[11]

In 1910, Dowding obtained extended leave to return to Britain and "cram" for the staff college's competitive entrance examination. Study certainly seemed to be called for, since at the time only seven places at Camberley were allotted to artillerymen. In the event, Lieutenant Dowding scored highly enough among applicants from the Gunners to become one of the youngest and most junior officers accepted for the 1912–13 class. Successfully arguing that the government should spare itself the expense of another round trip to India, Dowding secured an extension of his leave until his class began, in January 1912.[12] Dowding used some of this extraordinary, if not unique, seventeen and a half months of continuous leave to reconnect with his family. His youngest sibling, Kenneth, at this time introduced his older brother to the newly popular sport of skiing, which became an important part of both their lives.[13]

It was at Camberley that Dowding acquired the service nickname "Stuffy," which may have attached to him less for a reserved manner, or for his thoroughly conventional appearance, than for the unusual earnestness of his approach to professional military education. Perhaps because of his background as the son of an Oxford-educated schoolmaster, Dowding chafed at the intellectual mediocrity of the staff college. Certainly there was an element of sheer anti-intellectualism in the Camberley atmosphere; Dowding's nickname may well have been an echo among his peers of Field Marshal Lord Wolseley's notorious concern lest "bookworms" infest the officer corps. Late in life, Dowding claimed to have been an independent thinker from an early age—less inclined to defer to institutional conventional wisdom than his peers, less willing to accept argument from authority as a substitute for logic. For example, despite his fondness for mounted sports, he did not share the almost religious faith in the military primacy of the cavalry arm that pervaded Camberley.[14]

Far more important than the nostalgic attachment to horse soldiering, or the simple prejudice of the unread and unthinking, however, was the influence of those army leaders who, in the decade prior to 1914, devoted considerable brainpower to inciting a conservative reaction (what one historian has characterized as a "counter-reformation") against the technological transformation of the army. This movement was symptomatic of wider, cultural strains afflicting early twentieth-century Edwardian Britain. The happy certainties of the nineteenth-century Victorian era were steadily eroding. British elites, finding their economic wealth, their political power, their social influence, and their cultural values under threat, reacted defensively. In the case of the British military elite, this involved championing a human-centered, as opposed to a technological, understanding of the nature of war. By vigorously reasserting the primacy of traditional, martial virtues, military leaders might defy the implications of new technologies and avert fundamental changes in the profession of arms.[15]

In the early years of the twentieth century, therefore, military leaders in Britain, as elsewhere, adamantly insisted on the continuing validity of historic principles of war. They argued that the central problem of leadership and command in modern war was how to apply historically validated principles under novel conditions created by new technologies. The solution that military elites increasingly favored was moral leadership. Past wars, they asserted, had been won by moral force rather than physical force. Ascendancy over the enemy in battle was primarily the product of superior moral force (morale). In turn, superior morale, or moral ascendancy, was a product of superior leadership. Leadership being, inherently, the special province of the traditional elites, this principle thus had the highly desirable effect of renewing their claims to social usefulness, re-legitimating their positions of prestige and power. Hence the endlessly repeated avowal that, "moral force in modern war predominates over physical force as greatly as formerly."[16]

The more perceptive military professionals of the day, including Dowding's near-contemporary, Captain J. F. C. Fuller, were beginning to conceptualize the core problem of modern warfare as one of integrating "the human element" of war with the technological element. Yet even technologically oriented, younger officers like Fuller sometimes succumbed to the dangerous illusion that future wars would be won or lost on the psychological battlefield. Dowding's early aspiration to join the engineers suggests that he was interested in grappling with the technological challenges of modern warfare. Beyond that, however, his overall outlook suggests an empirically oriented mind, determined to make independent professional judgments based on the facts, as best he could determine them. Dowding's instinct was to resist the easy acceptance of prevailing attitudes, and challenge the conventional wisdom. This cast of mind would soon be manifested in a fateful decision to establish for himself the facts concerning one of the new technologies emerging during these years: aviation technology.[17]

Many senior military officers, including most influentially the chief of the Imperial General Staff (CIGS) General Sir William Nicholson, tended to dismiss the military significance of the first powered flights by heavier-than-air craft. Although the work of the Wright brothers and, after 1903, that of their rivals, evoked interest among political leaders such as the secretary of state for war, R. B. Haldane, not until late 1908 did the British government establish a subcommittee of the Committee of Imperial Defence (CID) on aerial navigation, to study the national-security implications. It was only in the spring of 1912, more than eight years after the first flight at Kitty Hawk, that a royal warrant established a flying corps, consisting of a military wing, a naval wing, and the Central Flying School (CFS). This prematurely "joint" organization was short-lived; the Admiralty quickly converted the naval wing into the Royal Naval Air Service (RNAS) under its own control and with its own flying school, leaving the military wing of the Royal Flying Corps (RFC) and the CFS to the Army Council.[18]

Dowding, newly promoted to captain in the Royal Artillery, after thirteen years of service, was more alert to the professional implications of these developments than most junior military officers, and far more open-minded than most senior officers. For example, Dowding's course instructor for a staff-college war game was either unaware of, or unimpressed by, the role that scouting aircraft recently had begun to play in the annual army maneuvers. Ridiculing Dowding for dispatching the imaginary aircraft included in his imaginary command to locate the equally imaginary enemy, he insisted that it was impracticable to use flying machines for operational reconnaissance. This experience convinced Dowding that properly trained staff officers should be equipped with some genuine knowledge of the military capabilities and limitations of aircraft. The RFC having just instituted a course to train military pilots open to officers under age forty with a civil pilot's certificate from the Royal Aero Club, he decided to qualify.[19]

Dowding arranged for private flying lessons with the firm of Vickers, which scheduled instruction in the early mornings, well before the staff college's gentlemanly starting-hour of 10:00 a.m. Exhibiting the same persuasiveness that had secured him a year and a half of leave, he somehow induced Vickers to defer payment of its fees until he was reimbursed by the army—something that would happen only if he first obtained his "ticket" from the Royal Aero Club, and then successfully completed the CFS course. Dowding's experience at Vickers' Brooklands Flying School typified the charming informality of the early days of aviation: his teachers included an aircraft mechanic who doubled as an instructor pilot, and he took the Royal Aero Club pilot's test after a total of less than two hours in the air—including passenger time. Dowding received pilot's certificate No. 711 on the same day in December 1913 that he officially "passed staff college."[20]

During the three-month CFS course at Upavon in his father's native county of Wiltshire, Dowding first encountered officers who would become the pioneering stock of the future Royal Air Force, and who were to have as great an impact on his life and career as on the development of British air power. Preeminent among these was a temporary lieutenant colonel known as "Boom" for the sound of his voice, which matched his outsized personality. Hugh Montague Trenchard was already leaving his mark on the infant Royal Flying Corps as second-in-command of the CFS. Dowding would later claim that Boom made little impression on him during his brief time at the CFS, but in the grim war years of 1914–18, Dowding would clash more than once with the opinionated and autocratic Trenchard. As one student of both men's careers put it, the relationship between Trenchard and Dowding proved to be a case of an irresistible force meeting an immovable object.[21]

In contrast to Dowding's unruffled early life, Trenchard had to overcome considerable emotional trauma and numerous setbacks just to begin his army career. When he was thirteen, his beloved younger sister died; when he was sixteen, his father's bankruptcy cost the Trenchard family its money, its home, and its social position. Not necessarily less intelligent than Dowding, the young Trenchard floundered at prep school; he failed to win admission to the Royal Naval College, Dartmouth; he twice failed the Woolwich entrance exam, and needed three tries to secure a regular infantry commission via militia service. Like Dowding, Trenchard learned regimental soldiering as a junior officer in India. Posted to South Africa after the outbreak of the Boer War, he was gravely wounded, but with amazing physical and psychological resiliency, recovered sufficiently to return to the fight. A decade later, Trenchard decided to escape routine, peacetime military duties by learning to fly. He never attended staff college.[22]

The struggles of Trenchard's youth, as well as the suffering he endured from his combat wounds and agonizing rehabilitation, seem to have strengthened his character, rather than breaking his spirit or souring his outlook on life. Entering middle age and approaching broader responsibilities, Trenchard was marked by boundless self-confidence and truly extraordinary perseverance. Nine years older than Dowding, Trenchard had won his RFC wings a year earlier, barely squeaking under the RFC age limit, and despite handling the stick of an aircraft with the same lack of finesse that characterized most of his earthbound activities. As few senior officers were prepared to risk not only their necks but also their careers in aviation, Trenchard was the most experienced army officer at the CFS. Almost from the moment he began the course, the school commandant delegated numerous administrative responsibilities to him. His subsequent assignment as adjutant and second-in-command of the CFS officially recognized a role he had already assumed.[23]

For his part, Dowding up to 1914 had enjoyed something of a charmed life. Dutiful he was, but without sacrificing the travel, athletic recreation, and select social contacts he valued. Dowding was also precociously skillful at levering out of the army bureaucracy the assignments he wanted. While he had displayed a commendable work ethic in mastering the artilleryman's trade and regimental soldiering, an unusual seriousness in preparing himself for staff duties, and an instinctive grasp of the military potential of aviation, Dowding had missed the experience of war in South Africa, in many ways a pivotal episode in the professional development of Dowding's generation of British army leaders. In a service buffeted by the turbulence of modernization and professionalization, there was a noticeable distinction between those rising leaders who had proved themselves on the battlefields of South Africa, and their contemporaries who had not.[24]

After he qualified for his wings in the spring of 1914, Dowding surprisingly asked that his name be placed on the RFC reserve list. The thirty-two-year-old army captain, veteran of rugged outposts in the Empire, and now pioneer military aviator, decided to revert to the Royal Artillery because his father thought flying was too dangerous. Unlike so many early military aviators motivated by thrill seeking or the romance of flight, Dowding had trained as a pilot not in search of adventure, but as a measure of professional self-development. Out of devotion to his family, Dowding deferred to his father's wishes, and began catching up on a dozen years of technical developments in coastal defense. Faced with the pleasantly daunting challenge of taking over a top-performing unit, a battery of six-inch guns on the Isle of Wight, Dowding reasserted his professional mettle as a gunner when his outfit scored a perfect twenty "hits" in competition.[25]

During the summer of 1914, Dowding, as was his habit, combined hard work with recreational athletics, although choosing golf, cricket, and tennis over fox hunting and polo. He also bought a used car, taking up the (in those days not necessarily less strenuous) pursuit of "motoring." Like many knowledgeable Europeans, however, Dowding expected trouble, writing his mother in late May: "I think we shall have an easy June, & then a mobilization in July." At the end of June, the murder of the archduke Franz Ferdinand, heir to the Hapsburg throne, set off a sequence of political reactions and military mobilizations during July; by the end of the month, all the Continental great powers were at war. At the beginning of August, Great Britain followed suit, dispatching to the aid of Belgium and France an expeditionary force including the bulk of the British regular army, less the army of the British Indian Empire.[26]

2

THE MAKING OF AN AIR OFFICER

1914–1918

Recalled to the RFC immediately upon mobilization, Dowding took charge of a transit camp for squadrons deploying with the British Expeditionary Force (BEF). After this initial and, most assumed, singular deployment, Dowding was detailed to salvage disabled aircraft left behind, and then sent to No. 7 Squadron at the already historic Farnborough Station, which was commanded at that time by "Boom" Trenchard. Under the then prevailing illusion that the war would be sharp but short, practically every officer remaining in Britain—including Trenchard—was pulling every possible string to get into action at once. Although it was obvious that trained and experienced officers were needed at home to sustain the BEF and maintain its lines of communication, and although Dowding no doubt realized that as one of the RFC's few staff-college graduates, he was for the moment at least, more valuable as an administrator than a frontline aviator, nevertheless he relentlessly "worried" Trenchard for a posting to the BEF.[1]

So relentless was Dowding that Trenchard finally did get him reassigned, to No. 6 Squadron, which was slated for deployment to France. Apparently intending to rebuke the very junior captain's importunity, however, Trenchard arranged for Dowding to go as a flight observer rather than as a pilot. Unfazed, Dowding leapt at the chance to go to the front, in whatever capacity. As he probably surmised when he accepted the transfer, under operational conditions it would not take him long to get his hands on the stick once more. During the six weeks as a back-seater in reconnaissance operations that followed, Dowding frequently experienced the supposed exhilaration of being shot at without effect, as well as the perhaps less agreeable experience of surviving two "smashes," fortunately without injury. Not surprisingly, attrition among the squadron's aircrew soon prompted Dowding's return to pilot status.[2]

Not limited to the duties of a frontline pilot for long, Dowding took on a variety of other assignments in quick succession while continuing to fly. The BEF's air component was rapidly expanding, and soon required a new echelon of command above the squadron level. Consequently the RFC began creating "wing" organizations, and during the fall Dowding was detailed to one of them as acting adjutant. In December, the insatiable demand for trained staff officers to manage the expansion led to his being pulled up to RFC headquarters at Saint-Omer for duty as a general staff officer grade 3. Just a few weeks later, however, he returned to squadron duty as a flight commander in No. 9 Squadron, which was stationed nearby. No. 9 Squadron was developing the use of "wireless telegraphy" for artillery spotting, and Dowding's background made him an ideal candidate for this assignment.[3]

Serving with No. 9 Squadron at Saint-Omer, Dowding experienced some of the squalor, if not the full horror, that befell millions of combat soldiers during the next four years. Rain and mud, combined with a lack of adequate shelter for either men or equipment, made for miserable working and living conditions. The equipment itself was so primitive that, at this early stage of the war, operational accidents posed a greater threat to aircrew than enemy action. Dowding himself crashed a new version of the famous Blériot monoplane, which had an unsuspected design flaw. Dowding attributed the accident to a fainting spell and scrupulously refrained from taking up passengers, but carrying capsules of amyl nitrite as an emergency restorative, he continued to fly. Later, after an accumulation of evidence, it was deduced that the engine exhaust of the new-model Blériot, not properly vented away from the cockpit, was causing pilots to lose consciousness.[4]

The hazards to which No. 9 Squadron was exposed also included its commanding officer, a major seconded from the Royal Engineers who was, it became increasingly apparent, beyond eccentric. Convinced that conditions in the squadron should be made more rather than less rigorous, he instituted predawn parades. More seriously, he refused to allow replacement of the wood-and-fabric wing structures of the squadron's aircraft, which were deteriorating owing to prolonged exposure to the elements. Dowding took advantage of the CO's absence on leave to order repairs, but on his return the major angrily demanded that the old wings be reinstalled. This order apparently attracted sufficiently high-level attention to bring about his reassignment to non-aviation duties. Shortly thereafter, two of the squadron's three flights were detached, and early in 1915, Dowding became commanding officer of a reorganized No. 9 Squadron, although he inherited from the old squadron little but its nameplate.[5]

Dowding's new No. 9 Squadron was to serve as, in essence, a "wireless" experimentation unit, stationed back at Brooklands. Unhappy at being sent home, Dowding nevertheless tackled the mission with energy and ingenuity, buoyed by promotion to the temporary rank of major in March, 1915. His new command possessed scanty equipment and minimal personnel, including no trained pilots but two knowledgeable, civilian technicians. Unwilling to wait for the slow and cumbersome official procurement process, together with Dowding they set about scrounging the components they needed to build a wireless telegraph set that was radically lighter, and therefore more practical for employment in aircraft, than anything in service. After successfully testing their lightweight wireless telegraph, Dowding's team moved on to build an air-to-ground radiotelephone, which Dowding himself successfully tested. Official skepticism and lack of support hamstrung the practical application of No. 9 Squadron's experimental work, however, fueling Dowding's skepticism regarding the functioning of the military establishment.[6]

In late July, Dowding's frustration with officialdom was relieved temporarily by a new assignment: commanding officer of No. 16 Squadron, operating under Trenchard as officer commanding (OC) First Wing. Warned by Trenchard of morale problems in his new command, Dowding worked to improve living conditions, which resembled those he had experienced at Saint-Omer six months earlier. Also eroding the flyers' morale was their realization that the senior army officers who controlled their fates still mostly lacked even an elementary grasp of the capabilities and limitations of airpower. The roots of the discontent, however, went far beyond No. 16 Squadron, or even the RFC and the army. Illusions of "a short and glorious war" had been destroyed, and all the belligerents were being forced to come to terms with the realities of a protracted struggle, for which they were intellectually and psychologically unprepared. Dowding had no recorded success in combating the resulting "cynicism" among his pilots by means of "personal magnetism" and inspiration.[7]

Amidst all these difficulties, Dowding's squadron did manage some noteworthy accomplishments. Although No. 16 Squadron could physically confirm only one German aircraft shot down during Dowding's period in command, the unit excelled in producing technical innovations that benefited the RFC as a whole, winning a competition to develop an attachment for mounting bombsights, cameras, and wireless equipment to aircraft. Dowding also contributed personally to the technical advancement of aviation during his tenure in command of No. 16 Squadron. While flying as observer with one of his squadron's best pilots, Dowding became one of the first aviators to identify the aeronautical phenomenon known as icing—and live to describe it. His forthright stance on another technical issue, however, resulted in a confrontation with his irascible commanding officer. The affair of the replacement propellers marked the beginning of what eventually became a serious estrangement between two strong-willed airmen.[8]

The trouble started with the shipment to No. 16 Squadron of some replacement propellers designed for an engine smaller than those with which its aircraft were equipped. The wing staff rebuffed his complaints, so Dowding took his objections to Trenchard. Boom insisted that engines of different sizes mounted the same prop. Dowding pointed out that the new propellers' hubs were the wrong size for his engines' shafts, and the bolt holes were in the wrong places. Trenchard then ordered Dowding to rebore the hubs and drill new bolt holes. Dowding carried out these orders, with such misgivings that he flew the first test flight himself rather than have one of his subordinates risk it. When Dowding reported the (fortunately) successful test flight to his commander, he was infuriated by Trenchard's response: "Oh, Dowding. I find that I was let down by our representative in Paris. The propellers won't do for your engines."[9]

The incident illuminates a central difference between the two men. Trenchard believed deeply that obstacles were things to be pushed aside, without delay, by whatever means might be at hand, and without regard to any risk of failure. In an early instance of his jealous defense of his own command prerogatives, Dowding was angered that Trenchard, over his protests as the subordinate commander directly concerned, relied on a demonstrably careless or ill-informed staff officer, as well as by the fact that when Trenchard discovered his error, he manifested no concern at having unnecessarily risked his subordinates' lives. Although not a trained engineer, Dowding had an eye for technical detail, and with his respect for empirical fact, consistently sought rational solutions to problems. Above all, Dowding deplored exposing subordinates to unnecessary risks. In Dowding's mind, Trenchard had failed to measure up as a leader. For his part, Trenchard dismissed Dowding's attention to detail as "pernickety primness," unbefitting a combat commander.[10]

Reinforcing Trenchard's unflattering view of Dowding's leadership was an awareness that Dowding was not a popular squadron commander. One of the unit's younger flyers later published a thinly veiled account of life in No. 16 Squadron that left little doubt that some, at least, of Dowding's subordinates found him not just unapproachable but almost repellent. The junior officers who disliked Dowding referred to him as "the Starched Shirt," criticizing everything from his "limp" handshake, to his "rather nasal" voice, to his walk, "like an angry ostrich, stepping high and pecking his head at each long stride." To them, the squadron's atmosphere was cold, full "of ill-feeling, of distrust, of envy and of hidden malice." Silence prevailed both on duty, and off duty in the officers' mess. All this Dowding's critics attributed directly to his individual personality, his "constitutional disability [*sic*] to inspire comradeship." Ironic, then, that a visit to the squadron by the famously inspirational Trenchard left the same officers almost equally unimpressed with both men.[11]

An age gap probably was a major part of the trouble: Dowding was still in his early thirties, but the typical frontline RFC pilot was a youth in his late teens or early twenties. Compounding the intolerance of extreme youth was the impatience of wartime, volunteer officers with the manners and methods of "regulars." Some of Dowding's subordinates perceived his manner (which, after all, even his staff-college colleagues had found "stuffy") as disdain for "scallywags" who never would have been commissioned in his old regiment. Moreover, as a career officer he was suspected of ambition, seeking to advance in rank by appropriating credit for the accomplishments of his subordinates. Even the fact that Dowding had abandoned the artillery for aviation was held against him: "gunners" were notoriously "brainy and fond of math." Dowding, at least in one man's opinion, displayed "none of that fire . . . essential in the leader of a good squadron."[12]

A further irony is that, during this period, Dowding's adherence to traditional standards of conduct reportedly gained him an exceptional degree of respect from the enemy's airmen. Incensed when British troops shot and killed the two crewmen of a downed German aircraft, he ordered their belongings returned across the lines, along with a message indicating the men's burial place. Dowding's reaction to the incident reflected not only an unusual ability to maintain his intellectual and ethical balance under the stress of war, but also considerable moral courage. In the nature of things, a military service locked in a death struggle with a powerful adversary generates immense pressures on members to overlook, if not actively justify, the misdeeds of comrades in arms. Dowding not only resisted that pressure but, going further, also took responsibility for a small but humane gesture toward the enemy, at a time of rising fury among his countrymen at the pain being inflicted daily on the nation by that enemy.[13]

Notwithstanding any doubts either his immediate superior or his subordinates entertained about him, the RFC evaluated Dowding as a sufficiently effective squadron commander to promote him to the (temporary) rank of lieutenant colonel at the beginning of 1916, and assign him to command the Seventh (Administrative) Wing, back at Farnborough. In his new position, he found the going surprisingly difficult when he attempted to interest top "public" schools in supplying officer candidates to the RFC. Apparently, many among the public-school elite in fact held the snobbish view of RFC officers attributed to Dowding himself by some of his former subordinates. Happily for Dowding, with the RFC racing to build up its strength in France ahead of a planned general offensive, he was already slated for combat command. That spring, Seventh Wing stood up a squadron, No. 70, equipped with the new Sopwith fighter. After leading No. 70 Squadron to France, Dowding assumed command of the Ninth (Headquarters) Wing.[14]

Ninth Wing was directly subordinate to the general officer commanding, RFC France (temporary) Major General Trenchard. With four squadrons assigned, Ninth Wing would act as the GOC's "strategic" force, conducting reconnaissance, interdiction, and air-superiority missions under his centralized control. During the fall and winter of 1915–16, when the German Air Service had begun operating large numbers of Fokker fighter planes that thoroughly outclassed available British aircraft, the RFC effectively had lost air superiority over the BEF's front. Although Trenchard consistently regarded support of the ground war to be his command's primary mission, nevertheless he had felt compelled to limit the number of close support and tactical reconnaissance missions in order to be able to launch formations large enough for self-defense. Now, Ninth Wing was to be Trenchard's chosen instrument for offensive counter-air operations designed to regain the initiative for the RFC, in advance of an impending ground offensive.[15]

As OC Ninth Wing, Dowding thus was cast in a significant, supporting role in one of the great and ultimately tragic dramas of the war. Originally conceived by the Allied high commanders as part of grandiose strategic concept, involving coordinated offensives by the armies of all the major Allied powers—Russia and Italy as well as France and Britain—by the early summer of 1916 the immediate objective had shrunk to a more modest goal: drawing German reserves onto the British front and relieving the pressure on the hard-pressed French defenders of Verdun. Still, General Sir Douglas Haig, newly appointed commander in chief of the BEF, preserved dreams of a breakthrough, to be followed by a war-winning battle of maneuver. To this end, the allies massed thirteen British and eleven French divisions for an assault on a narrow, twelve-mile section of the German front in the valley of the river Somme.[16]

During the run-up to the attack and the opening phases of the Battle of the Somme, the RFC experienced considerable success, stemming from its quantitative and qualitative preparations for the campaign. By the summer of 1916, the RFC deployed on the western front forces more than twice as large as in the previous year. The arrival in France of the Sopwith fighters during the spring of 1916 marked the operational debut of the first generation of true fighter aircraft produced by the British. The RFC also copied some innovations from the French air arm, augmenting its air-to-air firepower through attention to technical details such as improved machine-gun belts. Maintenance improved with the provision of aircraft hangars for forward airfields. A system of "contact patrols," which historian John Morrow described as "perhaps the most significant innovation in air operations during the Somme battle," yielded enhanced cooperation with friendly infantry in ground-assault operations.[17]

Success in the air, however, could not prevent catastrophe on the ground. The tragedy of the Somme can be summed up in a few, famous, but still staggering statistics: the British army suffered almost 60,000 casualties on the first day of the battle, including some 6,000 killed in the first hour. Overall British casualties in the Somme offensive, which continued for nearly five months, amounted to more than 400,000; total Allied casualties were more than 600,000. The British assaults utterly failed to break through the German defense-in-depth and gained little ground, at most making a large dent in the enemy front that forced the Germans to defend a longer line. In retrospect, British persistence on the Somme has been justified by some on grounds that the Allied Powers, with their vastly deeper well of manpower, were better positioned than the Central Powers—Germany and her allies—to win a war of attrition. As commander in chief of BEF, Haig was almost religiously determined to press the attack.[18]

Haig had no more committed supporter in his determination to maintain the offensive at all costs than his air-component commander. Trenchard fully shared the Edwardian assumptions about the nature of war that had shaped Haig's leadership and strategy. The two men were among the most unswerving, if not exactly unthinking, adherents of the doctrine that the moral element—morale, in fact—was decisive in war. Both men believed implicitly that the only way to secure moral ascendancy over the enemy was to attack. For Trenchard, the success of his offensive counter-air operations during the run-up to the attack and the opening phases of the Somme offensive not only helped to crystallize his core operational concepts of airpower but also, he believed, fundamentally vindicated his entire conception of warfare. As historian Malcolm Cooper observed, "The undoubted ascendancy gained over the Germans . . . served thereafter as the ideal" of air superiority in the minds of Trenchard and his followers.[19]

By far the most significant clash between Dowding and Trenchard now developed over the RFC commander's policy of "relentless and incessant offensive." Specifically, Dowding disagreed with the Trenchard policy of maintaining continuous, daylight fighter patrols over German-controlled territory, because this dispersion of forces allowed the enemy to attack with superior numbers at times and places of their choosing. Rather than contest his commander's policy in the midst of the campaign, however, Dowding instead challenged the rule forbidding senior officers from flying in combat. On July 11, Dowding personally led a mission, on which both he and his backseat flight observer were slightly wounded. As the RFC pressed its attacks in the battle space over the Somme through the summer and into the fall of 1916, Dowding grew increasingly concerned as losses mounted. The German airmen had regrouped, and were now holding their own—or better. The British ultimately lost some 500 pilots and 800 aircraft in the Somme campaign, against fewer than 400 German aircraft destroyed.[20]

The breaking point for Dowding came when he concluded that one of his units, No. 60 Squadron, would have to be temporarily withdrawn from operations. Trenchard acquiesced, but expressed exasperation in a private letter. Complaining that it was impossible to fight a war with "Dismal Jimmys" like Dowding for commanders, he resolved to find a replacement. At the end of the blood-soaked year 1916, Trenchard did replace Dowding as OC, Ninth Wing, with another temporary lieutenant colonel: Cyril Newall. That Dowding was superseded by an officer whom he had surprised and outmaneuvered in a peacetime exercise (when they were both very junior) was ironic, but signified little. More tellingly, the "brainy" former gunner had opposed with practical, common sense the half-baked theories of Trenchard, the supposedly straightforward, no-nonsense fighting man. Suspected by some subordinates of careerism and indifference to their concerns, Dowding risked his career in an effort to prevent his pilots' lives being sacrificed fruitlessly.[21]

Dowding went on to spend the last two years of the war as officer commanding training establishments, variously designated Southern Training Wing, Southern Training Brigade, and (by 1918) RAF Southern Group, as well as other various, senior administrative posts. Some solace for his banishment from combat command came on New Years' Day, 1917, when he was promoted to the temporary rank of full colonel. By no means, however, was his assignment to training merely a convenient "shelf" on which to store an unwanted senior officer. Early in 1916, Trenchard had sent home John Salmond, his most trusted senior operational commander, with orders to rectify deficiencies in pilot training. Based on requests from Haig, the Army Council in December 1916 approved yet another vast expansion of the RFC. During 1917–18, the effective management of flying training establishments was a top priority for the RFC; an essentially unlimited flow of personnel as well as matériel replacements had become a main pillar of the de facto war of attrition Haig and Trenchard were waging.[22]

If Trenchard thought that removing Dowding from France would stifle his "pernickety" criticism of RFC policy, Boom was promptly disabused. When Dowding discovered that training squadrons were being stripped of experienced pilots for deployment to France, he immediately pointed out, through official channels, that an adequate number of experienced airmen serving as instructor pilots was a precondition for, first, replacing the RFC's combat losses, and then building up its frontline strength. Not content with official protests, Dowding also wrote privately to an officer on Trenchard's staff, asking him to try to persuade the RFC commander to modify the policy. The staff officer showed Dowding's letter to Trenchard, and as Dowding later recalled, "That finished me with Trenchard," at least for the time being. Despite Boom's formidable disapproval, however, Dowding's usefulness as a top manager in the training arena had become sufficiently obvious that in June 1917 he gained a further promotion, becoming a temporary brigadier general.[23]

The most important development in the British air-war effort during 1918 was the formation of the world's first independent military air service. The impetus behind this controversial action was the failure of the two existing rival air arms, the RFC and the Royal Naval Air Service, to respond satisfactorily to German air attacks on British cities. Intermittent bombing by German airships (zeppelins) during the first two years of the war had been blunted when the British began operating true fighter aircraft in 1916. In 1917, however, the Germans began bombing with heavier-than-air craft (the Gothas), and the British public quickly lost patience with the inability of the armed services to mount a credible defense. By the fall of 1917, the government felt compelled to introduce legislation establishing a new executive department, the Air Ministry, to assume responsibility for the independent administration of the Royal Air Force as a separate armed service.[24]

The RAF was officially inaugurated on April 1, 1918 (a choice of date some considered "perverse"), with Dowding among the multitude of officers whose temporary, wartime appointments were transferred to the new service, without vacating their permanent commissions in the army and navy. Dowding was fortunate to serve in assignments at once important and remote from the ensuing, vicious infighting for control of the new service. Trenchard, recalled from France to become the first chief of Air Staff (CAS), resigned after just three months rather than work with the first secretary of state for air, Lord Rothermere, whom he had come to loathe even more than he despised most politicians. It was symptomatic of the farcical chaos at the top of the fledgling RAF that Trenchard, ostensibly having resigned because he opposed creating an "independent force" of strategic bombers, eventually returned to France and fought through the last months of the war in command of the Independent Force.[25]

The year 1918 saw the climax of the World War, but for Dowding personally it marked a beginning, rather than an end. In February, he married Clarice Vancourt, a cousin of his old commanding officer in No. 6 Squadron. The couple had first met in those distant, early days of the war at Farnborough. "She was," Dowding wrote of his wife, "always full of laughter and fun and gaiety." Clarice was the widow of a prewar army hero; Dowding became stepfather to her daughter, Marjorie. In January 1919 their son, Derek, was born. The fighting had come to an end a few weeks earlier, with the armistice effective at the eleventh hour of the eleventh day of the eleventh month of 1918. Amid the ruins of a Europe shattered by devastation on a scale few had foreseen four and a half years earlier, Hugh and Clarice began a new life.[26]

Neither starting a family of his own, nor the prospect of protracted peace, deterred Dowding from continuing his military career as an airman. The professional future was uncertain, however. Like so many officers temporarily elevated in rank by their services' wartime needs and their own accomplishments, Dowding had to wait for a permanent rank and assignment. Even Trenchard himself was on the roster of unemployed army officers (albeit at his own request) when, in January 1919, a mercurial and intensely controversial, forty-four-year-old politician named Winston Churchill, newly installed as secretary of state for war and air, asked him to return as chief of Air Staff. This unexpected comeback for Boom did not bode well for Dowding, given his fraught relationship with the once and future CAS. Nor was trouble slow to develop. When the Air Ministry soon afterward published its list of candidates for permanent commissions in the RAF, Dowding's name was absent.[27]

Dowding now faced an involuntary return to the Royal Artillery Regiment as a brevet lieutenant colonel. The Gunners' list was crowded with officers who had distinguished themselves in the war, and Dowding's professional qualifications as an artillerist were hopelessly out of date, even if he had preserved any interest in the army and its artillery branch, after four years of active service in aviation. At this juncture, Dowding's career was rescued from a dead end, if not indeed premature termination, by of all people, an admiral. Fortunately for Dowding, in his training commands he had come under the area command of Vice Admiral Sir Vyell Vyvyan, who had formed a favorable opinion of his professional ability. Moreover, having himself clashed with Trenchard during the war over policy and tactics, Vyvyan was not overly impressed by Boom's judgment; nor, having been a Royal Navy flag officer, was he in the least intimidated by the newly minted rank of air marshal.[28]

Vyvyan therefore repeatedly made an issue of Dowding's fate at the highest levels of the Air Ministry. Finally, in August 1919, Dowding received a permanent RAF commission, with the rank of group captain (equivalent to a full colonel). Not unnaturally, he resented having been left hanging, professionally speaking, for some nine months, and in later years put the blame squarely on Boom. Trenchard's advocates have rejoined that no direct evidence has ever surfaced to show that the CAS personally ordered Dowding's initial exclusion. Indeed, there is reason to conclude that the initial RAF officer list was not Trenchard's work: as CAS, he felt it necessary to correct other omissions, in addition to that of Dowding. Whatever the reason for the delay, Dowding now took his place as one of the senior officers of the tiny air service, just one-tenth the maximum size of the wartime force, which tenuously survived the government's drastic, postwar downsizing of the British military establishment.[29]

At thirty-six, Dowding was, like his RAF peer group, a young man for senior-officer rank by the standards of the twentieth-century military profession. Soldiers, sailors, and airmen alike belonged to a fated, professional generation born in the 1880s and early 1890s, old enough to reach senior leadership responsibilities, and even "flag" or general-officer rank, in the First World War, yet young enough to remain fit for active service and still greater responsibilities, in the Second. Group Captain Dowding's professional attributes included a foundation in regimental soldiering; training and experience as a staff officer; knowledge of basic airmanship, aviation technology, and combat air operations; deep experience of flying training and of large-scale, organizational management. He had exhibited moral as well as physical courage, and commitment to "service before self," as well as (for better or worse) a disposition to challenge some key characteristics of modern military service. Dowding had demonstrated fitness for high command in peace and war.

3 POSTWAR SENIOR LEADER 1919–1930

Dowding's postwar career began with eleven more months as a senior RAF administrator, varied by two brief spells as a temporary Area commander. Most of the shrunken RAF's few squadrons were deployed overseas; the dispositions of the units retained at home, sometimes referred to as the "metropolitan air force," can be explained by the RAF's roles and missions during this period. The fighter squadrons remained static, at stations around London; bomber squadrons operated from stations conveniently near Salisbury Plain, the traditional staging-ground for British army exercises. Stations near the coasts handled maritime responsibilities. These home stations and squadrons continued, as in the war, to be grouped into major commands by geographical area.[1]

In October 1919 Dowding was designated OC, 16 Group, but four months later he received a three-year appointment as OC, 1 Group, stationed at RAF

Kenley. In this assignment, his heaviest responsibility involved mounting the Royal Air Force Pageant (later the RAF Display), held annually at London's Hendon Aerodrome. The RAF Pageant was a prototype of the air shows that air forces around the world have used to display their prowess and generate public support. In retirement, Dowding—perhaps with tongue in cheek—would recall pageant days as the most anxious of his professional life. Dowding worked on the pageants directly under the air officer commanding, Inland Area, Air Vice-Marshal Sir John Salmond. "Jack" Salmond, a year older than Dowding, had been one of his flight instructors at the prewar Central Flying School. Having built a record of operational air command on the western front second only to that of Trenchard himself (some would say, second to none), Salmond was positioned eventually to succeed Boom as CAS.[2]

While Dowding was stationed at Kenley, tragedy struck with the sudden and shocking death of Clarice, after just two years of marriage. Dowding closed their household and moved back into his parents' home in Wimbledon, then still a suburb of London. His reputation for unsociability seems to date from the 1914–18 years of wartime command, but as a widower he became still more withdrawn, although the fact that he continued to find time, interest, and energy for polo and skiing argues against any notion that he led a monastic existence. The evidence does suggest that the death of his wife had a profound, emotional impact on him, leading him away from the conventional religious outlook of his Victorian parents and grandparents, toward increasingly unconventional notions of spirituality. At any rate, many who knew Dowding in the twenties and thirties viewed him as a man narrowly focused on his work.[3]

At the beginning of 1922, Dowding was promoted to air commodore, on par with the rank of brigadier general he had gained on a temporary basis more than four years earlier. A few months short of his fortieth birthday, he now achieved permanent air rank, the RAF equivalent of general-officer rank. Dowding was one of his service's most senior officers, on the edge of the tight, little inner circle that, with remarkable continuity, controlled the internal workings of the RAF for a full generation from 1918 through the first phase of the Second World War. The circle centered on Trenchard, naturally, given the positions he had occupied ever since 1915. All the interwar, RAF senior leaders had either worked directly with Trenchard as staff officers, or commanded operational forces as his immediate subordinates, or both. All owed their high positions during the decade of the twenties to selection by Trenchard.[4]

In addition to Jack Salmond, key figures in the RAF senior leadership included his older brother Geoffrey, who as commander of the air component of General Sir Edmund Allenby's army in the Middle East during 1917–18 had played a central role in defeating the forces of the Ottoman Empire. Edward Ellington, who had proved himself in wartime as one of the old RFC's most effective administrators, during the interwar years held several major RAF Area commands in succession. Robert Brooke-Popham, an influential planner and adviser on the postwar Air Staff, was responsible for standing up the RAF Staff College, Andover, as its first commandant, and returned to active duty as late as 1941 to face the Japanese as commander in chief in the Far East. A key member of Trenchard's senior staff in the late twenties was Cyril Newall, whose career had prospered after replacing Dowding in command of Ninth Wing in 1916, and who served from 1926 to 1931 in the powerful post of deputy chief of Air Staff, with direct control over the Directorate of Operations and Intelligence (DDOI).

On Brooke-Popham's original directing staff at Andover was Wilfrid Freeman, who became an influential link between the founding generation of RAF senior leaders and the younger generation already being groomed for the prominent positions they were to fill in the 1930s. The latter included Richard Peirse, Sholto Douglas, Keith Park, and C. F. A. "Peter" Portal, among the promising squadron leaders handpicked for the first RAF Staff College class; another squadron leader who caught Trenchard's eye during the war, Arthur Tedder, was detailed to the Naval Staff College. All of these officers, together with squadron leaders Trafford Leigh-Mallory and "Jack" Slessor, who served Trenchard in the late twenties as writers and planners, went on to feature prominently in the climacteric of 1938–40. Dowding stood on the edge of this Trenchardist inner circle, but he was not part of it; nor did the quality of his relations with the rising, next generation of RAF leaders bode well for the future.[5]

More than one edgy encounter with Tedder, a Trenchard protégé and a close friend of Freeman, contributed to the bad blood between Dowding and the RAF's leadership elite. On one occasion while serving in Dowding's group, the self-assured young squadron leader clashed abrasively with his air officer commanding over preparations for an exercise. Later, tapped by Trenchard to lead a short-notice deployment to the eastern Mediterranean as a result of a sudden crisis in the Middle East, Tedder cut corners and ignored regulations in efforts to ensure that his unit had all the equipment and spare parts it needed—much as Major Dowding had done for No. 9 Squadron, back in 1915. Air Commodore Dowding, however, declined to overlook the irregularities. Despite the outstanding success of Tedder's crisis deployment, Dowding asked the Air Ministry to take "disciplinary action." Friends of Tedder in high places managed quietly to smother the complaint without damage to his career, but he never forgave Dowding.

The discord between Dowding and Tedder reinforced negative views of Dowding as a man without either "human sympathy or imagination" that were already circulating at the top of the RAF. Tedder also accused Dowding of "petty" vindictiveness, apparently believing that Dowding's actions were payback for his earlier opposition to Dowding's ideas. Yet Dowding displayed precisely the qualities of human sympathy and imagination in protecting another of the service's rising stars, Sholto Douglas. When a court of inquiry attributed a fatal accident to squadron-level maintenance failure, the Air Ministry directed Dowding as Group AOC to bring Douglas, the acting squadron commander, before a court martial. Dowding refused, on the grounds that the failure had been due to orders issued by the substantive squadron commander, not Douglas. Dowding's stand was both courageous and unselfish, given that the issue had arisen before his own permanent commission was confirmed.[6]

In sharp contrast with his opposition to Trenchard's wartime doctrine of maintaining a continuous offensive, Dowding's postwar friction with the Trenchard circle resulted from conflicts of temperament and personality, rather than substantive policy differences. RAF leaders during these years had strong incentives to hang together in defense of the policies, programs, and doctrines developed by the Air Staff, in view of the ongoing, interservice struggle for resources and control of air roles and missions. Dowding fully shared the anxiety of his peers regarding the political threat to the RAF. Churchill and his immediate successors at the Air Ministry, together with Trenchard and his staff, were forced to devote much of their time to fighting off proposals for dismembering the RAF that continued to flow from the War Office and the Admiralty. Prime Minister David Lloyd George finally asked elder statesman and former prime minister Arthur Balfour to arbitrate the competing organizational claims of the three services.[7]

Coincidentally, but usefully for the RAF, while Balfour was studying the problems of overall defense organization, rising diplomatic tensions with Great War ally but historic rival France highlighted the extent to which Britain's home air defenses had nearly disappeared. All three services were suffering from the effects of the so-called Ten Year Rule, which Lloyd George had established to shape defense budgets on the assumption that Britain would not face another major war within ten years. The RAF could reasonably claim to have been hit hardest by the postwar budgetary constraints. Lacking the well-established infrastructure of the older services, the RAF under Trenchard had deliberately chosen to spend scarce funds on personnel and on facilities directly supporting training and education, rather than on aircraft and consumable goods supporting immediate readiness. Thus by early 1922, the RAF possessed only three fully operational squadrons at home as against some six hundred French aircraft within potential striking distance of London.[8]

Balfour's report convinced the Committee of Imperial Defence that the air-defense issue required stronger political oversight, and it set up a standing subcommittee to address the problem. Meanwhile, however, the defense establishment and the entire government came under intense political pressure over government spending and waste. War-weary Britons resented the cost of European and imperial commitments, fervently wishing to concentrate on home affairs. A weakened prime minister was forced to create an investigating committee to identify potential savings, convened under the leadership of businessman-politician Sir Eric Geddes. Spurred by its chief, the Air Staff devoted weeks of effort to convincing Geddes that the army and navy offered more promising hunting ground for wasteful spending than the much smaller RAF. Geddes's committee eventually recommended cuts in defense expenditures so drastic that they became known as "the Geddes axe," but Trenchard's timely, patient, proactive work helped direct the blows of the axe mostly elsewhere than the RAF budget.[9]

Continuing international tensions reinforced the Air Ministry's case that the RAF already had been downsized too much for safety. As a result, the 1922 budget debates in the House of Commons favored the RAF, and that summer the Lloyd George government announced plans to increase the home air-defense forces to five hundred aircraft. These commitments, however, emanated from a failing administration. In October 1922, Conservatives led by Andrew Bonar Law and Stanley Baldwin ousted it from office, and Bonar Law formed a new, business-dominated Government dedicated to "economy," meaning fiscal conservatism. No friend of either Trenchard or the principle of an independent air force, Bonar Law promptly set up a parliamentary committee "to settle the issue" of defense organization with an eye toward "economy." As far as the RAF was concerned, the effect of this new group, known as the Salisbury Committee, was to unsettle the decisions of the previous government.

At this juncture, cancer removed Bonar Law from the scene. In May 1923, Baldwin inherited the premiership, the Salisbury Committee, and the air-defense issue. A month later, the new prime minister used the occasion of an interim report from the Salisbury Committee to deliver a surprisingly saber-rattling speech, and on June 26, the government announced a five-year program to build a fifty-two-squadron "Home Defence Air Force." The Air Staff developed the fifty-two-squadron requirement based on numerical parity with the current strength of the French metropolitan air forces. Plans for implementing the program were "roughed out" by Brooke-Popham and other Air Staff members, while Trenchard took a month off to recover from his political battles. Execution of the program would involve the staffs of the Area commands, now including Dowding, who relinquished command of 1 Group early in 1923 to become chief staff officer, Inland Area.[10]

At the Uxbridge headquarters of Inland Area, Dowding served under one of the RAF's most experienced Area commanders, the colorful air vice-marshal J. F. A. Higgins, who had succeeded Jack Salmond as air officer commanding. The Higgins-Dowding era at Uxbridge in 1923–24 coincided with a period of discussion among RAF leaders regarding the proper composition of the newly authorized Home Defence Air Force. It is essential to bear in mind that when civilian policy makers and military planners in the 1920s spoke of the Home Defence Air Force, they not only specifically included offensive bombing aircraft as well as defensive fighters, but also regarded the striking forces in the bomber squadrons as the most important element of air defense. Now that the government had established an overall requirement for forces, RAF leaders had to decide what proportion of the fifty-two squadrons should be allocated to fighters and to bombers, respectively.[11]

A central premise of the interwar RAF's theory of airpower doctrine was that the only way to defeat an enemy's bombing offensive was with a more effective bombing offensive of one's own. The experience of the Great War had taught British airmen that, although sound air defense could impose costly attrition on an enemy, it was not technically feasible to decisively defeat a serious bombing offensive by defensive means alone. It followed, therefore, that decisive results—victory—would go to the side that mounted and sustained the more effective bombing campaign. Nevertheless, some experts pointed to technological advances that, by improving early warning and communications, would enable defenders to turn the airspace over the defending country into a battle space. Even Geoffrey Salmond began to question a central article of the airpower faith: that unlike surface forces, air forces need not engage and defeat an enemy's military forces in order to break the enemy state's will to resist.[12]

Although Trenchard expressed concern that the senior leadership of the RAF appeared to be dividing into "offensive" and "defensive" factions, in fact a consensus quickly formed that development work on effective air defenses should share priority with development of the bomber force. Consensus was possible because, as one Air Ministry official put it, "Everybody wants to get a maximum into the offensive, and a minimum into the defensive. The only difference of opinion is as to what constitutes the minimum which can be usefully employed in the defensive." Despite the efforts of "Peter" Portal, then a young staff officer, to answer this question by applying intellectually sophisticated concepts such as marginal utility, ultimately the RAF adopted a classic, split-the-difference compromise between the numbers advocated by "bomber purists," and those advanced by the air-defense experts. Arbitrarily, one-third of the Home Defence Air Force would consist of fighter squadrons, and two-thirds bomber squadrons.[13]

Even as work on air-defense issues intensified, Dowding was given a still higher profile post, confronting problems of far more immediate, strategic, and political concern. In his new assignment, Dowding again served as chief staff officer to Higgins, who once again had succeeded Jack Salmond, this time as air officer commanding-in-chief, Iraq. In that nascent and troubled state, from the fall of 1924 to the spring of 1926, Higgins and Dowding together helped guide the evolution of the RAF concept of air policing. It was an effort with consequences for the political survival of the RAF, which had attracted support from otherwise indifferent, skeptical or hostile politicians by promising effective substitution for conventional military and naval methods of colonial control—gunboats and punitive expeditions—at lower cost. Cost was the vital factor; the war had left Britain with more extensive imperial commitments, especially in the Middle East, and diminished resources.[14]

Efforts to employ air forces in colonial control operations were as old as the airplane. Leading the way had been the Italians in Libya beginning in 1911, and the British, on the frontiers of the Indian Empire in 1915 and 1917, and in Darfur in 1916. After the war, the surviving European empires were materially weakened. At the same time, one of the indirect effects of the 1914–18 struggle, and particularly of the wartime exploitation of liberal idealism by the Allies, was the political mobilization of subject peoples around the world. For Britain, 1919–20 saw an explosion of troubles in an arc of instability extending from the Indian North-West Frontier (now Pakistan) and Afghanistan, through the Middle East, and back home to Ireland in the United Kingdom itself. It was in the context of this so-called crisis of empire that the RAF achieved a small but fateful success.[15]

In Somaliland early in 1920, a mere eight aircraft appeared to succeed where the army had failed for years in dispersing the forces of Mohammed bin Abdulla Hassan (known as "the Mad Mullah"), almost overnight relieving the British administration of that territory of a chronic security problem, at a fraction of the cost of a conventional, punitive expedition. Seizing upon this apparent demonstration of the effectiveness of air substitution, Churchill asked the CAS for a plan to control Mesopotamia (as the British then referred to Iraq) by airpower. The former Ottoman Turkish provinces of Mosul, Baghdad, and Basra had been conquered by British imperial forces during the war, and were governed by Britain after the war under a mandate from the League of Nations. More than 100,000 British and Indian troops and four years of costly fighting had been required to oust the Ottoman army from the provinces; in 1920, over 34,000 British imperial troops remained in occupation.[16]

Before Churchill could secure approval of Trenchard's plan over opposition both within the War Office and in the Cabinet, the situation on the ground deteriorated suddenly and sharply. In the summer of 1920, a popular insurgency swept Iraq, led by the ever-dangerous combination of Shia clerics and former (in this case, Ottoman) regime functionaries and military officers. The insurgency inflicted painful casualties on the British imperial forces, to the acute political embarrassment of the government in London. Churchill, always strong for decisive action in a crisis, urged both troop reinforcements and air operations to restore British control. The government was extremely reluctant to send in more troops, and indeed, had downsized the army to such an extent that few reinforcements were immediately available. A limited number of British and Indian troops, assisted by a few RAF squadrons, fought through the summer and into the fall, stabilizing the situation by October 1920.[17]

Churchill now developed a two-pronged, political-military strategy aimed at undercutting the grievances that had fueled the insurgency, thus reducing the likelihood of its recurring. He insisted on substituting airpower for ground forces, to reduce the friction and resentment caused by a large military footprint, to conserve British manpower, and not incidentally to save money. At the same time, Churchill also advocated creating a new state, a kingdom of Iraq, with Faisal bin Al-Hussein bin Ali El-Hashemi, a descendant of the hereditary grand sharifs of Mecca, as monarch. Churchill hoped by these means to cloak the British imperial position with a system of indirect rule, such as had been successful in India and Egypt. The RAF and its unique capabilities were integral to this dual, political-military strategy of indirect rule, but not until his move from the War Office to the Colonial Office was Churchill in a position to convert his vision into official Government policy.[18]

On October 1, 1922, Jack Salmond became the first air officer of any nationality to hold chief command of all the military forces in a country, the first airman to serve as, in effect, a joint-forces commander. Salmond's two years as commander in chief in Iraq registered in London as a brilliant success. Salmond successfully maintained Iraq's internal stability and external security, somewhat to the surprise and very much to the chagrin of the Imperial General Staff, which had warned the government that the RAF, with its immature senior leadership and even more immature staff system, would be in over its head. The climax of Salmond's tenure in Iraq was an impressive demonstration of the precision effects of airpower. His air-ground teams suppressed several groups of Turkish-sponsored rebels that had been destabilizing British control of Iraq's Kurdish northern region, and more importantly deterred a potential overt military intervention by Turkey.[19]

Higgins and Dowding thus had big shoes to fill when they took over Iraq command in 1924, and soon confronted a recurrence of the Turkish challenge. In late September, large numbers of "marauders" were detected infiltrating into the area around Mosul. RAF Iraq launched air attacks which inflicted hundreds of casualties before it was discovered that the supposed "irregular" infiltrators were actually Turkish regular army troops, undertaking another covert operation aimed at securing control of Kurdistan for Turkey. Some British political authorities, as well as the client regime of King Faisal, wanted to pursue further counterattacks, which might have escalated the confrontation into full-scale war between Britain and Turkey. Higgins, however, was confident that his prompt if inadvertent counterattack would deter further Turkish adventures, and events bore out this assessment. After the League of Nations eventually worked out a settlement, Trenchard drove home the lesson with evident relish, admonishing the Cabinet:

> The great temptation which confronts commanders handling the air arm is its power of immediate action of an overwhelming and decisive character. . . . The A.O.C. was altogether proof against this temptation . . . keeping off the Turks and yet tiding over a crisis whilst the League of Nations made up their minds.

Taking up Trenchard's hint, the Committee of Imperial Defence and the Cabinet duly praised the judgment and restraint shown by the military command in the theater of operations. Some credit for the success of the Iraq Command in the 1924–25 crisis must flow down to Dowding, whose working relationship with "Josh" Higgins was close and harmonious.[20]

In the aftermath of the Mosul crisis, Iraq Command had to deal with only relatively low levels of chronic, internal unrest, especially in predominantly Kurdish areas. As he had been during the war, Dowding was concerned with "just conduct" by his own forces in the "small war" in Iraq. When Higgins's departure on leave put Dowding in temporary command, he boldly announced a modification in bombing policy: villages were not to be bombed without warning. Dowding's initiative was the more striking because one of his predecessors, Air Commodore L. E. O. Charlton, who had served as chief staff officer to Salmond in Iraq, had resigned in protest over the policy of bombing recalcitrant villages. Charlton's gesture failed to deflect either Salmond, Trenchard, or the London Government from the policy, but Higgins acquiesced in Dowding's decision, and left the new warning policy in place upon his resumption of command.[21]

Dowding's year and a half as chief staff officer in Iraq was enlivened by at least one personal adventure. While flying in a three-ship formation near Sulaimanaya, he was forced down by engine trouble. The district recently had been roiled by the arrest of a local notable, but Dowding and his mechanic were granted hospitality and taken under protection by the wife of the detainee, in a most unlikely episode. A squadron of cavalry extricated Dowding and the aircraftsman but, as Dowding lacked the power of royal clemency, his benefactor's husband had to remain imprisoned. In the spring of 1926, Dowding's work in Iraq ended with a summons home, for duty on the Air Staff in the key post of director of training. It was his first assignment at the Air Ministry, but he was to spend nine of the next ten years there, at the center of RAF policy making.[22]

Dowding returned home to international and domestic environments that had changed significantly since the immediate postwar years. On the one hand, the international situation seemed the most benign for decades—since at least the turn of the century. The Treaty of Locarno in December 1925 had raised hopes of a genuine settlement and resolution of the outstanding international issues arising out of the World War. On the other hand, strain on the British financial system continued to increase, generating increasing domestic social discontent and political crisis, culminating in a paralyzing general strike and a ruinous coal strike during 1926. Under these circumstances, it seemed reasonable to reduce the financial strain by cutting defense expenditure. Consequently, the British government decided, among other economy measures, to stretch out the RAF's fifty-two-squadron Home Defence Air Force program over another seven years, now aiming for completion only in 1935.[23]

Although the pace of expansion slowed, RAF commanders and staffs still faced the challenges of training personnel, both ground crews and pilots, to man the new squadrons that had been stood up during the previous two years. As director of training, Dowding had to find a way to work with Trenchard; possibly to the surprise of both men, he did so with no new friction. Dowding even gained the somewhat grudging respect of the RAF's household deity. Historian Mark Andrews has suggested that Trenchard's attitude toward Dowding may have been influenced by a perception of his junior adopting a "superior" attitude, based on his loftier educational attainments. A simpler explanation, given their respective temperaments, is that the friction arose from "Stuffy" being characteristically pedantic, while Boom was characteristically intransigent. In any case, on one much-noted occasion in the late twenties, Trenchard rumbled at him "I don't often make mistakes about people, Dowding, but I made one about you."[24]

Dowding was less successful in winning over members of the younger generation of RAF leaders, two of whom served in succession as his principal deputy. Sholto Douglas maintained his close relationship with Trenchard while handling Dowding with circumspection, and even some flattery. Arthur Tedder, appalled at the prospect of serving under Dowding, remained uncompromisingly hostile.[25] Trenchard's belated endorsement was key to Dowding's future advancement to the highest level of RAF leadership, but the gap in understanding that persisted between Dowding and the generation of officers who would fill the leading Air Staff positions and the key operational commands in 1940 foreshadowed troubling limits on his future effectiveness as an air officer commanding-in-chief (AOC-in-C). Dowding, it appears, neither integrated into the Trenchard tribe, nor developed his own following. His failure, or refusal, to build a structure of political support within the senior officer ranks left him overly reliant on formal, positional authority as he continued to rise in the service hierarchy.

Whether because of the achievements of the Higgins-Dowding leadership team in Iraq or a new, personal regard for Dowding's qualities, in late 1929 Trenchard gave him his first independent command as an air officer. Arab resentment at growing Jewish immigration to Palestine exploded in bloody riots during the summer of 1929. On two days' notice, Trenchard dispatched Dowding with orders to assume "executive command" of all British forces in Palestine-Transjordan, and report within two weeks "the smallest force that would suffice" to restore order. Trenchard was handing Dowding, recently promoted to air vice-marshal (major general equivalent) an extraordinarily difficult assignment. RAF leaders at the time were well aware of the limitations of air control of insurgencies in urban settings. Further complicating an already daunting situation, the senior British political official in Palestine, High Commissioner Sir John Chancellor, remained the nominal commander in chief of the armed forces in the mandate, as he pointedly reminded Dowding when the air vice-marshal arrived in-country.[26]

Displaying a previously undisclosed political skill, Dowding began by carefully cultivating good relations with the prickly high commissioner. With a refreshing combination of political sensitivity, personal modesty, and plain common sense, Dowding approached the intractable Arab-Jewish conflict with even greater caution. As his friendly biographer Basil Collier put it, "Where Palestinian politics were concerned he had the open mind which, in all but the crassly stupid, accompanies an almost total lack of knowledge or prior interest." After a necessarily brief survey, Dowding's estimate of the situation focused on two elements: first, a weak intelligence-gathering system, and second, poor administration and discipline in the police services. To Trenchard's satisfaction, he recommended improvements in these areas and against the dispatch of military reinforcements. Returning to Britain at the end of 1929, in the New Year Dowding took on one of the peacetime RAF's more prominent assignments, as air officer commanding, Fighting Area, Air Defence of Great Britain.[27]

In 1924, the RAF had centralized under Fighting Area Headquarters (FAHQ), responsibility for command and control of all fighter aircraft and ground forces assigned to the Aircraft Fighting Zone. The AOC and staff of FAHQ thus became the first major command devoted exclusively to the air-defense mission, with control of all resources assigned to that mission.

In the mid-1920s, FAHQ was able to draw on the Great War experience of a number of senior leaders, still active, who had hastily improvised British defenses against the German air attacks. Pioneers of air defense such as E. B. Ashmore and F. V. Holt passed on their lessons learned to junior officers such as Squadron Leader Keith Park, who in later years referred to the senior leaders of that era as the "masters" of airpower. As a wing commander on Dowding's FAHQ staff in 1930, Park took his first steps in paying forward their legacy to the generation of 1940.[28]

FAHQ thus began building up British air defenses not from zero, but on the foundation of a well-developed system, already proven under war conditions. Based on the lessons of recent history, its efforts focused during the late 1920s and early 1930s less on defining threats and devising operational concepts, and more on refining the organization and integrating new technologies, especially in the areas of communications and signals intelligence. The professionalism with which the ADGB and FAHQ during this period not only promoted innovation through pathbreaking work in the new science of operations research, but also tested their concepts of operations and new equipment in large-scale, annual exercises, has won considerable praise. It should be noted, however, that Dowding's view of these exercises was quite different. Years later he described the 1930 exercise, in which his command played a leading role, as having been "a farce," because of conditions created by decisions and rulings from the Air Staff.[29]

Dowding was particularly incensed because the exercise rules not only forced his aircraft to fly predictable routes, but also awarded the bombers' defensive armament two fighter kills for every bomber downed by a fighter. Dowding found a way to disrupt the script, with a large-scale replay of the sort of imaginative tactics he had utilized against Cyril Newall in their long-ago days as junior officers on the North-West Frontier. Sending scouting aircraft to trail the enemy bombers back to their bases, Dowding then followed up with rapid counterattacks that destroyed them on the ground. The umpires were forced to rule Dowding's counterattacks tactically successful, but his colleagues resolutely ignored the larger, operational significance of air-to-air interceptions. The possibilities for successful defense through a combination of defensive counter-air operations, and limited, offensive counter-air operations, garnered little interest in the face of the undiluted orthodoxy of decisive attack by unescorted bombers.

Dowding's postwar decade was a period of continued professional growth, despite the staggering blow of his wife's death. In addition to deepening his experience of operational-level command, he gained direct insight into the problems of high command as a senior Air Staff officer (chief of staff) to an air officer commanding-in-chief. The RAF finally capitalized on Dowding's experience in wartime training commands, while he, in turn, learned to negotiate the folkways of Air Staff and Air Ministry power, in the process managing to repair his professionally vital relationship with Trenchard.

Dowding's assignment in Iraq and his brief, temporary duty in Palestine expanded his professional experience with exposure to counterinsurgency warfare and high level, political-military relations. This Middle East experience, albeit limited, illustrates a pioneer airman confronting enduring problems of airpower employment against insurgency, and his efforts at solutions underscore his continuing concern for just conduct in war under operational conditions radically different from those of great-power warfare in Europe. The end of the postwar era saw Dowding's career come full circle, with a return to home-defense operations, and to Area command, an essential stepping-stone for advancement to the very top of the service hierarchy. Dowding continued his professional advance without sacrificing either his independence of judgment, or the odd streak of unorthodox creativity in operational problem solving that set him apart from many of his professional peers.

4

THE AIR COUNCIL

1930–1933

On September 1, 1930, "Stuffy" Dowding returned to the Air Ministry, joining the Air Council as air member for supply and research (AMSR), once again succeeding his former chief, Air Marshal Higgins. By historical coincidence, it was nine years to the day before the German invasion of Poland began the European war that escalated into the Second World War. The Air Council was the RAF equivalent of the Royal Navy's legendary Board of the Admiralty, and the similar, though less well known, Army Council. Its members included two politicians, the secretary and the under secretary of state for air; a senior civil servant, the permanent under secretary of state for air; and four or more active-duty RAF officers styled "air members," including the chief and the deputy chief of Air Staff, the AMSR, and the air member for personnel (AMP).[1] Subject to the authority of the Cabinet and Parliament, the Air Council was the RAF's policy-making body.[2]

As AMSR for nearly four and a half years, Dowding was the air officer responsible, under the CAS and the secretary of state for air, for the whole of the matériel side of the RAF establishment: the equipment element in the organization, training, and equipping of the service. Dowding spent his first two and a half years working in this capacity under the leadership of Jack Salmond, Trenchard having finally relinquished his appointment as chief of Air Staff after a tenure of just under eleven years, to be succeeded by his longtime heir presumptive. For the most part highly regarded as an operational commander, and personally popular—contemporaries and historians alike have stressed his good looks and "charm"—Salmond did have his critics,[3] who considered him an intellectual lightweight with an overinflated reputation and a proclivity for backstairs intrigue. Nevertheless, after Trenchard's departure he was the best-known senior air officer, overshadowing contemporaries such as Dowding.[4]

In the 1930s, the stable acquisitions process bequeathed by Trenchard to the RAF was first unsettled, and then swept away by powerful, external forces. Dowding and his Air Council colleagues confronted unprecedented problems. Worrisome changes in the international environment, combined with near-revolutionary changes in technology, drastically altered the RAF's organizational and senior leadership challenges. Internationally, the hopeful "spirit of Locarno" dissolved into bitter wrangling at the preparatory sessions for the International Conference on the Limitation of Armaments, to be convened at Geneva, Switzerland. The failure of the Geneva Disarmament Conference, revealing the impossibility of reconciling Germany's demands for what it called "equality of rights" with France's conception of its national security requirements, marked an early turning point on the path to another European war. Simultaneously, the global economy collapsed into the Great Depression, drying up financial resources at the very moment when rapid innovation in electrical and aeronautical engineering promised huge performance returns on investment in technology.

Dowding's debut in his new role was inauspicious. Just one month after he joined the Air Council, British aviation suffered a major disaster with the crash of the airship R-101 (a technologically innovative version of the zeppelin concept) on its inaugural passenger flight. Fatalities included Director-

General of Civil Aviation Sir Sefton Brancker, and the incumbent secretary of state for air, Lord Thomson of Cardington. Like the in-flight explosions of the German airship *Hindenburg* and the US space shuttle *Challenger* in later decades, the R-101 disaster was both a policy and a public-relations nightmare for the government concerned, not only calling into question the safety of a major aeronautical program, but also the basic competence of the responsible government agencies. Dowding himself shared official responsibility: he had signed the new airship's certificate of airworthiness just two days before the fatal flight. Making things worse, if possible, when the news broke upon a shocked Cabinet, the CAS was out of touch in his remote country cottage.[5]

Dowding never tried to dodge his share of blame, stating with typical bluntness, "I was wrong not to insist on much more extensive trials and tests," and explaining with painful candor that he had been "in my new saddle for only a few weeks" when called upon either to endorse or halt a project in which the Air Ministry, the Government, and the British public had invested great hopes. He himself laid no claim to the specialized expertise required to evaluate the technical controversies surrounding the airship's design, although characteristically, he participated personally in R-101's final, sixteen-hour test flight. Over the course of what was by this point a thirty-year military career, Dowding had developed an ingrained wariness of official wisdom in the areas of strategy and organization. Reflecting that, "I was not sufficiently self-confident to set my personal opinion against that of the technical experts," the R-101 disaster added a new dimension to his chronic skepticism.[6]

Almost incredibly, a week after systemic failure claimed the lives of, among others, not only one of Britain's most famous aviation experts, but in addition, the Cabinet member at the head of his own ministry, the chief of Air Staff pressed Dowding to authorize a flight to the Middle East by R-101's sister ship (albeit of a different design) the R-100. That Salmond would make such a request in the midst of national shock over the crash, just two days after the memorial service for the dead, and well before the technical investigations and the official inquiry could even begin, forcefully illustrates the strength of the political and economic interests behind the airship program. The terms in which the CAS conveyed his request, "I am personally anxious the R-100 should do the trip," speak volumes about the RAF's "Trenchardist" leadership culture, Salmond's character, and the integrity that led Dowding to say "no."

It seems likely that Dowding's intransigence regarding the airship program in the aftermath of the R-101 disaster helped consolidate a reputation among his peers for negativity and lack of team spirit, and it is certainly possible that it permanently affected his relationship with Salmond, especially if—consciously or unconsciously—the CAS took Dowding's stance as reflecting poorly on his own integrity. (It should be noted that, in later years, he specifically disclaimed having been subjected to "pressure" to authorize the fatal flight of R-101.) The AMSR's internal dissent broke into the open, and created public controversy, with his testimony before the official inquiry. Newspapers reported that, "Vice Marshal [*sic*] Dowding alone of all today's witnesses did not think the ship was in shape for her first long voyage." Dowding's testimony before the inquiry is evidence that "pernickety primness" had been forged by the fires that consumed R-101 into a steely resolve to speak the truth as he knew it, "though the heavens fall."[7]

Not only did he make no effort to evade or mitigate his own responsibility in the disaster, he drew attention to facts that brought into question his own knowledge and judgment. For example, Dowding testified that the airship captain did not follow his direction to complete previously postponed full-power tests immediately after liftoff. Other testimony noted that there was no written order for a further test, and experts opined that the captain had exercised good judgment in not improvising a stress test at the outset of a long-endurance flight. Overall, the general impression given by the inquiry report is that the handoff of responsibility as AMSR from Air Marshal Higgins to his successor was unfortunately timed, and that the Air Ministry Research Department allowed the R-101 program managers to cut corners in testing, in order to inaugurate passenger service on time. The inquiry panel specifically concluded that this happened, in significant part, because the program managers, in their turn, were overconfident.[8]

More broadly, the R-101 disaster and its disturbing sequel highlight the wickedly complex interaction of bureaucratic, political, economic, technological, and strategic challenges facing Dowding and his Air Council colleagues. Dowding's most important share of the broader challenges facing the service was adapting the RAF to the ongoing revolution in aircraft design, which saw monoplanes supplanting biplanes, and metal replacing wood and fabric in construction. Adaptation involved a gradual, but ultimately decisive break with the service's Trenchard-era standards and practices regarding the acquisition of technology. As early as 1924, specialists on the Air Staff warned that aircraft acquisition, and indeed the entire British aircraft industry, were being hamstrung by the Air Ministry's uneconomical proliferation of excessively restrictive technical requirements. Trenchard and his deputies blocked major acquisition reforms during the 1920s, but on Dowding's watch the Air Ministry began to publish general specifications that embodied statements of "ideal" performance characteristics tied to operational requirements in place of highly detailed design requirements.[9]

During Dowding's tenure as AMSR "the whole attitude of the service" toward the acquisition of technology changed, although change came neither easily nor quickly to the Trenchard-ist Air Ministry. When in 1933 Dowding sought "to cut development times by half," by consolidating operational requirements for new aircraft and informally circulating them to industry before formally soliciting bids, it took the Air Council until 1935 to give the idea final approval. As AMSR, he had to tread carefully around the opinions and preferences of successive chiefs of Air Staff and their inner circles of advisers. Not only colleagues such as the deputy chief of Air Staff (DCAS) but also relatively junior officers holding key portfolios, such as flying operations and director of operations and intelligence, were empowered to critique AMSR plans, policies, and decisions, and promote their own ideas, in practice circumscribing Dowding's nominal mandate. Getting results would depended at least as much on his patience and negotiating skills, as on formal, positional authority.[10]

Sometimes Dowding himself utilized delaying tactics. On taking over as AMSR, he inherited a bureaucratic stalemate regarding the specification for a follow-on to the Bristol Bulldog, one of the RAF's standard, biplane fighters. Desire for substantially increased speed and a better field of vision for the pilot pointed toward adopting a monoplane design; fears that industry was not ready to produce a reliable, military monoplane, combined with the increasing uncertainty of future funding from the Treasury, suggested that taking what one could get immediately was the better part of wisdom. Dowding, however, was in no hurry to push development of yet another generation of biplanes. Accepting the risk of waiting, he teamed up with his sometime rival Newall, then deputy chief of Air Staff, to buy time for monoplane development to mature. Together, they persuaded the CAS to postpone the decision regarding a Bulldog replacement.

Part of the problem was conflicting priorities. As air member for supply as well as research, it was Dowding's responsibility to balance a host of industrial-production factors against desirable technical innovation. Attempts to exploit the acquisition process to promote technical innovation sometimes clashed with efforts to nourish struggling aircraft manufacturers with procurement contracts. Since the end of the Great War, the Air Ministry had doled out contracts among the few potentially viable aircraft-manufacturing firms at least as much to, in effect, subsidize the industrial base of British airpower, as to meet current aircraft requirements. The AMSR also had to reckon with the political power as well as the market position of Britain's aircraft manufacturers, notably exerted through an industry trade association known as SBAC (Society of British Aircraft Constructors). SBAC could, and did, take its members' complaints to the Cabinet when Air Staff endeavors to improve acquisition processes encroached upon what the businessmen considered their due.[11]

After nearly a year of patient bureaucratic maneuvering, Dowding secured approval of a specification that was open to "low wing" monoplanes as well as biplanes, and to both air-cooled and liquid-cooled engines. From this historic Specification F.7/30,[12] issued in September of 1931, flowed the development stream that eventually resulted in the RAF's acquisition of high-speed monoplane fighters, as well as the intimately related development of new types of high-performance aircraft engines, such as the Rolls Royce engine that would evolve into the world-famous Merlin. In a practice he would continue as air officer commanding-in-chief of a combatant command, as AMSR Dowding allowed considerable independence to his principal subordinates, such as the director of technical development (DTD). While the Air Staff struggled to reconcile operational requirements and rapidly evolving technological potentialities, the DTD was working closely with Hawker Aircraft and Supermarine Aviation on advanced designs following on from the initial responses to Specification F.7/30.[13]

The foregoing does not mean that the RAF's—or Dowding's—path to acquiring the high-performance fighters of 1940 was straight, clear, or short. Throughout the early 1930s the Air Staff and the Air Defence of Great Britain (ADGB) command were deeply embroiled in a debate over the intertwined issues of fighter-aircraft characteristics and fighter tactics. Many of the RAF's most senior and influential leaders, including successive AOC-in-Cs of ADGB— Sir Edward Ellington, Sir Geoffrey Salmond, and Sir Robert Brooke-Popham—were convinced that the only feasible approach to defensive counter-air operations was to use the concentrated fire power of fighters in mass formations to "break up" incoming bomber formations. Discounting single-seat aircraft because of their inability to fight in formation, they called for two-seat fighters featuring movable machine guns. Essentially, these veterans envisaged fighters of the future as faster versions of World War One vintage aircraft such as the Bristol F2.[14]

Compared to many of his colleagues, Dowding was much more impressed by the tactical potential of the single-seat, monoplane fighter with fixed, forward-firing guns. Indeed, the Air Staff actually opposed the multi-gun fighter, predicting poor aerodynamic performance. The AMSR was unbeguiled by visions of fighters cruising in mass formations and using enemy bomber formations for target practice, probably because he relied on the results of practical experiments, rather than "vision," to inform his thinking regarding future requirements. Dowding's "air firing trials" produced statistical evidence that a single-seat fighter with multiple, forward-firing fixed guns was actually more likely to score fatal hits on enemy aircraft than the gunner in a two-seater firing a movable, twin machine gun. Promotion to the rank of air marshal (three-star or lieutenant general equivalent) in January 1933, should have fortified Dowding's ability to drive home his conclusions, but the hand of fate intervened to give the RAF a new chief of Air Staff with a contrary agenda regarding fighter development.[15]

The New Year's 1933 personnel moves saw Jack Salmond, after just three years in office, hand over as CAS to his brother Geoffrey. Unfortunately, within days the latter was diagnosed with terminal cancer. To succeed him, the secretary of state for air, Lord Londonderry, eventually selected Ellington, apparently by virtue of seniority. Jack's retirement at the early age of fifty-two, together with Geoffrey's untimely death, not only cost the RAF the services of two of the most experienced, and arguably the two most successful, operational-level combat commanders in its short history, but also catapulted to its head an officer with no experience of wartime operational command, and almost no personal experience as a flyer. Ellington was perhaps the RAF's most accomplished senior staff officer and administrator, but some insiders worried that "Uncle Ted," as he was known in the service (whether affectionately, or dismissively, or both) lacked the force of character necessary in the top job.[16]

A particular problem for Dowding was that the new CAS, having served not only as ADGB commander, but also as director of aircraft production and research in 1919–20, clung tenaciously to his well-developed, albeit obsolete, ideas regarding air-to-air combat and fighter aircraft. Uncle Ted immediately reversed the development priority for a single-seat fighter with fixed, forward-firing guns, and funded his own pet project: a two-man fighter with dual controls and fore-and-aft gunnery positions. The CAS's design concept, which fully justified his self-conscious comment that, "I do not expect that the first attempt will produce a very satisfactory machine," was never built. Instead, the Air Staff eventually persuaded him to abandon his wildly impractical idea of a push-me–pull-you fighter with crewmen at opposite ends of the fuselage alternating as pilot and gunner, in favor of the only slightly more plausible concept of a "turret fighter" whose pilot would concentrate on flying in formation while a crewman aimed the guns.[17]

The ultimate outcome of the obsession with aerial combat between mass formations of bombers and fighters was to be the Boulton-Paul Defiant, which featured no fixed, forward armament and a gunner literally trapped in a four-gun turret behind the pilot. The turret could traverse forward to fire over the pilot's head, but its guns could not be depressed to fire either directly ahead, or forward and downward. The tactical concept was that formations of Defiants would cruise along beneath enemy bomber formations, picking them off from below. Unsurprisingly, in actual combat the turret fighter concept failed catastrophically. Not only did the weight of the turret preclude the speed and agility necessary to bring its weapons to bear on high-performance enemy aircraft; its four machine guns were in any case hopelessly outclassed by the firepower of its rivals. The brutal attrition suffered by the Defiants in 1940 fully validated Dowding's prediction that this aeronautical monstrosity would be helpless against single-seat fighters.

The AMSR, along with some of the sharper minds on the Air Staff, also understood that the coming generation of fast, multiengine, monoplane bombers, each self-defended by multiple machine guns as well as armor plating, would make difficult targets even for heavily armed, high-performance fighters. They perceived that the key to future fighter effectiveness would be somehow to combine maximum speed, rate of climb, and agility with maximum firepower. With the monoplanes coming off the drawing boards promising vastly increased speeds, Dowding and his colleagues sought a corresponding increase in firepower, by either multiplying the longstanding, standard fighter armament of twin machine guns, or by substituting 20 mm cannon for the machine guns. Dowding recognized that the "cannon fighter" would provide optimal firepower, but problems with the reliability, size, and weight of available cannon (including the weight of the ammunition) pushed him toward choosing eight fixed, forward-firing machine guns as an interim solution.[18]

By the fall of 1934 two firms, Hawker and Supermarine, had each produced designs Dowding was willing to purchase in prototype. In a remarkable instance of serendipity, the need to meet the eight-gun specification by accommodating four in each wing inspired Supermarine's Reginald Mitchell to give his design its famous elliptical wings, vastly improving the aerodynamic performance of the Spitfire. Colin Sinnott, having exhaustively and persuasively analyzed the acquisition of the Spitfire and Hawker Hurricane prototypes, concludes tartly that Dowding, "did not consult the Air Staff" before placing the orders. It was thus Dowding's initiative, based on the work of his subordinates in the AMSR Directorate of Technical Development, which produced this famous and critically important leap forward in RAF fighter performance. The telling contrast between this historic achievement, and the record of British bomber development in the decade of the 1930s, underscores the failure of Dowding and his colleagues to achieve a similar, timely advance in bomber development.[19]

Shortly after becoming AMSR, Dowding presented a specification for a high-speed aircraft carrying double the bomb load of the RAF's current, standard day bomber. So-called day bombers traded heavy bomb and fuel loads for speed and/or defensive armament; night bombers sacrificed speed for bomb load and range, flying under cover of darkness to improve their chances of evading interception. Carrying heavy loads of both bombs and fuel, as well as defensive armament, ammunition, and multiple crewmen, meant big aircraft. Just as Dowding's "high speed development work" had led eventually to the Hurricane and Spitfire, approval of the specification for a high-performance, multi-role bomber as early as 1930 might well have set in motion timely development of long-range, "heavy" bomber types that could have been operationally effective in the conditions of 1939–41. In this case, however, facing objections from Air Staff Flying Operations (F.O.1) "that the proposed aircraft was unduly large," Dowding backed down.

Although RAF leaders recognized the advantages of bombers capable of both day and night operations, F.O.1 favored giving priority in bomber development to speed, to help neutralize the threat of interception. Increasing operational range did not seem particularly urgent; for imperial defense and colonial control missions the Air Staff still preferred compact aircraft easily transported by ship. Such views were not quite so myopic as they may seem in light of later events. Neither imperial Japan nor fascist Italy was on the march; Germany was still effectively disarmed under a parliamentary regime committed to peaceful revision of the Versailles Treaty. Conditioned by memories of the Dreadnought-building naval race a generation earlier, which many believed had contributed to the outbreak of war, British foreign policy emphasized nipping in the bud a potential race to build bigger, better bombers. While disarmament negotiations were underway at Geneva, therefore, the British government suspended bomber procurement, and imposed a weight limit on new designs.

In addition to the potential political backlash against proposals to develop heavy bombers, technical and financial factors reinforced the reluctance of Dowding and his colleagues to press the issue. The Air Staff consistently overestimated the physical and psychological effects of bombing; and consequently, it tended to discount the significance of heavier bomb loads, much as they discounted the importance of increasing bombers' operational radius.[20] As Dowding himself correctly anticipated, moreover, British aircraft manufacturers resisted investing the vast amounts of capital required, not only to solve the complex design problems posed by next-generation, multiengine, long-range heavy bombers (and transports) but also to expand and retool the aviation industrial base in order to produce such behemoths. Despite the burgeoning potentialities of the ongoing revolution in aeronautical technology, therefore, all these varied considerations seemed to validate the RAF's go-slow approach to bomber development.

In the circumstances, the Air Staff naturally, if unimaginatively, thought in terms of replacing aging aircraft with somewhat faster, but otherwise generally similar, types.[21] Three of the five aircraft operational in Bomber Command at the beginning of the Second World War, the Handley-Page Hampden, the Vickers Wellington, and the Fairey Battle, developed out of initial specifications issued during this period. The Hampden was a relatively capable bomber for its day, with a top speed of 265 mph and a 4,000-pound maximum bomb load, although its small, cramped fuselage—a result of the Government's arbitrary weight limit—limited its operational usefulness. The slower Wellington (top speed 235 mph) could carry a slightly more robust 4,500 pounds of bombs, and its larger airframe proved highly adaptable; successive, upgraded models operated effectively as "medium" bombers throughout the war. Neither aircraft, however, possessed the combination of range and bomb load needed for strategic bombing operations against Germany.[22]

The most ill fated of the RAF's prewar bomber acquisitions was the 1932-vintage Battle. The specification that led Fairey Aircraft to tender this design was for a high-performance, monoplane bomber. Dowding pinned his hopes for "high performance" on the development of a new engine, the Griffon, which unfortunately was not produced in time to be married to Fairey's airframe.[23] Thus, like so many aircraft developed during the aeronautical transformation of the thirties (including its fighter equivalent the Defiant) the Battle proved obsolescent upon delivery for service. Even when equipped with the versatile Merlin engine, the Battle possessed neither sufficient range and bomb load for strategic bombing on the one hand, nor the speed and maneuverability for tactical attack roles, on the other. In May of 1940, eight squadrons of Battles attained an awful immortality in RAF history, losing thirty-five of sixty-three aircraft in an inexpressibly brave, utterly futile effort to prevent German panzer divisions from crossing the Meuse River.

The constraints that nearly stultified British bomber development slowly began to lift as the Geneva Disarmament Conference staggered toward eventual collapse, and Britain's vulnerability to air attack erupted into a hotly debated domestic political issue. Airpower actually seemed to be elbowing aside sea power as the central pillar of national security. Conservative Party leader Stanley Baldwin summed up the national anxiety in November 1932, with a remark in the House of Commons that, quoted or misquoted, and often misattributed, has reverberated through the history of airpower: "No power on earth can protect the man in the street from being bombed . . . the bomber will always get through." Winston Churchill, officially a Conservative although excluded from the coalition National Government formed in 1931, chided his nominal Leader for a speech that "led to no practical conclusion," but Baldwin in fact had accurately summarized the informed public's understanding of the situation.[24]

Educated public opinion in Britain linked two political assumptions together with one military assumption to form a widely shared chain of strategic reasoning: (1) failure to reach international agreement on arms limitation would result in an arms race; (2) an arms race would lead to another great war; and (3) in the next great war, Britain would be exposed to devastating air attack. Within the mental framework created by these assumptions, British leaders struggled to cope with the erosion of the post–World War international order. Then, in January 1933, what a well-placed army officer on the staff of the Committee of Imperial Defence described as the "ultra-nationalistic, saber-rattling Nazi government" came to power in Germany. The increasingly apparent failure of international "conference diplomacy" to achieve positive results, combined with the unnerving apparition of Adolf Hitler as German chancellor, impelled British leaders to reassess defense force structure requirements comprehensively for the first time since the early 1920s.[25]

To develop a new planning basis, the Committee of Imperial Defence

(CID) spun off a Defence Requirements Committee (DRC) composed of representatives from the Army, Navy, Air Force, Foreign Office, and Treasury, charged with identifying "the worst deficiencies" in Britain's defense posture, and proposing remedies. Working through the winter of 1933–34, the DRC readily agreed that, notwithstanding the clear and present threat posed by Japanese expansionism to British economic interests and imperial security, "Germany must be regarded as the ultimate danger." Despite this already daunting global threat environment, however, the DRC report suggested only modest modernization and infrastructure improvements for the Navy; preparations for an updated version of the small British Expeditionary Force of the pre-1914 era (approximately equivalent to two army corps); and completion of the RAF's fifty-two-squadron Home Defence Air Force, whose development had been on hold since 1931, along with ten additional squadrons for imperial defense, and a further ten squadrons for expansion of the Naval Air Arm.[26]

The bland prose and moderate terms of the DRC report concealed contentious and possibly irreconcilable differences regarding the capacity of all three services to carry out their prescribed roles and missions. Concerning the RAF, two issues stood out. First, the DRC simply deferred the whole question of fighters for the defense of England's industrial midlands, the north of England, and Scotland—areas that would be within range of "modern" bombers operating from bases in northwestern Germany, to say nothing of the worst-case scenario of German bases in the Low Countries. A second, related problem was that a new BEF, implicitly intended to once again help defend the Low Countries and northwestern France, would need an air component. The DRC report assumed this would be supplied out of the resources of the Home Defence Air Force. Amid the open skepticism of his fellow chiefs of staff and the dismay of his Air Ministry colleagues, Ellington endorsed this assumption.

Ellington's gaffe provoked consternation because the air officers still envisioned the Home Defence Air Force as primarily a strategic bombing force with a deterrence/second-strike role, not to be frittered away in tactical support of ground forces. Accordingly, they insisted that the RAF could not supply an air component for a new BEF out of the Home Defence Air

Force's projected fifty-two squadrons. Literally at the last minute, when the DRC was meeting to approve its report, Ellington had to concede, humiliatingly, that his colleagues were demanding that he redo his sums. The issue of the RAF's proper size and composition thus became entangled with the prospect of once again dispatching a BEF to defend from German attack the same ground liberated at the cost of nearly a million British dead less than a generation earlier. The failure to persuasively articulate the RAF's position created a fateful political vacuum at the center of the defense policy-making process.[27]

As air member for supply and research, Dowding was, second to Ellington, on the hottest of Air Council's hot seats during this crucial period, for it was during this period that Dowding's "supply" portfolio came to encompass some of the most strategically critical and politically charged issues in British national defense policy. By the end of 1933 the longest-tenured member of the Air Council, as one of the handful of senior air officers best placed to shape the destiny of the RAF at a defining moment in its institutional history, Dowding must bear a full share of the Air Council's collective responsibility for the collective leadership failures in the period that Churchill later memorably described as the "years for the locusts to eat."[28]

5
THE AIR COUNCIL
1933–1936

Sir Hugh Dowding—as he became when appointed a Knight Commander of the Order of the Bath in the fall of 1933—at age fifty-one was within reach of the top of his service. In the bureaucratic profession of modern military service, three years represented a normal-length senior-officer assignment. To this point, what did the RAF have to show for the Supply and Research Department's years under Dowding's leadership? It is tempting to conclude very little, other than protracted wrangling over innumerable obscure, bureaucratic processes that had yet to yield much in the way of material results. What would become the best-known accomplishment of Dowding's first three years as AMSR, acquisition of the Hurricane and Spitfire fighters, was still months away even from flying prototypes. Unknown, and indeed to this day still unmeasured, was his contribution to the expansion scheme that ultimately would form the skeleton of the later, wartime RAF.

Amid the Air Ministry's continuing struggle to articulate a coherent position regarding its own force structure, overall defense policy making took a fateful turn with a decisive intervention by the chancellor of the exchequer, Neville Chamberlain. If the mood of the nation was massaged and manipulated by Baldwin, a master of therapeutic politics, such energy and direction in national security affairs as the National Government possessed came from Chamberlain, a historical figure almost universally recognizable, and almost universally misunderstood. The clichéd image of a naïve senior citizen with the wardrobe of a Victorian-era bank manager and a matching demeanor belies the reality of a politician with a ferocious will to power. Lacking expertise or experience in international relations or military policy, Chamberlain made up the deficiency with sheer self-confidence and assertiveness, as well—to be fair—as a proclivity for hard work, a capacity for logical thought, and a talent for rigorous argumentation: all qualities in short supply among his political contemporaries.[1]

Consequently, by the mid-thirties Chamberlain came to dominate British politics and policy making, imposing clear priorities on a wavering Cabinet and a disjointed military establishment. Assisted by the permanent secretary to the Treasury, Sir Warren Fisher, Chamberlain systematically exploited his authority over the Government's budget to rewrite the "deficiency program" put forward by the Defence Requirements Committee. Envisioning airpower not as one essential component of a joint defense force, but rather, as a cost-effective alternative to surface forces, the chancellor argued for slashing the expensive improvements the DRC had proposed for the navy, and especially those proposed for the army, not only on grounds of economy but also of strategic focus. Chamberlain produced an airpower centered plan, calculated not only to save money, but also to preclude the risk of Britain once more being drawn into a "continental commitment" of ground combat forces in another European war.[2]

Having previously summed up Britain's position with a typically categorical insistence that, "today financial and economic risks are by far the most serious and urgent that the country has to face and . . . other risks have to be run," Chamberlain rejected broad-based rearmament. The chancellor instead focused defense policy on what he, like most other Britons at the time—very much including Churchill—considered the most deadly, indeed the only really mortal, military threat: the possibility of a massive, all-out air attack on Britain at the outset of a future war. However unfortunate for Britain's overall military capacity to defend the totality of its imperial interests, Chamberlain's conception of national military strategy seemed to be good news for the RAF. Ironically, however, uncritical air-mindedness was to rebound unhelpfully not only on Chamberlain's fiscal conservatism, but also on Air Staff dogmatism. The RAF would prove incapable of justifying faith in the magical properties of airpower.

Concern over current and projected numbers of aircraft in the RAF inventory grew into a political mania, with the pause in RAF expansion attracting increasingly strident condemnation in the press and in parliament.[3] Seeking to placate the critics, in March of 1934 the Government promised the House of Commons that no nation would be allowed to outbuild Britain in airpower. The Government thus de facto committed itself to maintaining air parity with Germany, generally understood to mean roughly equal numbers of first-line military aircraft. Consequently, secret intelligence received shortly thereafter indicating that Germany's undeclared but well-known air rearmament was already on pace to outmatch the planned RAF expansion thrust the Cabinet onto the horns of a dilemma: a prominent minority of the Government's own supporters in Parliament began lining up to insist that the air-parity promise was at risk, yet both the Treasury and, surprisingly, the Air Ministry, opposed rapid, all-out air force expansion.[4]

The rapid pivot in political attitudes toward rearming and expanding the RAF was nowhere better illustrated than in the reaction when the National Government eventually presented its air expansion program to Parliament. Based on a July 1934 plan that the RAF called "Scheme A," the numbers in this and in the numerous, later RAF expansion schemes were—perhaps intentionally—thoroughly confusing to nonexperts. The Air Ministry's initial proposal, a five-year program, would have doubled the existing 42 home-based air squadrons to 84, while significantly altering the balance between bomber and fighter squadrons in the Home Defence Air Forces, from 2:1 to 4:3 (48 bomber squadrons and 36 fighter squadrons). The latter change flowed from increasing external demands for Fleet Air Arm and Army Cooperation aircraft, rather than from any change of doctrinal heart by the Air Staff regarding the relative importance of bombers and fighters.[5]

Critics at the time (and since) castigated the relatively modest increase in offensive striking power promised by Scheme A, which included just 9 more bomber squadrons than had been projected in the still-incomplete, 1923 program. Churchill, in his imitable style, scorned the legislation as "tiny, timid, tentative [and] tardy," but Chamberlain championed the Treasury belief that Britain could not financially sustain large-scale rearmament over an extended period of time. Churchill also deplored the staid pace of the proposed program, slated for completion in 1939. Sweeping aside assurances from Government spokesmen, Churchill insisted that the still officially unacknowledged German air rearmament would outstrip British strength in the air within two years. For its part, the Air Ministry rejected the whole concept of rapid, massive expansion of its force structure. Was the root of the matter, as some historians have suggested, the stultifying effect on innovation of "Trenchardist" institutional conservatism?[6]

Under Trenchard in the 1920s the RAF developed firm doctrinal precepts, techniques, and procedures for dealing with the organization, training, and equipment of air forces. Clearly his protégés and successors, regarding their standard operating procedures as best practices, found it difficult to think outside the mental box they had created for themselves. Even if the National Government had been willing to find ways and means to pay for it, RAF leaders believed, rapid expansion would be inherently flawed, capable of producing only an unsound, "shop window" force. Partnering with industry to assimilate new aviation technologies, expanding airfields and other infrastructure, recruiting and training a new generation of ground support personnel as well as pilots, developing new tactics as well as new command-and-control techniques, and finally, absorbing practical experience and integrating all these elements into operationally effective airpower, required time—years of institutional maturation.[7]

As a result of such overly rigid assumptions about the development of force structure, Air Ministry planning excluded the possibility that an air force could undertake rapid, large-scale expansion without sacrificing long-run quality. Well within Churchill's predicted two-year window, however, the Air Ministry consensus proved to have been a miscalculation of nearly catastrophic proportions. Indeed, the whole course of events stands as a classic object lesson in the dangers of assuming that an enemy, or a potential enemy, cannot or will not do something, simply because it is something that you cannot, or will not, do yourself. Some, at least, of the Air Ministry resistance to more rapid expansion likely emanated from Dowding, who up to 1935 was the Air Council member most directly concerned, and who had a long record of strong and consistent commitment to what he considered to be empirically tested, functionally rational organizational processes.

While quantitative expansion was being self-retarded, qualitative progress slightly accelerated as Dowding and his colleagues reached, and crossed, a watershed in bomber development. First, a new deputy chief of Air Staff, Sir Edgar Ludlow-Hewitt, proposed doing away with the distinction between day bombers and night bombers, and instead building a force of dual-use, light, medium, and heavy bombers.[8] A few weeks later, Ellington acknowledged that the German walkouts from both the League of Nations and the negotiations on international arms limitation had changed the political calculus of British defense policy. A key Air Staff planner, Group Captain Arthur Harris (subsequently renowned as "Bomber" Harris) argued straightforwardly that Britain needed bombers with the range to strike critical targets in Germany from bases in the United Kingdom, as well as similar targets in Russia, from bases in India. Dowding brought the issue to a head by formally requesting removal of the weight limit on bomber designs.[9]

Dowding's concerns at this time centered on "the very superior performance of the Heavy Bombers in the possession of certain other powers," including but not limited to the United States. He also stressed the importance of accelerating the overall pace of aircraft acquisition. Ellington responded by instructing Dowding to give the aircraft manufacturers greater leeway in designing new bombers, and even proposed buying examples of the latest American types as a shortcut. Dowding promptly dispatched his director of technical developments to the United States, meanwhile soliciting tenders from selected British aircraft manufacturers, in an effort to encourage the sort of design competition that seemed to be working well for the US Army Air Corps. Dowding's efforts met concerted opposition from leading members of the Society of British Aircraft Constructors (SBAC) who, as "Uncle Ted" commented wryly to Dowding after a particularly contentious meeting, had "frequently pressed for a free hand [but] now are afraid of receiving it."[10]

Information gathered in the United States regarding new design work by the Martin and Boeing Aircraft companies led Dowding's staff to begin rewriting bomber specifications, based on a new set of operational requirements, which included a 2,000-pound bomb load, a 2,000-mile range, a 230 mph top speed, and three defensive gun positions—characteristics (except for the weaker defensive armament) very similar to the Boeing prototype soon to become world-famous as the B-17 Flying Fortress. The Air Ministry circulated these new requirements in May of 1935, some nine months after the US Army Air Corps launched the design competition that led to the B-17, and just two months before the initial flight test of Boeing's prototype, Model 299. Unlike the USAAC development project, which was publicly justified by a vaguely defined (and by the US Navy much contested) coastal defense mission, the RAF specification was explicitly, if secretly, keyed to a specific, strategic bombing mission: attacking Germany.

The first fruit of the Air Ministry's 1934–35 bomber development push was the Armstrong-Whitworth Whitley, a prototype of which flew early in 1936, and which began delivery for squadron service a year later, becoming the RAF's first operational, monoplane heavy bomber. Armstrong-Whitworth achieved this remarkably speedy design-to-delivery cycle partly by revising plans originally drawn up to meet a specification for a dual-use, troop transport/bomber, and partly by making ease of construction a priority. The result was, unlike its better-known, American contemporary, a twin-engine design that sacrificed speed and range, as well as strength of defensive firepower, in order to carry up to 7,000 pounds of bombs. Despite its limitations, however, Whitleys accounted for much of what little actual weight of explosives Bomber Command could (optimistically speaking) deliver on target at the outbreak of war in 1939. To Whitleys fell the honor of carrying out the RAF's first long-range bombing missions against both the German and the Italian mainlands.[11]

At the light end of the RAF's mid-thirties bomber acquisition spectrum was the Blenheim, a military adaptation of a fast, six-passenger transport offered to the Air Ministry by Bristol Aircraft. The ministry, with unusual flexibility, responded to the offer by writing a specification to fit the characteristics of Bristol's design, which consequently became operational as the Blenheim in the spring of 1937. Although later, improved models of the Blenheim, like various upgrades of the heavier Wellington, proved operationally effective in numerous wartime roles and missions, neither they nor any of the other aircraft that together made up Bomber Command's front-line strength of 992 in September 1939 were adequate strategic bombers. Despite these advances, astoundingly for a service that based its institutional identity on the concept of strategic air attack, at the outbreak of hostilities the RAF lacked aircraft with the necessary combination of bomb load, range, speed and defensive armament to carry out serious bombing operations against the German enemy.[12]

Making every allowance for the financial and industrial realities that continued to hamstring planning for an immediate surge in heavy-bomber production, the Air Ministry's failure during 1935–36 to accelerate development, at least as far as the prototype stage, remains puzzling. Political leaders continued to believe in a credible, British strategic bomber force as the best deterrent to another German war, and perhaps even a lever for appeasement negotiations; the RAF leadership maintained the theory that, in the event of war, long-range aerial bombardment would be the correct employment for airpower; yet neither gave practical effect to their convictions. Arthur Harris, among others, continued to warn of the inadequacies of the RAF bomber force for a German war, yet the Air Ministry failed to launch a concerted effort to produce a great leap forward until the so-called "ideal bomber" study, begun after Dowding left the Air Council in the spring of 1936.

Over and above giving an all-too-modest impetus to heavy-bomber development, the salient accomplishment of Dowding's last two years on the Air Council, on par in historical importance with his acquisition of the Hurricane and Spitfire fighters, was his role in igniting a revolutionary transformation of military technology. Popular culture in the 1930s was filled with speculation, mostly of a science-fiction nature, about transformational weapons—death rays and the like. In those days, government officials and military staff officers in many countries devoted a surprising amount of unproductive time to investigating claims by professional visionaries and amateur inventors, partly to satisfy political sponsors of said visionaries and inventors, but also at times, it seems, to quell uncomfortable feelings that they might be spurning the next Thomas Edison or Orville Wright. Dowding, the very archetype of the no-nonsense decision maker impervious to such considerations, was quick to recognize and seize a moment of genuine opportunity.

As Churchill's caustic, parliamentary response to Baldwin's famous phrase, "the bomber will always get through" illustrated, the middle-aging statesman was growing restless, dissatisfied with airpower orthodoxy. Lending the weight of expert opinion to Churchill's suspicions of RAF dogma was a leading Oxford scientist and administrator, and Churchill intimate, Frederick Lindemann. A famously aggressive controversialist in scientific and technical matters, with special credibility in the domain of aviation due to his important, technical discoveries while flight testing during the World War, when Lindemann utilized the upper-class Englishman's megaphone, a letter to the *Times*, the challenge to RAF assumptions regarding bomber supremacy became unignorable. In November, 1934, the Air Ministry's director of scientific research, a civil servant named Henry E. Wimperis, sent a memorandum to the secretary of state for air, Lord Londonderry, as well as Ellington and Dowding, warning that dynamic changes in technology were affecting the capabilities and limitations of airpower in unpredictable ways.

Arguing that the technological dimension of airpower required systematic and focused oversight from the very top of government, Wimperis advocated forming a group of independent science advisors, with direct access to the Committee of Imperial Defence. Wimperis's initiative represented his own judgment regarding the urgency of the RAF's overall research and development needs, but it also reflected steadily intensifying external pressure. Largely in accordance with Wimperis's proposal, the CID created an Air Defence Research subcommittee. In December, the Air Ministry followed suit with its own Committee for the Scientific Survey of Air Defence (CSSAD), chaired by another eminent scientist and university administrator, Henry Tizard. At Dowding's insistence, the CSSAD was placed under his authority as air member for research and development. At its first meeting, in January 1935, the CSSAD (soon better known as the Tizard Committee) reviewed a paper on the air-defense potential of an early warning technique known as "radio reflection."[13]

Championing the use of radio reflection for air-defense early warning was physicist Robert Watson-Watt. Radio direction finding, or RDF (later universally referred to by the American acronym *radar*, for radio direction and ranging), represented an evolutionary advance in technology with revolutionary military consequences. Tizard's panel immediately grasped the significance of Watson-Watt's paper, and asked Dowding to allocate £10,000, a modest sum equivalent to something like $1 million in today's money, to build a prototype. Dowding in this case indeed proved "stuffy." In a move characteristic of his empirical, incremental approach to innovation, he insisted on a practical demonstration with existing laboratory equipment before he would authorize the expenditure. An improvised experiment at the BBC's Daventry shortwave radio station succeeded in tracking an aged Heyford bomber at ranges up to eight miles, which so satisfied Dowding that he expansively promised Wimperis "all the money he wanted," before recovering himself to add, more typically, "within reason."[14]

After the Daventry test, the Tizard Committee moved quickly to develop RDF technology and apply it to air defense. Having firmly established his control of the Air Ministry's work on RDF, Dowding zealously defended its independence throughout the ensuing bureaucratic-political infighting, of a sort typical of large-scale, governmental undertakings. Such protection was much needed: the bureaucratic-political challenges were formidable, and could easily have prevented Britain from developing radar in time to be militarily useful by 1940. With fine, historical irony, one obstacle Dowding had to maneuver around was none other than Winston Churchill. Still excluded from the Cabinet, nevertheless from his famous front-row seat "below the gangway" in the House of Commons Churchill exercised considerable, and after 1935 growing, influence in defense matters. Churchill thought the RDF project, along with other air-defense research and development projects, should be placed under the centralized control of the CID subcommittee, of which he just happened to be a member.[15]

At face value, such centralization seemed to represent a reasonable way of organizing defense research and development, but implementing Churchill's ideas would have complicated the Air Ministry's ability to coordinate the technical development of radar with its application to air defense. Of particular concern to Dowding and Tizard was the near-certainty of disruption by Lindemann, Churchill's friend and ally, but Tizard's archrival. "The Prof," as Churchill called him, resented both Tizard's position as CSSAD chairman, and the fact that work on RDF was displacing research on infrared detection, Lindemann's favored solution to the aircraft-warning problem. Churchill–Lindemann made a formidable team, which during the coming war frequently flattened opposition by the governmental science establishment (including Tizard) on important issues. In the case of RDF, however, the rival team of Dowding-Tizard displayed remarkable bureaucratic skill, sidelining Lindemann and neutralizing Churchill. Consequently, RDF development proceeded rapidly, and the RAF began field-testing its first radar station at Bawdsey, in September 1936.[16]

Dowding's key victory in what today would be called interagency governmental politics did not fully translate into success in the internal blood feuds of the RAF leadership. At the beginning of 1935, his job was essentially cut in half: he remained on the Air Council, now designated air member for research and development (AMRD), while a new post, "air member for supply and organization," was created to handle procurement. Adding spice to the situation, if not exactly insult to injury, the designated AMSO was none other than Cyril Newall. The Air Ministry's official history suggests that the decision reflected the need to focus leadership at the highest level on the transformation of aeronautical technology. And indeed, Dowding himself in later years seemed to agree that R and D on the one hand, and procurement on the other, each had become such large, complex enterprises that it was logical to assign to each a senior air officer as its chief executive.

Without necessarily contradicting the official account, it is, however, also correct to observe that the Air Ministry was thus assigning Newall what seemed at the time much the more immediately important area of responsibility. In the mid-thirties, the focal point of Government concern regarding airpower policy was not the quality of aircraft design, but the problem of "bridging" from peacetime production capacity to the required prewar and wartime levels of output.[17] The alteration in Dowding's responsibilities was, in fact, an early tremor in a much wider shake-up in Air Ministry leadership.

Lord Londonderry was to be forced out as secretary of state for air, in part because of perceived personal and political shortcomings, but also in part as a handy scapegoat for the Cabinet's collective failure to adequately address critical aircraft-procurement issues. Coincidentally, Londonderry's replacement, Sir Philip Cunliffe-Lister (soon to become Lord Swinton), was a longtime friend and sometime political patron of Newall.[18]

Hitler's announcement of the official reestablishment of the German air force in March of 1935, together with his boast that the new Luftwaffe already stood at "parity" with the RAF, transformed the National Government's long-running air-force policy dilemma into a domestic political crisis of the first magnitude. In May, the Cabinet publicly acknowledged previously secret estimates that the new Luftwaffe had actually been inaugurated with a 50 percent quantitative superiority over the RAF's metropolitan air strength. The Government dealt with the resulting domestic, political uproar by presenting to parliament the RAF's expansion "Scheme C." Scheme C was first in a series of disingenuous revisions of the RAF's expansion program designed to prevaricate with the Government's air-rearmament problems. Giving the appearance of massive commitments of resources to air-force expansion, the Government simulated responsiveness to parliamentary and public opinion, while actually allowing the Air Ministry to continue the slow, steady expansion that constituted its preferred course of action.[19]

As secretary of state for air, Swinton brought back to the Air Ministry the Scottish engineer, businessman, and political wire-puller, Lord Weir, who reached his interwar apogee of influence, as "industrial adviser" at the Air Ministry. Both men were close political associates of Stanley Baldwin, who in the spring of 1935 was about to begin his third and final tenure as prime minister. After bringing in Newall to backstop the lightly regarded Ellington, the four constituted an unofficial, inner decision-making group within the Air Ministry. Appointed to implement the group's decisions as director of production was a Weir protégé, Henry Disney. An ex-World War pilot, Disney lacked any obvious technical expertise in the industrial aspects of aircraft production, but his personal relationship with Weir made him a suitable front man. If Swinton and Weir thought that Newall, regarded by colleagues as "pleasant," would be more amenable to these new arrangements than Stuffy Dowding, there is no reason to suppose that they were wrong.[20]

Sweeping and substantive changes to RAF organization ensued during the first half of 1936. The umbrella organization Air Defence of Great Britain, which for more than a decade controlled all the RAF's home-based forces, was abolished, along with the even longer-standing Area commands under it. In place of ADGB, the Air Ministry created a series of functional commands, starting with Bomber Command, Fighter Command, and Coastal Command. Fighter Command would assume the functions formerly belonging to the old Fighting Area and Inland Area commands. Thus the responsibilities of the air officer commanding-in-chief, Fighter Command, would largely parallel those Dowding had held briefly as AOC, Fighting Area, in 1930. As a commander-in-chief, however, the new chief of Fighter Command would be directly responsible to the Air Council through the CAS. Ironically, in light of his next assignment, Dowding emerged as the most senior opponent of this "functional" reorganization of the service.[21]

Dowding considered centralizing in functional commands administrative control of what today would be termed "force sustainment" to be illogical and unworkable. While he agreed with the service consensus that wartime command and control of both offensive and defensive operations (in twenty-first-century parlance, the "strategic attack" and "defensive counter-air" missions) was too much for a single AOC-in-C, he believed that it would be equally impossible for the heads of the new functional commands to master all the crucial, administrative details down to the station (air base) and squadron levels. Even worse, crisscrossing Britain in the effort to administer their far-flung units, the functional AOC-in-Cs would be unable to exercise the "centralized control" that was, in airpower theory, the essence of operational-level air command. Conversely, Dowding also feared that depriving group commanders of control over their own logistics while leaving personnel under their control was a recipe for organizational chaos. He therefore strongly—and unavailingly—opposed the new structure.[22] After the stress test on the functional commands resulting from the Munich crisis, the Air Ministry was forced to admit officially that Dowding's judgment on this point had been correct.[23] At a minimum, the speedy reversal of the procurement reorganization is evidence that just eighteen months' experience sufficed to convince the Air Ministry that the division of responsibility had been a bad idea.

Long afterward, Dowding claimed that he was sent to Bentley Priory in the spring of 1936 to organize the new headquarters of Fighter Command with the understanding that, after a year, he would return to the Air Ministry as the next chief of Air Staff. To the detached observer, any expectations of the top job Dowding may have entertained seem, fairly obviously, to have been wishful thinking based on little more than his seniority, as well, perhaps, as kindly Uncle Ted's reluctance to crush the illusions of a longtime colleague. Newall had had "a good war," in 1914–18, helping to pioneer long-range, strategic bombing in the Royal Flying Corps, in the process leapfrogging Dowding in stature as an operational commander. In hindsight, it seems plain that in moving Newall from deputy chief of Air Staff, to AOC Middle East, and then back to the Air Council, RAF leaders were grooming him to be Ellington's successor. Splitting the AMSR's responsibilities may well have had a secondary purpose, beyond placing aircraft production firmly in the hands of Swinton and his coterie: gently downsize Ellington's role while pushing Newall forward and Dowding aside.[24]

Neither at the time, in some remarkably astringent correspondence with Ellington, nor in recollections for his authorized biographers, did Dowding attempt to conceal his chagrin on learning, early in 1937, that he would be passed over for CAS. In evaluating Dowding's later claim of having been misled it should be noted that the published excerpts from the correspondence do not explicitly make this complaint. The correspondence gives a unique insight into Dowding's psychology. For perhaps the only time prior to his retirement, he let slip his stoic mask of officership, revealing a man buffeted between a strong sense that he should behave with impersonal logic, and an even stronger need to express feelings, not only of disappointment, but of injustice. Viewed retrospectively across the events of 1940, Dowding's four and one-half years building Fighter Command and leading it into battle have come to seem, as he himself later suggested, a providential convergence of the man and the historic mission. Yet in 1936, the assignment looked very different. In the eyes of professional airmen, the new Fighter Command was distinctly secondary in importance to Bomber Command.

Dowding's fellow air marshals doubtless thought he had been safely relegated to Captain of the Second Eleven. Despite his conflicted status within the RAF elite, however, seniority and organizational prominence in January 1937 brought Dowding recognition from his service commensurate with his position: the final military promotion of his career, to air chief marshal, equivalent to a "full" or four-star general. The wider British establishment followed suit. Shortly after His Royal Highness the Duke of York (the first airman in the British royal family), succeeded to the throne as King George VI, the new monarch appointed Dowding one of his principal aides-de-camp. This position, which made Dowding the RAF's symbolic representative at the new Court, together with His Majesty's bestowal of the Grand Cross of the Royal Victorian Order (then as now a personal gift of the sovereign) may have been intended to help console Dowding for his failure to reach the very top of his service.[25]

Dowding's record as a member of the Air Council may appear in the guise of mere bureaucratic housekeeping, with disproportionate time and effort devoted to fine-tuning procedures and organizational processes. Certainly he was sensitive—perhaps oversensitive—to the importance of functionally rational organizational processes. Instinct may have led him to capitalize on the "high speed development project," but it was empirical testing that prompted his resistance to acquiring more biplanes in the early thirties, as well as, later, resistance to procuring a turret fighter. As a senior leader, Dowding was at his best when wielding positional authority to identify, empower, and protect his most productive subordinates, whether the staff of the Directorate of Technical Development fostering the evolution of Supermarine's racing machine into the Spitfire fighter, or the physicists and engineers turning radio reflection into an operational, aircraft-warning system. Dowding's leadership style was most effective when he teamed with a senior subordinate like Tizard, a considerable, professional figure in his own right.[26] All the abilities developed, knowledge gained, and skills honed in thirty-six years of military service were now to be tested and proved in Dowding's four and a half years as air officer commanding-in-chief, Fighter Command.

6

FIGHTER COMMAND

1936–1939

Beginning in the summer of 1936, Sir Hugh Dowding guided Fighter Command's development into an effective integrated air-defense (IAD) system. While the RAF's serial aircraft expansion schemes of 1930s were constantly overtaken by events and never completed as planned, the supporting ground infrastructure for Scheme A was put in place, on time, between 1937 and 1939. Simultaneously, elements of the old Air Defence of Great Britain (ADGB) were reoriented from defense against an attack from France to confront attack from Germany, with the Civilian Observer Corps and the Army Antiaircraft Artillery forces under the operational control of Fighter Command. An unprecedented network of control rooms and communications landlines developed out of the command, control, and communications (C^3) system created for ADGB, augmented by the "filter room" concept that evolved between 1925 and 1935 to prevent control rooms being swamped by floods of unprioritized data. The most important new element of the system was, of course, radar.[1]

"Inventing radar," one author mordantly observed, "was easy: any genius could do it." Dowding's contribution was not genius, as the word is conventionally understood, but rather a broad vision, based on years of command and staff experience, of both the air-defense problem and the practicable solutions, as well as a steady determination to patiently work through the manifold difficulties of implementing the solutions, and a willingness to make himself unpopular at the Air Ministry, if necessary, to secure the resources he considered necessary to accomplish his mission. Dowding not only had to integrate technology and personnel, but also drive the development of tactics, techniques, and procedures. Within weeks after he became AOC-in-C, processes Dowding had set in motion while on the Air Council began to mature. Over the next four years, he accomplished what Luftwaffe leaders would fail to achieve: institutionalizing innovation in a stable organization.[2]

The stand-up of Fighter Command coincided with a decisive turning point in the long, political struggle over the British response to the reemergence of German airpower. While the British defense establishment recognized from the inception of the Nazi regime that Hitler meant to carry the Weimar-era evasion of arms limitations to its logical conclusion by, among other things, building and operating a world-class air force, from 1933 until 1936 RAF leaders consistently downplayed the scale of the German airpower challenge. Even after Hitler in March of 1935 openly proclaimed the establishment of the Luftwaffe on a level of parity with the RAF, the Air Staff assumed that the Germans would not exploit their industrial potential in order to secure maximum quantitative advantages, but rather would concentrate on maximizing technical and operational efficiencies. During the first half of 1936, however, the Air Staff gradually discarded this, in effect, best-case scenario.[3]

By the fall of 1936, new and deeply pessimistic intelligence assessments forced the Air Ministry to accept in substance, if not in all details, what critics such as Churchill and the permanent under secretary of state for foreign affairs, Sir Robert Vansittart, had been arguing for years. Hitler was in the process of acquiring the largest, most capable air force he could build, as fast as he could build it. Even worse, it was judged to be beyond British air-industrial capacity to match the German expansion. The Government thus fell irretrievably into default of its pledge to Parliament and the nation to maintain air parity with Germany. Britain faced a rapidly approaching strategic danger zone of indefinite duration, in which it would be forced to deal with the political-military consequences of overall German air superiority. Concern mounted that, if war came under these circumstances, Germany could exploit its air superiority to deliver a knockout blow against Britain at the outset of hostilities.[4]

As AOC-in-C, Fighter Command, Dowding was among the national leaders charged with drawing up policy and strategy blueprints to address these dire prospects. In October 1936, the Committee of Imperial Defense commissioned yet another special committee, this time under Dowding's chairmanship, to conduct a comprehensive review of air-defense policy. The CID directed Dowding's panel to define the characteristics of an "ideal" air defense of Britain, meaning by "ideal" simply that their report should identify military requirements without regard to the budgetary considerations that previously had constrained such studies. One factor affecting calculations was the RAF's ongoing restructuring of its basic, tactical unit for fighter aircraft on the basis of 14 rather than 12 aircraft per squadron. Dowding's committee recalibrated the home-defense requirement for fighters to 45 squadrons, which yielded 630 aircraft, compared to 432 in the 36 12-plane fighter squadrons (out of the projected total of 84 home-based squadrons of all types) planned under Scheme A.[5]

Significantly, Dowding's estimate of requirements, like those the Air Staff and Air Ministry, assumed a potential German striking force of 1,700 bombers. His committee also confirmed the findings of previous studies that the German threat required changes in the deployment of British air defenses. Much concerned to create defense in depth for the industrial midlands of England, as well as metropolitan London and the Home Counties, Dowding's committee recommended, in addition to "plugging gaps" in currently planned air defenses, pushing them further north, to Edinburgh and Glasgow. The ground-based elements of this proposed expansion incited protracted debate, because these elements, although assigned to the operational control of Fighter Command as part of the integrated air-defense system, were organized, trained, and equipped by the army. The Government assumed that men and guns added to ground-based antiaircraft defense would have to be subtracted from resources allocated to other army roles and missions.[6]

Emblematic of the importance of the antiaircraft forces within the British army during the late thirties was the assignment, as Dowding's first Antiaircraft Artillery (AAA) commander, of the famously acerbic but exceptionally able Alan Brooke, then a newly promoted lieutenant general, but long a star among his generation of army officers. Dowding and Brooke were near contemporaries, the latter having graduated from "The Shop" (the Royal Military Academy, Woolwich) two years after the accelerated graduation of Dowding's class. Both were originally commissioned in the artillery after falling short of a coveted place with the engineers, but while Dowding defected to the newborn Royal Flying Corps, Brooke rose to prominence as a gunner, in 1935 becoming the army's inspector of artillery, and in 1939 receiving the honorific title of a Colonel-Commandant of the Royal Artillery. Dowding and Brooke, both renowned for being "difficult," appear to have experienced no difficulties with each other, perhaps because Dowding consistently refrained from micromanaging high-performing subordinates.[7]

More than a year passed while the services and the Cabinet grappled with implications of the report submitted by Dowding's committee in February 1937, apparently paralyzed not only by the need to set priorities, but also by the sheer scale of the problem. The report called for more than doubling the number of Antiaircraft Artillery batteries and nearly doubling the number of searchlight batteries. With the regular army committed to generating mobile expeditionary forces for imperial defense, and with the specter of a continental commitment in Europe once again looming in the background, the home-based antiaircraft forces would have to come from the Territorial Army (roughly the equivalent of the National Guard in the United States). The War Office and the Imperial General Staff, having already agreed to convert two of fourteen planned Territorial Army divisions to antiaircraft defense, resisted effectively limiting the Territorial Army's mobile forces to just ten divisions.[8]

Therefore, although the CID accepted the results of the Dowding committee's review in principle, in practice the outgoing Baldwin and incoming

Chamberlain Cabinets hesitated to act, for reasons of "manpower as well as money." Without conscription—a nonstarter in terms both of foreign policy and domestic politics—there were few signs the Territorials could fill the ranks of even the planned, two antiaircraft divisions, let alone two more. As for money, an attempt by Chamberlain in his final weeks as chancellor to fund rearmament with a "flexible" tax scheme provoked a backlash from Conservative Party supporters in financial elite of the City so furious that for a moment it actually seemed to threaten his succession to Baldwin at No. 10 Downing Street. Although probably caused more by his own secretive, high-handed policy-making methods than any particularly crushing financial burden he was proposing, this unsettling episode reinforced Chamberlain's preconceptions regarding the urgent need to restrain the upward spiral in defense costs.[9]

In early 1937, Sir Thomas Inskip, who since the previous March had shouldered the anomalous burden of a "minister for the coordination of defence" without a Defence Ministry, tried to induce the armed services to cost out their long-term rearmament plans. The result, unsurprisingly, was a three-way escalation in service demands, with the Air Ministry envisioning ninety squadrons of heavy bombers by 1943. Inskip's reaction to this seemingly fantastical apparition was an audacious assault on the RAF's whole theory of airpower. Influenced by, among others, the strategist-pundit B. H. Liddell Hart, Inskip suggested that, "at the outset of a war our first task is to repulse a knock-out blow within the first few weeks, trusting thereafter to defeat the enemy by a process of exhaustion, resulting from our command of the sea." By this circuitous path, the new Chamberlain Government was drawn toward increasing reliance on a defensive counter-air strategy as the least unattractive of the perceived options.[10]

Even after more than three-quarters of a century, the grand strategy of the Chamberlain Government continues to arouse bitter controversy, in which arguments regarding the capabilities and limitations of Dowding's Fighter Command have always been central. Less than a year after inaugurating Fighter Command, Dowding presented a fully formed strategic appreciation of his command's wartime mission in a lecture to the RAF Staff College. Dowding's estimate of the situation largely coincided with the strategic views of the new prime minister and the defence minister, resting as it did on the same strategic intelligence. Without ever naming Germany, Dowding made it clear that Fighter Command expected to confront a strategic air offensive by a continental European "Totalitarian State." Dowding's main concern was to prevent such an enemy from scoring a "knock-out blow," either by terror bombing of London, or by air interdiction of Britain' sea lines of communication leading to "paralysis of our food supply."[11]

Significantly, Dowding's lecture explicitly discounted invasion as either a short-term or a long-run threat, although he warned that the RAF must be prepared for the possibility that the enemy, instead of going for the knockout blow immediately upon the outbreak of war, might instead opt initially for a counterforce campaign aimed at destroying British airpower, leaving Britain helpless to prevent either terror bombing, or air interdiction of vital shipping lanes.

British intelligence estimated that Germany was poorly positioned economically for a long war. Chamberlain and Inskip assumed that, in the circumstances, Germany's best hope of avoiding a long war it could not expect to win would be an early knockout blow to Britain, which was peculiarly vulnerable to a concentrated, strategic air attack. From these strategic assumptions, the CID leapt to the conclusion that the Luftwaffe was, in fact, being organized, trained, and equipped for the purpose. Therefore, they reasoned, defensive forces in Britain capable of repulsing a strategic air attack, and thus imposing a protracted war on the Germans, might deter Hitler from going to war with the Western democracies in the first place. Chamberlain and Inskip also calculated that such a defensive force would be both cheaper, and easier to build quickly, than balanced, air-sea-land forces large enough, and sufficiently well-equipped, to meet the German armed forces in a continental war on anything like equal terms.[12]

The Chamberlain/Inskip conclusions rested on a combination of faulty intelligence, weak analysis, and extensive mirror-imaging. British intelligence on the German economy was riddled with gaps and inaccuracies, and conclusions regarding Germany's economic war potential were often far wide of the mark. Moreover, in assessing the strengths and weaknesses of Germany's position, British leaders tended to use their own measures of national capabilities and limitations, rather than try to understand Hitler's worldview and its implications for German policy. At least since 1929, British governments had regarded financial and industrial conditions as their national center of gravity, and developed both domestic and foreign policies accordingly. As a result, they conceptualized a possible conflict with Germany in terms of binary alternatives: a short war won by a knockout blow delivered against Britain by the Luftwaffe, or a long war of economic attrition won, as in 1914–18, by the superior resources of the Allied coalition.[13]

Finally Head of Government, Chamberlain was fiercely determined to bring the force structures of RAF and the other services into line with his strategic priorities. Yet, while rejecting massive expansion of Bomber Command, the Government approved no additional squadrons for Fighter Command until 1938, after the German-Austrian Anschluss provoked another fit of public anxiety over potential air attacks. Facing another near revolt among Government supporters in the House of Commons, Chamberlain first offered a further round of promises, to "increase . . . some parts of the [defence] programme, especially . . . the Royal Air Force and the anti-aircraft defences," and then, after still more savaging by Churchill and other critics, tossed Swinton and Weir to the wolves. Yet for all the parliamentary drama, the actual planning target for home air defense that the Government established in 1938, 34 fighter squadrons of 16 aircraft each, amounted to 86 fewer fighters than the 630 requested by the Dowding Committee more than a year earlier.[14]

In addition to the Chamberlain Government's continuing parsimony, Dowding also had to battle poor judgment by the Air Staff, notably in the persons of the assistant chief of Air Staff Sholto Douglas, and Douglas's key subordinate, the influential, ambitious, and fast-rising "Jack" Slessor (deputy director, Plans) as well as the deputy director (Home Operations) Donald Stevenson. As late as 1938, not only was Slessor still clinging to the old, Trenchardist theory that fast bombers could successfully evade fighter interception, the three combined to fight a seemingly perverse, rearguard action in favor of the two-seat Defiant turret fighter, even as squadron delivery of Dowding's high-performance Hurricanes and Spitfires began. The understandable—albeit horribly wrong—reason for Douglas's insistence on equipping nine of Dowding's squadrons with Defiants was that, with procurement under the direction, successively, of Newall and then the highly regarded Air Marshal Wilfrid Freeman,[15] the Air Ministry had rush-ordered hundreds of them to fill out its window-dressing expansion schemes.[16]

Once again, as in the early thirties, aircraft acquisition and procurement issues were intimately bound up with thinking about future tactics. Even with Hurricanes and Spitfires flying in actual squadron service (and for that matter, with the German Messerschmidt 109 actually demonstrating its combat prowess in Spain) Douglas, Slessor, and Stevenson were still recirculating the tactical arguments of first-generation airmen like Brooke-Popham, Ellington, and Ludlow-Hewitt, including the bizarre insistence that single-seat fighters with fixed, forward-firing guns would only be able to attack "from dead astern." Once again it was Dowding, the pre–World War aviator, who demolished the shopworn arguments of his contemporaries, now issuing from a younger generation with, supposedly, up-to-date technical knowledge and experience.[17]

Suggestions that the Defiants were procured as long-range escort fighters smack of post facto rationalization, since (*a*) they lacked the range for deep penetration of enemy airspace; (*b*) they were designed for formation attacks on enemy bomber formations, not to engage enemy fighters; and (*c*) at the time they were procured, the Air Staff refused to admit that bombers needed escorts. Dowding managed to bid the Air Ministry down to six squadrons of Defiants, but his efforts to confine them to training, "where they will do the least harm" (the sort of remark with which Dowding frequently stored up future trouble for himself) were unavailing.[18]

During his early months as AOC-in-C, Dowding's approach to the complex problem set of fighter tactics was to open up the subject for debate within his own command. When he lectured at No. 11 Group Headquarters, Uxbridge, for example, he offered far more questions than answers. Biographer Vincent Orange meticulously cataloged the tactical issues Dowding raised practically at the outset of Fighter Command's history. The lecture challenged the audience to anticipate how the prototypical performance of the next-generation fighters would translate into operational performance in actual squadron service. In accepting the conventional wisdom of the day that pilots were likely to reach—and exceed—their physical breaking points in the air before the new machines reached theirs, he further challenged his airmen to envision how the man-machine pairing might be made combat effective. Perhaps most importantly, Dowding highlighted the interplay of two weapons systems: the strengths and weaknesses of advanced fighters against those of next-generation bombers.

Dowding bluntly posed the question of which tactical approach, the sharpshooter aiming for a critical point such as cockpit, engine, or fuel tank, or the shotgun-style riddling of entire aircraft, would be more effective. The question related directly to the RAF's official, doctrinal position on formation flying in combat, the product of a traditionally British, collective policy-making body, the Air Ministry's Air Fighting Committee. Adherence to the RAF's standard, three-aircraft fighter formation known as the "Vic," later universally condemned as mindless conservatism, did have a logical basis: it made sense on the assumption that the key air defense problem was how most efficiently to bring massed firepower to bear against hostile bomber formations, not how individual fighters could best engage enemy aircraft one-on-one. The underlying assumption remained that enemy bomber formations would be unescorted by fighters. In effect, the Air Fighting Committee failed to come to terms with the tactical differences between air-defense interception, and air-superiority combat.[19]

Dowding wanted tests and exercises to examine both bomber vulnerability to interceptors and the viability of escort fighters. He was particularly interested in the question of how protecting aircraft vitals with armor could affect air-to-air combat. Because of the reorganization of the RAF's "metropolitan" forces into functional commands, however, Dowding needed the cooperation of Bomber Command to stage realistic tests and exercises. Although Ludlow-Hewitt, his brother AOC-in-C, was willing to go along, the Air Ministry systematically obstructed horizontal cooperation, insisting on the Air Staff's role in coordinating the activities of the two commands. In addition to the obvious, bureaucratic motive of preserving its institutional role, the suspicion arises that the Air Staff's resort to the bureaucratic practice known as slow rolling arose from fears that the proposed tests and exercises might challenge the effectiveness, if not indeed the possibility under existing conditions, of bombing operations opposed by "modern" fighter interceptors.[20]

Fighter Command's second-anniversary present was the appointment of newly promoted air commodore Keith Park as Dowding's senior Air Staff officer (SASO). In a not unrepresentative instance of the personnel malpractice seemingly endemic to modern military institutions worldwide, the Air Ministry's original moves for summer 1938 had included Park going to operational command in Palestine, and "Bomber" Harris to Fighter Command Headquarters. Only by chance was the Air Ministry deflected from thus pounding two unique (and, at least in the case of Harris, grotesquely ill-fitting) pegs into the wrong slots. By pure serendipity, a reversal of assignments set both officers on tracks to historically significant service. Combining the right professional experience and the right temperament, Park's influence on Fighter Command's organizational development would be second only to Dowding's. For the next twenty months and beyond, Park would prove a near-perfect interpreter and implementer for Dowding, while retaining an independent judgment that would well serve both men, and the RAF.[21]

In the summer of 1938, fear of a knockout blow from the Luftwaffe was a major factor in sustaining parliamentary support for Chamberlain's handling of the Czechoslovak crisis and the infamous Munich conference that September. Whether or not at this point Britain and France should have called a halt to Hitler's serial aggression continues to be a fiercely contested issue. Some argue that the strategic position of a potential anti-German coalition at that time would have been far more favorable than the conditions that faced the Allies a year later. Those who maintain, to the contrary, that the Allies were even less well prepared for war in 1938 than in 1939, point to RAF Fighter Command for their most important and compelling evidence. Although it was—and is—a gross distortion to formulate a strategic assessment without regard to the co-relation of opposing forces, Fighter Command's lack of operational readiness was real.[22]

Only six of Dowding's squadrons had, as yet, received their promised new monoplane fighters; the planned chains of radar stations were incomplete; newly assigned personnel had yet to master their jobs; and the whole organization had not yet undergone the months of sustained drills, practices, and exercises that alone could weld Dowding's array of units into an integrated system. For its part, however, the Luftwaffe of 1938 was incapable of mounting sustained, large-scale air operations against Britain from bases in Germany and, in any case, was almost completely committed to central Europe for the duration of the Czech crisis. To continue the parallel: the Luftwaffe's prospective ability by the summer of 1939 to launch follow-on operations against Britain like those it undertook in the summer of 1940, would have depended on imponderables, especially the behavior of France and the Soviet Union during 1938–39. What is measurable, however, is Fighter Command's significant strengthening relative to its prospective opponent between September 1938 and August 1940.[23]

In the troubled aftermath of the Munich conference, the Chamberlain Government hastily raised Fighter Command's expansion target to 50 squadrons (46 for home defense, 4 allocated to an expeditionary air component). The allotment of aircraft to fighter squadrons now totaled 736, as compared to 630 in the Dowding committee's "ideal" scheme of 1937. During the next year, Fighter Command's ever-expanding responsibilities led to the promise of a further 7 squadrons, specifically dedicated to new tasks on Britain's maritime periphery, thus raising the overall entitlement to 57 fighter squadrons. In effect, during 1938 the Government recognized the failure of Britain's weak bomber threat to deter German aggression and, implicitly, defaulted to the national military strategy of initial air defense combined with air force counteroffensive that Dowding had advocated in 1937.[24] While the Air Staff continued to reject strategic defense as a long-term policy, in the Munich aftermath, the Air Council did accept the immediate need to strengthen Fighter Command.[25]

It was around this time, in the fall of 1938, that Dowding made his most important, strategic choice: rather than deploy his fighters evenly across his front, he concentrated his main strength in No. 11 Group, whose area of responsibility (AOR) covered London and the Home Counties of southeastern England. No. 12 Group, whose AOR covered central England ("the industrial Midlands") was half the strength of its southern neighbor. No. 13 Group in the north of England and Scotland was smaller still, and not until March 1940, was No. 10 Group formed to provide limited fighter cover for the vital ports and naval bases of southwestern England. Dowding decentralized control of operations to his group AOCs, confining his headquarters to strategic matters. Shrewdly, he anticipated that once active operations began, managing the flow of information to and from the Air Staff, and through it, to and from the Government, would itself become almost a full-time job.[26]

After Munich, there was little doubt in the minds of British military leaders that war with Germany was "a matter of time, and not too much time." There was considerable doubt, however, whether Dowding would be one of the commanders in that war. The previous summer, the Air Council had given him a year's notice that his current appointment would end in June 1939. They also forewarned that he would be offered no further active-duty appointment. Neither of these decisions was exceptional. Three years was a normal tenure of command, which argued for replacing Dowding in mid-1939; the fact that he would then have slightly less than three years to serve before mandatory retirement at age sixty, argued against giving him a new appointment. Moreover, for the former AOC-in-C of Fighter Command, any posting other than Bomber Command or chief of Air Staff—neither due to come open—would have been a letdown.[27]

Then, in February 1939, Newall telephoned to say that although the *Evening Standard* newspaper was reporting Dowding's planned relief by Air Marshal Sir Christopher Courtney, the Air Ministry had decided against making a change "during the present year." Some weeks later, Dowding was informed in writing that he was to retire in March 1940. Courtney's subsequent injury in an aircraft accident led to a misimpression that the scheduled change of command had been deferred for that reason. Actually, the Air Ministry never gave its reasons. In such circumstances it is not unusual, however, for a Government wishing to avoid prematurely losing the services of a successful, senior officer to extend his final assignment for an additional year. Viewed in this light, the mystery is less the extension of Dowding's tenure at Fighter Command, than why Courtney slipped from the command track. The latter never attained high command, yet exceptionally, was retained on the Air Council throughout the coming war.[28]

An underappreciated function of a senior military leader like Dowding in the 1930s is shaping the cultural norms of the service. As a first-generation British airman, having reached general-officer rank in the Royal Flying Corps during the World War, carried "air rank" for almost the entire history of the

RAF, and been entrusted with inaugurating of one of the RAF's first functional commands, Dowding should have been a prime example of a culturally influential service founder. A routine, apparently trivial duty such as a visit to a service school, speaking to the graduating class and presenting awards to outstanding graduates, illustrates his approach to such softer aspects of institution building. As a member of the Air Council Dowding addressed the 1934 graduating class at RAF Cranwell, and addressed the 1936 graduates while engaged in standing up Fighter Command. On both occasions, the audience included many of "the Few" who, by 1940 would constitute his "veteran" pilots.[29]

Service-school graduation addresses are usually occasions of thinly veiled tedium. Still, what senior leaders choose to say, and not to say, on such occasions can have considerable, long-term effect on organizational culture, especially if a particular message is consistently—and collectively—reinforced over time. Channeling the public-school prize-givers of his Victorian youth, Dowding lauded the cleanliness of the school's workspaces, and victories over Sandhurst on the playing fields. He was particularly concerned with avoiding accidents, sternly warning against recklessness. The implicit reprise of Baldwin's old motto—Safety first—may seem a strange message for future combat aviators, and probably exasperated any self-identified, hunter-killers in the audience. Dowding's real message, however, was one of professionalism, defined in terms of attention to detail and the careful application of expert knowledge, but delivered in the authentic voice of Victorian moralism. Quoting the New Testament ("a little leaven leaveneth the whole lump") he admonished the new officers, "See to it that you are good leaven."[30]

In peacetime, Dowding would visit Fighter Command stations to discuss aircraft characteristics directly with the pilots. Peter Townsend, who later became one of the most famous Battle of Britain pilots, recalled an occasion when Dowding arrived at Townsend's station to find the men covered in soot because of work in progress. Many another senior military officer would have exploited the situation to create a jocular, personal connection with his frontline fighting men, but Dowding's lack of obvious humor and spontaneous repartee turned it into an uncomfortable staring contest. Townsend's account of the incident, filtered through his and his readers' knowledge of all that happened subsequently, seems gently, almost affectionately teasing, but Townsend's portrayal of Dowding's demeanor and leadership style differs only in tone, not in substance, from that of his former subordinate in No. 16 Squadron more than twenty years earlier. Dowding seems to have treated these expeditions as fact-finding missions rather than inspirational theater.

Dowding's concern to hear from the pilots directly may have been related to disappointing reports on the performance of the first Hurricanes and Spitfires to enter squadron service, which fell short of speeds expected, based on their prototypical performance. At the behest of Fighter Command, the Air Ministry found ways and means of improving performance, including utilizing imported, American-refined high-octane aviation gasoline, and installing variable-pitch propellers. Despite such successes, however, Dowding grew increasingly frustrated that every material improvement seemed to require fighting and winning a bureaucratic battle with the Air Staff and Air Ministry. With two of the three (arguably) most important such issues—providing hard-surfaced, all-weather runways for the Fighter Stations, and limited armor protection for fighter aircraft—Dowding had little success before the outbreak of war. Even the request to install bulletproof windscreens required a personal intervention by the AOC-in-C, which was received in a manner that Dowding considered both technically ignorant and professionally discourteous.[31]

In another, critically important case, that of so-called self-sealing fuel tanks, Dowding subsequently blamed himself for the lack of timely action. He later explained that, after he left Air Ministry Research and Development for Fighter Command, a miscommunication developed between himself and the engineers working on improving the safety of the fuel tanks. The engineers reported repeated test failures, but Dowding didn't realize that what they were failing to produce was crash-proof tanks. He, in turn, failed to communicate the importance of achieving the technically less-demanding goal of bullet-resistant tanks, which could be—and later were—produced by coating the interior of the tanks with sealant. It was only after numerous, horrific burn injuries to Hurricane pilots in 1940 that self-sealing tanks were rushed into service. Dowding blamed himself, but it seems almost incredible that no one else, either at Fighter Command or in the Air Ministry, noticed the technical discrepancy before the war.[32]

Meanwhile, the Air Ministry's work on radio direction finding (RDF) was systematically solving an immense array of technical problems with astonishing speed, based on a remarkable, official willingness to defer to the expertise of the scientists, engineers, and technicians actually engaged on the work. Equally important was the decision of administrators including Watson Watt and A. P. Rowe to aim for adequate products tomorrow, rather than, on the one hand, demanding something (anything) today, or, on the other hand, waiting for delivery of an ideal product sometime in the indefinite future. The first operational radar stations were built in 1938, and by 1939 enough of a system ("Chain Home") was in place for Fighter Command to begin exercising it operationally. The data stream from RDF in these early days was highly unreliable, particularly as to altitude and the number of contacts or "bogeys," exacerbating the long-recognized problem of how to filter data so as to ensure that it reached the operational commanders in usable form.[33]

Continuing in Fighter Command the approach to a solution pioneered by the old ADGB command, Dowding worked closely with his SASO, Keith Park, to improve the tactics, techniques, and procedures as well as the equipment employed by the plotting-room crews. In a rare (for him) instance of doctrinal purity, however, the AOC-in-C adamantly defended the principle known to airmen as "centralized control, decentralized execution," indignantly rejecting Air Staff proposals to give each group its own filter room. Perhaps considering that Dowding, in his determination to resist unwarranted interference with his organization, was in this case being not just firm in principle but overly rigid in detail, Park played an essential role in paving the way for a rational outcome. He also initiated expansion of the operations room at Bentley Priory into an operations block, with twin plotting rooms in addition to a central filter room. As always, Dowding proved responsive to a practical demonstration of a practical plan.[34]

Another instance of Dowding's responsiveness to the fusion of technological and operational innovation was to have far-reaching, long-term consequences, securing for Britain a global lead in the development of airborne radar. Even in the early stages of RDF's development, Henry Tizard's Air

Ministry committee already had begun to think though the implications of its potential success. One implication was that an enemy repulsed in daylight likely would turn to night attacks. After once again sifting through a plethora of impractical, science-fiction-type schemes, as early 1936 the Tizard Committee began low-priority work on adapting RDF technology to night interception. Their solution was a radar small and light enough to be carried onboard a night fighter, to guide the pilot though the final stage of interception. By the summer of 1939, development reached a point at which a prototype night-interception radar (known as AI) could be demonstrated for the AOC-in-C.[35]

Crammed into the cockpit of a single-engine Battle along with a sergeant pilot and one of the radar's developers, E. G. Bowen, Dowding flew off into an early morning June sky with a black cloth covering the canopy to simulate night flight. After a radar-guided interception perhaps a little too close for comfort, and a landing that certainly lacked finesse (it broke the aircraft's tail frame) Dowding met for some two hours with the test pilots, discoursing enthusiastically on the way ahead. The AOC-in-C expressed a firm conviction that night air defense required a heavy fighter: a twin-engine, high-endurance aircraft with a crew of two or three (depending on the practicality of combining the roles of radar operator and navigator) and a powerful armament. Bowen, an experimental physicist leading the AI radar development team, later recalled his surprise at the clarity and sophistication of Dowding's thinking, at this early stage, regarding the interplay of technological and tactical difficulties in night interception.[36]

Among other things, after his AI radar test flight in the undersized and underpowered Battle, Dowding appreciated the need for an aircraft better suited to the radar-interceptor role. He quickly identified Bristol's new Beaufighter as the right platform for the AI radar. Unfortunately, the Beaufighter prototype was still weeks away from its maiden flight, and far from mass production. As a stopgap, therefore, he settled for a Bristol Aircraft type in current production, the Blenheim. Within days, two Blenheim light bombers arrived at the RAF's Martlesham research establishment to be fitted with AI radar. Moreover, based on Dowding's assessment of the Martlesham developments, the air-defense subcommittee of the CID approved "highest priority" for the development of radar-guided night-fighter equipment and tactics. Orders were issued to convert thirty Blenheims into radar-equipped, night fighters—with a thoroughly unrealistic completion date of September 1, 1939.[37]

The RAF's summer 1939 exercises demonstrated distinct progress in operational effectiveness, at least on the part of Fighter Command. Headquarters at Bentley Priory was beginning to get a grip on the filtering problem, aided by invention of a practical device for distinguishing friendly from hostile radar contacts, known as IFF (identification friend or foe). A beginning had been made on low-altitude radar coverage ("Chain Low"), and the radar system had been networked together with the longstanding Observer Corps of ground spotters providing coverage inland from the coast into an integrated system. The AOC-in-C was unhappy with a lack of progress on antiaircraft artillery, searchlights, and balloon barrages, but it was satisfied with No. 11 Group's interception rate of 60 percent, although No. 12 Group lagged both in interception and radar effectiveness. Acting as Dowding's enforcer, Park clashed over the exercise results with the No. 12 Group AOC, Air Vice-Marshal Trafford Leigh-Mallory, in a mild foreshadowing of infamous, future conflicts between the two over organization and tactics.[38]

Leigh-Mallory has attracted violently contrasting assessments of his quality as a senior air officer. It is clear that he possessed the kind of "leadership" qualities that attracted the loyalty of the junior officers who worked, and fought, under him. Douglas Bader, who would become world-famous during the coming war as the RAF's double-leg-amputee fighter pilot, "found him a great leader," who was "tough, enthusiastic, and completely honest with his juniors." Some of Leigh-Mallory's fellow senior officers were, however, a different story. Wilfrid Freeman, who fancied himself an arbiter of senior-officer performance standards, recorded a highly negative opinion. To be sure, Freeman had a highly negative opinion of almost everybody, but in 1944 Leigh-Mallory, as commander of the air component of the Allied Expeditionary Force during preparations for D-Day of Operation Overlord, managed to alienate even the infinitely patient "Ike" Eisenhower. It is particularly noteworthy that the final straw for Eisenhower was a faint whiff of disloyalty to the Supreme Allied Commander.[39]

Dowding clearly laid down his operational-level, commander's intent regarding a central question: should operational effectiveness be measured by rate of interception, or—to put it bluntly—by kills? Dowding realized that the fighting would resolve itself into one-on-one combats, but above all, he was determined not to overexpose his fighters, emphasizing the importance of maintaining a reserve to cover the refueling and rearming of each wave of interceptors. The AOC-in-C warned that, consequently, Fighter Command would have to accept numerical inferiority at the point of attack, brushing aside Air Ministry inquiries regarding attacks by multiple squadrons in "wing" formations. The squadron would remain the basic, operational unit for fighter operations, although Dowding did not entirely rule out cooperation by two or more squadrons in the counterattack role. Despite his carefully reasoned arguments, however, the allure of a decisive battle of annihilation won by massed, fighter formations lingered in the minds of many senior air officers.[40]

In thrashing out the details of air-to-air combat tactics, Dowding allowed Park to take the lead for Fighter Command as a participant in the work of the Air Fighting Committee. Park thought the exercises up to 1938, employing as they did mostly obsolete platforms, were essentially useless in framing tactics for future operations with high-performance monoplanes. Crucially, Park wanted to test alternatives to the Vic, the three-aircraft tactical unit flying in V formation. Park's criticism of the 1939 edition of the Air Ministry's *Manual of Air Tactics* was remarkably prescient, rebutting the assertion that "low-flying bombers . . . [would] enjoy 'comparative immunity' from anti-aircraft fire," and correctly predicting that "dive-bombers were particularly vulnerable to fighters." Like the USAAC (but unlike Bomber Command) he stressed the consequences of breaking up bomber formations. Finally, warning that tactical development must take into account the possibility that enemy bomber formations might have fighter escorts, he prepared for Dowding's approval a training guide, "Fighter Command Attacks, 1939."[41]

Park's guidebook stressed initiative and teamwork, analyzing all the essentials of the art: exploiting the vulnerabilities of specific, enemy aircraft types; effectively maneuvering between cloud and sun; and "above all" seizing the initiative to gain the advantages of surprise. Park's approach to developing tactics and training seems to have been correct, and Dowding backed him. Why, then, was Fighter Command initially outclassed tactically by the Luftwaffe fighter forces in the spring of 1940? Before the war, neither Dowding, Park, nor anyone else knew exactly what Fighter Command would be up against. Luftwaffe operations in the Spanish Civil War were suggestive, but clearly not to be taken too literally as precedents. Tactical imagination, like that displayed by Park, was essential, but it was difficult to model imaginative tactics under restrictive training regulations issuing from the Air Ministry. Moreover, Bomber Command either could not, or would not, provide the representative bomber formations necessary for realistic exercises.[42]

7

COMMAND IN WAR

1939–1940

British attitudes hardened after Munich. The initial burst of joy at avoiding war quickly dissipated, replaced not so much by shame at the fate of "a distant people, of whom we know nothing," as by foreboding that far from "peace in our time," what had been gained was only a short interval for overdue preparation. When Britain and France issued guarantees of support to Rumania and Poland, Hitler's likely next targets, few Britons doubted that next summer's end would see, not just another diplomatic crisis, but another European war. By now Dowding's son Derek, having joined the RAF in 1937, was a fighter pilot serving under his father's command. That summer, the father summoned his stepdaughter to "prepare . . . to do something," seeing to it that she joined up as well, as a member of the newly created, and at the time unpaid, Women's Auxiliary Air Force (WAAF).[1]

The prime minister's radio address announcing Britain's declaration of war on the morning of September 3, 1939, was immediately followed by the sound of air-raid sirens wailing across London. At the Churchills' town home, Clementine "commented favourably upon German promptitude and precision," while her husband, noting "slowly rising thirty or forty cylindrical balloons . . . gave the Government a good mark for this evident sign of preparation." Actually, both sirens and balloons represented an opening fault for Dowding's system; the Luftwaffe was fully occupied elsewhere on that fateful Sunday. The false alarm, triggered by a single, stray passenger plane bearing a member of the French military mission to his post in London, may have had something to do with Dowding's resolve to keep air-raid warnings directly under his personal control. Much worse than simple embarrassment followed, with a series of incidents including a friendly fire tragedy, "the Battle of Barking Creek."[2]

Based on erroneous contact reports from coastal searchlight batteries at dawn on September 6, Fighter Command controllers laid a plot tracking a (nonexistent) German raid in the Thames estuary. The Antiaircraft Artillery opened fire, and when fighters scrambled to intercept, they were misidentified on the radar plots as more incoming raiders. Spitfire and Hurricane pilots attacked each other's aircraft, with two of the latter destroyed. Subsequently, pilots blamed poor ground control, although arguably, the controllers were the only ones who did what they were supposed to do with the data at their disposal. The chaos in the control-room plots was due to the Chain Home radars having been put into service without a simple, but essential, technical guard to prevent bounce-back, reverse echoes. Elsewhere, ground observers, AAA gunners, and pilots had all flunked basic aircraft identification. Recriminations naturally followed, but acquiring operational experience under war conditions was bound to be painful.[3]

Dowding's most frequent engagements during the so-called Phony War, the seven months between the fall of Poland and the German invasion of Scandinavia, were fought against business as usual in the Whitehall bureaucracy. Some issues were impersonal. There was, for example, no reason other than interservice jealousy why the Antiaircraft Artillery units that would fight under Dowding's operational control should have their positions assigned by the deputy chiefs of Staff Committee. Other issues give every appearance of having all-too-personal origins. As with aircraft production in 1935, for instance, Dowding's colleagues developed a sudden interest in reorganization when it was recognized that a function under his control had gained critical importance. After assigning one of Dowding's juniors, Air Marshal Sir Philip Joubert de la Ferté, "special duties" overseeing RDF, the Air Ministry proposed placing RDF under an independent command. Dowding had to quash this preposterous idea, ostensibly intended to improve the filtering of the data stream to his control rooms.[4]

Working with his reliable partner Henry Tizard, Dowding established that the fundamental causes of the problems Fighter Command was experiencing with RDF were administrative, rather than operational. Unsurprisingly, ad hoc administrative structures, and the largely civilian technical personnel running them, were proving unsuited to direct and sustain what was fast becoming a new combat element, later known as electronic warfare, during wartime operations by a major command. Moreover, at the outbreak of war the original Air Ministry Research Establishment (AMRE) that had developed RDF split into no fewer than eight parts with differing chains of command. To ensure unity of command and effective integration of technical services with combat arms, a new RAF formation designated No. 60 Group was created to exercise overall administrative control of the radar-related components of electronic warfare, in the direct line of Dowding's chain of command as AOC-in-C, Fighter Command.[5]

Struggle continued over fulfilling the Government's commitment to meet Fighter Command's needs. Dowding's main complaint was that, at the outbreak of the war, his command was still eleven squadrons short of the number officially accepted as necessary to meet a potential German air offensive. Taxed with urgent demands from the army and the navy for air support, unwilling to abandon the RAF's institutional commitment to the primacy of Bomber Command, the Air Ministry found it extraordinarily difficult to meet all these requirements. The limitation had long since ceased to be financial; the key constraint now was the time required to expand production capacity. By the winter of 1939–40, Fighter Command was approaching its expansion targets, but with six fighter squadrons deployed in support of the BEF, and four more held in readiness for deployment, Dowding still considered himself skirting the edge of adequate numbers, leaving no margin for error, or the accidents of war.[6]

Following a hint from the Air Ministry that Fighter Command might not reach its expansion goals for another year, Dowding rhetorically hammered the Air Council: "I must put on record my point of view [that] the Home Defence Organization should not be regarded as co-equal with other commands, but that it should receive priority to all other claims." Dowding's sonorous assertion was unlikely to have gone down well, either with his RAF colleagues, determined to expand Bomber Command as fast as possible; the army leadership, acutely conscious of the underdeveloped condition of the BEF; or with political leaders who formerly prioritized home air defense, but now focused on buttressing the Anglo-French alliance. And indeed, dispassionate strategic analysis suggests that, in the existing circumstances, the alliance was in fact the center of gravity of the war, and the soundest, British course of action was to directly strengthen the immediate combat potential of the Allied forces on the Continent.[7]

The nastiest technological surprise of the war's first phase was the Germans' so-called magnetic mine, which initially threatened to interdict passage of merchant shipping through Britain's home waters, as well as the use of economically vital ports. By virtue of his position and seniority, Dowding had to address the issue as part of Britain's interservice high command, participating in the intricate network of committees through which it functioned. At a Navy–Air Force meeting on November 25 regarding this unexpected and potentially disastrous threat, Dowding was either the pragmatic realist of the group, or "Dismal Jimmy," depending on one's taste, pointing out that effective countermeasures inevitably would encounter "teething troubles and delays." As it happened, a technological solution to the magnetic mine crisis was devised and implemented quickly, but Dowding's attitude reveals intellectual and temperamental qualities that fatefully affected his approach, when primary responsibility for handling a similar crisis fell to him.[8]

During all this time, when, as he had previously written—truthfully, if scarcely tactfully—to the secretary of state for air, Sir Kingsley Wood, "I have dealt with or am in process of dealing with . . . vital matters which generations of Air Staff have neglected," Dowding expected to turn over his command

and retire from active duty in March. For some reason, the Air Ministry waited until March 30 to notify him that his tenure as AOC-in-C, Fighter Command, would be extended again, this time to mid-July. Official and unofficial prognosticators were forecasting offensive moves by both sides with the coming of spring, and indeed, the Allies were debating launching limited operations in Scandinavia within the next two weeks. None of this, however, seemed likely immediately and directly to involve Fighter Command in major combat operations, and in any case, as Vincent Orange observed, the coming summer could scarcely have been expected to bring a quiet period for the rescheduled change of command.[9]

Dowding might be thought fully entitled to vent—if not explode—over the Air Council's cavalier treatment of his personnel status during the three years before the war. In wartime, however, it is both commonplace, and often necessary, for assignments from the lowest to the highest to change with neither notice nor explanation. Ironically, during this period Dowding had been making some personnel changes of his own, affecting some of the most senior officers under his command. In December, Air Vice-Marshal William Welsh had replaced Air Vice-Marshal Leslie Gossage as AOC of No. 11 Group. This appears to have been a routine personnel move. Gossage, having commanded the group for more than three years, since the inception of Fighter Command in the summer of 1936, was promoted to acting air marshal and elevated to the Air Council as air member for personnel.[10]

Nevertheless, such a transition only four months into the war, and before any serious fighting, suggests at a minimum that the Air Council and the AOC-in-C shared a higher regard for Gossage's administrative talents than his demonstrated potential for wartime, operational leadership. And when only three months later Welsh was, in his turn, superseded by an officer some five and a half years his junior in air rank, there is a strong inference that Dowding, searching for an air officer he judged well fitted for the most critical operational post in Fighter Command, rather than the Air Council, was responsible for the change. This inference is buttressed by the continuing upward trajectory of Welsh's career, becoming an AOC-in-C, first at Technical Training Command and then Flying Training Command. Did Dowding's thoughts go back to 1916, when Trenchard, as RFC commanding general on the western front, contrived a similar, noncombat "promotion" for the inconvenient CO of Ninth Wing?[11]

Clearly, Dowding was right not to settle for less than, in his opinion, the best available AOC for No. 11 Group; perhaps less obviously, he was also was right not to retain in operational command any officer who did not enjoy his unqualified confidence. Events proved his selection of Keith Park to command 11 Group triumphantly right. Literally promoted from hospital, where he had been recovering from an appendectomy, Park was so junior he had to be given temporary rank as "acting" air vice-marshal. During twenty months as Dowding's SASO, Park had emerged as the RAF's preeminent expert on defensive counter-air operations. An immensely hard worker who managed to be both an independent thinker and a pillar of support for his AOC-in-C, Park possessed an unexcelled grasp of Dowding's operational concepts. By no means a personal follower, nevertheless, almost uniquely among next-generation air-rank officers, Park forged with Dowding a professional bond of trust and confidence.[12]

Dowding's abrupt and unexpected advancement of Park was not universally popular. Leigh-Mallory, for one, seems to have resented being retained in the second-string role of No. 12 Group AOC despite being well senior to Park. In addition to any possible personal resentment, moreover, Leigh-Mallory continued to clash with Dowding and Park over organization, operational strategy, and tactics. Some claim Leigh-Mallory pushed dissent to the point of disloyalty, if not outright insubordination. Long afterward, Park recalled Leigh-Mallory openly vowing to oust Dowding from his command. There are two ironic lessons here: first, Dowding's disregard for Welsh's and Leigh-Mallory's personal feelings was as fully justified, under the circumstances, as the Air Council's disregard of Dowding's. The difference was that, unlike the Air Council, Dowding made up his mind and then acted decisively to put his man in place. This, in turn, highlights the second irony: Dowding, to his cost, failed to act with similar decision in dispatching his Leigh-Mallory problem.[13]

The organizational puzzles confronting the RAF leadership during the Phony War exploded into strategic crisis with the German spring offensives of 1940. Fighter Command was called upon to deploy two squadrons to Norway in April, and four more to France (making a total of twelve deployed) on May 10. As increasingly desperate demands for help poured in to the Government in London, Dowding fought to retain his remaining squadrons at home to protect "the security of the base." This struggle is often portrayed as a contest between Dowding's military necessity, and the political imperative of supporting—and being seen to support—the French in their hour of trial. It is not widely understood that not only the politicians, but also "Peter" Portal, newly installed as AOC-in-C of Bomber Command, and A. S. Barratt, AOC-in-C, British Air Forces in France, insisted upon deploying Fighter Command resources to try to protect their exposed bomber forces.[14]

It might be taken as testament to the hold that doctrines of strategic attack exerted over even so pragmatic an airman as Dowding that, at this critical juncture, he suggested to the War Cabinet launching Bomber Command against the Ruhr as "the soundest action which we could take in the present situation." Trenchard himself could not have said it better. But behind this apparently doctrinaire recommendation lay a hidden agenda at once subtle, bold, and unorthodox. British leaders expected serious bombing of Germany to trigger retaliation against British targets. The French expected any retaliation to target them, and as a consequence, they consistently obstructed such attacks.[15]

Dowding made it clear more than once during the early months of the war that he considered Fighter Command would have the advantage against Luftwaffe operations conducted over Britain from bases in Germany. If the Germans could be lured or goaded into such operations, it would simultaneously relieve some of the pressure on Allied ground forces, reduce Fighter Command's operational exposure, and increase that of the Luftwaffe bomber forces.[16]

On May 13, the Chiefs of Staff Committee directed Dowding to strip thirty-two Hurricanes from home-based squadrons to replace combat losses in deployed squadrons. The next day, French premier Paul Reynaud urgently requested deployment of ten more British fighter squadrons. His appeal went to Churchill, now his opposite number, who had replaced Chamberlain as British prime minister and had begun forming a new, all-party governing coalition on May 10. Discussing Reynaud's plea with his newly chosen War

Cabinet of Chamberlain, Halifax, and parliamentary Labour Party leaders Clement Attlee and Arthur Greenwood, Churchill reflected, "we should hesitate before we denuded further the heart of the Empire." Later that day he cautioned the French that while the British "would continue to give full assistance . . . [we] could not unguard ourselves beyond a certain point." Defining that point—and sticking to it—posed an agonizing dilemma that would bedevil the prime minister and his colleagues for the next six, awful weeks.[17]

On May 15, the Chiefs of Staff brought Dowding and his colleague Sir Richard Peirse (just promoted to the newly created position of vice-chief of Air Staff) to their regular morning meeting with the prime minister. Addressing Churchill, Dowding warned that, "If more fighters were taken from him . . . they would not achieve decisive results in France, and he would be left too weak to carry on over here." He went on to assert forthrightly, "Provided no more fighters were removed . . . he was confident that the Navy and the Royal Air Force would be able to keep the Germans out of this country." An RAF staff officer present as a member of the War Cabinet secretariat later described Dowding's famous intervention: "He was factual and to the point, the professional airman stating expertly and concisely a case that had to be made. There was no room for rhetoric."[18]

The War Cabinet then convened and, after hearing from the chiefs of staff and the airmen, agreed with the prime minister that "no further fighter squadrons should for the present be sent to France, and . . . [that] the Prime Minister [should] so . . . inform Monsieur Reynaud." Conveying this news to Park, Dowding displayed a combination of innate caution, and skepticism born of long years of experience with political-military affairs. "Appeals for help," Dowding predicted, "will doubtless be renewed with increasing insistence and I do not know how this morning's work will stand the test of time."[19] In the same spirit of caution and skepticism, the next day Dowding wrote what was to become a famous letter, formally placing his position before the Air Council:

> I would remind the Air Council that . . . my strength has now been reduced to the equivalent of 36 Squadrons. . . . I believe that, if an adequate fighter force is kept in this country . . . we should be able to carry on the war single-handed for

> some time, if not indefinitely. But, if the Home Defence Force is drained away in desperate attempts to remedy the situation in France, defeat in France will involve the final, complete and irremediable defeat of this country.

That same morning, the CAS briefed his fellow Chiefs of Staff on a renewed demand, this time from the French generalissimo, Maurice Gamelin, for ten more fighter squadrons, "at once," without which "the battle would be lost." Newall then rather illogically proposed sending four squadrons. The Chiefs of Staff Committee endorsed Newall's proposal, and the prime minister put it to a meeting of the War Cabinet that followed, suggesting as well, preparing to deploy the two fighter squadrons assigned to defend the Royal Navy's main operating base at Scapa Flow. At this point, Sir Archibald Sinclair, the newly appointed secretary of state for air, reminded the War Cabinet of the previous day's warnings from Dowding, adding that "'sending any [more] fighters out of the country' would ... be 'a very serious risk ... contrary to the advice' of the officer 'responsible for the defence of this country.'" Then, like Newall, Sinclair illogically accepted sending four. The War Cabinet agreed.[20]

Churchill reversed his attitude of the previous morning, and pressured the War Cabinet for action "to support the French morale and give them a chance to recover themselves," not only based on Reynaud's and Gamelin's insistence that victory or defeat hung in the balance, but also on news that the French army had begun retreating from its main line of resistance, which "would expose the British Army to far more serious risks." Now at stake was the survival of not only the Anglo-French coalition, but also that of the BEF, which as in 1914 included most of the British army's fully trained and equipped maneuver forces. On May 19, the prime minister once again reacted to the increasingly precarious position of the BEF, issuing prescient orders to prepare air cover for the possible, cross-Channel evacuation of the BEF. At once, all but three of the British fighter squadrons in France began to withdraw for "reorganization."[21]

To No. 11 Group, Dowding assigned Fighter Command's most urgent mission yet: providing air cover for the evacuation of the British and French troops trapped in a "pocket" around the French port of Dunkirk. As he planned in peacetime, the AOC-in-C left control of operations to his group

AOC. Dowding's principal contribution at this stage was to shield Park from impractical demands by the Air Staff for "continuous patrols in strength" in the Dunkirk battle space. With both Newall and Churchill unfavorably critiquing for the benefit of the War Cabinet his (admittedly very conservative) estimates of the situation, Dowding allowed Park to demonstrate the effect of maintaining a moderate average strength by leaving short intervals between patrols, rather than try to explain that, in the circumstances, patrols could be either "strong" or "continuous," but not both. The quickly apparent success of Park's battle management evidently persuaded the Air Staff and the War Cabinet to refrain from further attempts to interfere.[22]

The nine-day Dunkirk air battle resulted in a relatively narrow, 3:2 victory for Fighter Command in air-to-air combat, with 132 German aircraft destroyed (262 claimed) set against losses of 99. What mattered most, however, was that the duel for air superiority helped divert the Luftwaffe from its interdiction mission: preventing the extraction of more than 300,000 Allied troops, including most of the BEF. According to the diary of "Jock" Colville, an aristocratic, young foreign service officer detailed to work as a secretary in the prime minister's office, by June 2 Churchill's "main energies" were refocusing on "consolidating . . . home defences, [and] conserving . . . air strength." Yet at the same time, the prime minister still considered it "vital to sustain French morale and give no excuse for collapse." Dowding played an important role in another critically important War Cabinet meeting on June 3, which debated undertaking a new deployment of forces to France.[23]

Melodramatic accounts of this meeting have an unbending Hugh Dowding defying Winston Churchill, thus saving Fighter Command from defeat, and Britain, if not Western civilization, from destruction. The script for this melodrama was composed by Lord Beaverbrook, present at the meeting in his new character as minister of aircraft production. Beaverbrook later furnished the brilliant but congenitally mischievous historian, A. J. P. Taylor, a faintly rancid tale that Churchill's War Cabinet "quailed" when Dowding put down his pencil in a gesture of exasperation. At the end of his life Dowding, apparently tempted by the pedestal erected for him by his admirers, gave the Beaverbrook-Taylor story an equally mischievous half denial. Dowding's own story was that he showed Churchill a specially prepared chart, graphically illustrating that two more weeks of the current loss rate would leave Fighter Command with no Hurricanes at all. Dowding's chart did not, however, end the matter, but merely prolonged the War Cabinet's agony of decision.[24]

The War Cabinet decided, boldly in view of the near catastrophe that the original BEF had only just barely escaped with severe losses in men and crippling losses in equipment, to send to France three fresh divisions that had been preparing for deployment. These forces also had to be extracted from the Continent, with heavy losses, within two weeks. Debate on further air force deployments continued on June 4, with Newall repeating Dowding's warning of the previous day: aircraft losses in the continental fighting had so weakened Fighter Command that, without "a respite," it could not sustain a defense "against a concentrated air attack for more than forty-eight hours." Eventually, the War Cabinet decided to bring up to full strength the last three British fighter squadrons in France, but to deploy no more squadrons to the Continent. In addition, with the illogicality born of desperation, they directed Dowding to commit several more squadrons to the fighting in France, operating from bases in southeastern England, refueling at French airfields, but returning to their home bases at night.[25]

When, two days later, the Wehrmacht began its final offensive of the 1940 campaign in France, Churchill yet again desperately sought ways and means of responding to a final wave of French demands for air cover. There was growing resentment among British political and military leaders at French blame casting, together with growing alarm at the degraded state of Fighter Command, but not until the evening of June 8 did Churchill send Reynaud the telegram finally and for good turning off "the Hurricane tap." Both blame and resentment missed the point; never during May or June would commitment of even the whole of Fighter Command have sufficed to win theater air superiority on the Continent for the Allies, a point Churchill himself later made explicitly in the House of Commons. On June 17, Premier Paul Reynaud and his cabinet resigned. Marshal Henri Philippe Pétain formed a new cabinet without the constitutionally required sanction from the now-dispersed Senate and Chamber of Deputies. The French Third Republic, de facto, had ceased to exist. Pétain immediately sued for an armistice.[26]

At the end of May, many Britons had been as stunned by the so-called blitzkrieg in western Europe as the French, but the Dunkirk "miracle" began a psychological transformation. The BEF's return created such a wave of euphoria that Churchill felt a need to warn, "Wars are not won by evacuations." This strange feeling of "lunatic relief" in Britain grew stronger with the final collapse of French military resistance, and for once, Dowding resonated in tune with popular emotion, writing personally to Churchill, "Well! Now it is England against Germany, and I don't envy them their job." It was a defining moment in his relationship with the new prime minister. Churchill admired physical courage; perhaps even overvalued its more extreme manifestations as a qualification for high command. But above all, Churchill demanded lieutenants with moral courage; men who, like himself, would "never, never, never give in, except to convictions of honour and good sense."

Dowding's message came to Churchill as "a word in season," because Fighter Command's capabilities now became an essential pillar of Churchill's political-military argument for carrying on the war. Two of Churchill's most famous speeches, delivered in the House of Commons on June 4 and June 18, world-renowned for passages of oratorical brilliance and inspirational appeal, also conveyed a hard core of military analysis intended to build parliamentary support and undergird his strength in the politically decisive arena, the War Cabinet. The prime minister employed the full measure of his rhetorical ingenuity to give Parliament and the nation hope that airpower, effectively employed, might neutralize even overwhelming land power. Destruction or capture of the Anglo-French forces in the Dunkirk pocket had been a grand strategic objective of the highest order, he pointed out; it was reasonable to assume the Luftwaffe made a maximum effort, but failed to secure local air superiority.

In Churchill's narrative, the RAF had won "a victory inside [the] deliverance" of Dunkirk. Fighter Command had demonstrated qualitative superiority over the Luftwaffe's fighters, inflicting losses of "three or four to one" on the numerically superior enemy. Underscoring the operational advantages of a battle in British airspace, as compared to the fighting over French territory, the prime minister expressed his confidence that for all its size and power, the Luftwaffe would prove unable to secure the air superiority over Britain that, he asserted, was prerequisite for a successful invasion. Finally, he claimed that, based on the Luftwaffe's heavy losses in "the Battle of France," Fighter Command was "stronger at the present time relatively to the Germans."[27]

Only after thus laying a foundation of pragmatic, if optimistic, military analysis did Churchill close his June 18 speech with one of the most quoted perorations in all of English oratory, seeking to infuse Britain's struggle with a transcendent, historical meaning. In words that instantly entered the political liturgy of the West, he conjured into being a name the world would associate with the coming air campaign, in cadences that would forever link Dowding's casually modern young pilots awaiting the onslaught, to the archers and chivalry of Henry V on the eve of Agincourt, to Elizabeth I's "trained bands" awaiting the Spanish Armada, to Nelson's sailors off Cape Trafalgar:

> What General Weygand called the Battle of France is over. I expect the Battle of Britain is about to begin. Upon this battle depends the survival of Christian civilization. Upon it depends our own British life, and the long continuity of our institutions and our Empire. The whole fury and might of the enemy must very soon be turned on us. Hitler knows that he will have to break us in these islands, or lose the war. If we can stand up to him, all Europe may be free and the life of the world may move forward into broad, sunlit uplands. But if we fail, then the whole world, including the United States, including all that we have known and cared for, will sink into the abyss of a new Dark Age made more sinister, and perhaps more protracted, by the lights of a perverted science. Let us therefore brace ourselves to our duties, and so bear ourselves that, if the British Empire and its Commonwealth last for a thousand years, men will still say, "This was their finest hour."[28]

Churchill's confidence—at least regarding a campaign to maintain air superiority at home—like Dowding's, had considerable material justification. In combat over the Continent, Fighter Command had evidenced sound organization and training, excellent equipment, and even better morale, reflecting Dowding's success as a peacetime institution builder. The price, however, had been high, with eight squadrons rendered combat-ineffective; eleven more were nonoperational, undergoing reequipment with new fighters.[29]

New challenges would now test the resilience and flexibility of Dowding's organization in reconstituting combat effectiveness, while redeploying to deal with the new strategic geography created by the German advance to the North Sea and Channel coasts. The approximately five hundred fighters lost would be replaced through an already increasing rate of production; more dangerously, associated personnel losses meant replacing experienced pilots mostly with novice flyers. Facing renewed demands for point defenses around aircraft and aircraft engine factories, even under pressure from the prime minister and the Chiefs of Staff Dowding steadfastly refused to upset the carefully calculated balance of his position by large-scale reinforcement of No. 11 Group. Shifting some antiaircraft guns and balloons to southern ports, repositioning some fighter squadrons closer to the northern end of the Channel, and relocating a few squadrons to the south coast and the west of England, Dowding provided against new angles of attack now open to the Luftwaffe, without unbalancing his overall defensive scheme.[30]

Confronted with a sudden, radical change in the strategic environment, Fighter Command exemplified an effective learning organization, with an organizational culture of attention to technical detail and an innovative spirit. Conversion of Spitfires and Hurricanes to constant-speed propellers accelerated, partially offsetting the incorrect, prewar estimates regarding the likely conditions of air-to-air combat. Also important in keeping Fighter Command's efforts focused on the coming campaign was Dowding's refusal to waste limited time and scarce resources on ventures with low probability of success, including a Churchill-Lindemann favorite, the "Parachute and Cable Rocket, whereby wires held up by parachute were to be sent up by rocket. . . . If an enemy aeroplane ran into the wire, a second parachute opened, forming a fatal drag on the aeroplane wing." Dowding commented drily that the device was "not of any value," thus presumably contributing once again to his reputation in the Air Ministry as "such a difficult chap to deal with."[31]

Dowding was by no means blameless in the long-running, escalating, and potentially dangerous friction between Fighter Command, on the one hand, and the Air Staff and Air Ministry, on the other. As one of the RAF's most senior, active-duty officers, an AOC-in-C with nearly a decade's prior service on the Air Council, Dowding was one of the service leaders best situated to take a judicious, if not detached, view of the perilous situation. Presumably, Dowding fully understood the extraordinarily complex organizational puzzles the staff and the ministry faced, not least of which was the institutional stress resulting from the accession to power of Churchill's Coalition Government, which to many members of the British governing elite felt at the time less a traditional, British change-of-government than, almost, a regime change.[32] And of all the bureaucracies in the Whitehall governmental establishment, the Air Ministry may have had the most to fear from Churchill as prime minister.

It had been partly due to the polemical effect of Churchill's unrelenting criticism of the RAF and the Air Ministry that, across the decade of the 1930s, each secretary of state for air in succession—Lord Londonderry, Lord Swinton, Sir Kingsley Wood, and finally, Sir Samuel Hoare—was in his turn discarded. The Ministry of Aircraft Production only came into being because even the Whitehall establishment finally was forced to acknowledge the inadequacy of the "production of armaments, particularly aeroplanes," and the Air Ministry's lack of "efficiency or ability to 'get a move on.'" When, on May 10, Churchill received the Sovereign's commission to form a new Government, the names of Sir Archibald Sinclair and Lord Beaverbrook were among the first he proposed to the King. Both men were to have a major impact on the remainder of Dowding's tenure as AOC-in-C of Fighter Command, as well as on the timing of his departure from command.[33]

Sinclair, a wealthy member of the Scottish gentry, as leader of the historic but shrunken Liberal Party in the House of Commons, had a reasonable, partisan claim to a modest place in the new coalition. Because of his friendship with Churchill, forged when they served side by side in the trenches of the western front, Sinclair might have been thought to pose a threat to the status quo at the Air Ministry as its new secretary of state, but proved to be nothing of the kind. Prim and earnest but lacking forcefulness, with scant ministerial experience and no airpower expertise, he tended to accept Air Staff advice and adopt the perspectives of his colleagues on the Air Council, advocating their causes both in Cabinet and in the House. He seems never to have independently assessed Dowding's strengths and weaknesses, but was led into attempting to liquidate his colleagues' perceived Dowding problem, even at the risk of antagonizing Churchill.[34]

Beaverbrook's appointment as minister of aircraft production was more singularly tied to a personal relationship with Churchill, also dating from the First World War era. Among the few things the 1st Baron Beaverbrook had in common with Sinclair, other than Churchill's friendship, were wealth and a taste for politics. A Canadian-born, self-made millionaire, as Max Aitken he built a newspaper empire, exploiting the money and influence on public opinion it generated to lever his way into British governing circles. Unlike Sinclair, this "newspaper baron" was a man of immense personal force. A magnet for, as well as a generator of political intrigue, during the winter and spring of 1940. Trenchard, and Trenchard disciples such as "Jack" Salmond, saturated him with strident criticism of almost the entire top echelon of RAF leaders, including both Newall and Dowding. (That the officers they condemned had all been placed on their respective paths to the top of the service by Trenchard is an irony worth emphasizing.) A far stronger character and shrewder politician than Sinclair, after taking charge of the MAP Beaverbrook skillfully exploited RAF factionalism for his own advantage.[35]

As head of a department carved out of the Air Ministry, Beaverbrook inevitably found his efforts to assert his own ministerial control opposed by Sinclair and Newall. Beaverbrook's instinctive response to this opposition was an ad hominem offensive against both men, openly scorning the former as "a thoroughly bad minister," and dismissing the chief of Air Staff with malicious wit: "He was an observer in the last war, and he has remained an observer ever since."[36] Based on his private briefings from RAF insiders, Beaverbrook would have been well aware of Dowding's prickly relations with Newall, and cannot have failed to identify in Dowding a potential, bureaucratic ally. Certainly it would have been entirely consistent with Beaverbrook's personal, business, and political style, for him to handle Dowding on the basis of the principle, "the enemy of my enemy is my friend."[37]

Planting a seed of future trouble for Dowding, however, was the appointment of Salmond as Beaverbrook's director of armaments production. Less than a year Dowding's senior in age, owing to his rapid advancement to high command during World War I, Salmon had progressed through the "air" ranks roughly a decade ahead of Dowding. Unlike Dowding, he had culminated his RAF career with appointment as chief of Air Staff (1930–33) and subsequent promotion to Marshal of the Royal Air Force. By 1940, however,

Salmond had soured into an increasingly harsh, even unbalanced, critic of his successors in RAF leadership. Despite his lack of technical expertise—exacerbated by seven years' disengagement from the practical work of the Air Ministry—and lack of direct knowledge of the RAF's functional commands, which had only existed since 1936, Salmond's hypercritical attitude, together with his rank, personal connections, and the fading echo of his public reputation, made him from Beaverbrook's point of view a valuable confederate.

Although Beaverbrook's ad hoc, politicized, personalized, and above all, devious approach to management was the polar opposite of Dowding's professional, systematic, empirical approach, Dowding still responded positively to the new minister. Dowding's notorious inability to "get on with" the powers that be mostly involved conflicts with bureaucrats, both civilian and uniformed. From at least the time he reached air rank, Dowding displayed an awareness of the critical importance of political-military relationships. He seems to have handled most politicians he encountered, and in the final stages of his career the public, with some care and skill. Having clashed with Churchill and Lindemann over RDF development, in the last months of peace he had been shrewd enough to try to mend fences, with what today would be called a "strategic communications" effort, showing off the successful application of the most advanced radar technology. On this seemingly shallow foundation, the statesman and the commander later would build a short-lived, but consequential, relationship.[38]

During the Battle of France the Chiefs of Staff Committee and the War Cabinet initially showed signs of impatience with repeated warnings from Dowding (Dismal Jimmy?) regarding attrition of Fighter Command assets. During the first week in June, however, detailed statistical analysis of Fighter Command's degraded operational readiness, and the time required to restore it, prompted Churchill to demand explanations from Sinclair. The prime minister suspected the problem arose from the "inflexible set-up of Flying Training Command," and despite Air Staff assurances relayed by Sinclair, Churchill continued to badger his secretary of state for air on the subject, suggesting changes to RAF pilot training and assignment policies, among other things, and repeatedly asking when Dowding's demands for pilot transfers from the Fleet Air Arm would be met. The prime minister's growing dissatisfaction boiled over at an emergency conference on June 21, convened to address the German *Knickebein* radio-navigation system, codenamed "Headache" by the British.[39]

The prospect of the Luftwaffe bombing accurately even at night or on cloudy days was deeply disconcerting, not only because it would greatly expand the offensive potential of the German bomber force, but also because the RAF's experimental, radar-guided antiaircraft batteries and airborne radar for night fighters were not yet operationally effective. A young experimental physicist named R. V. Jones intervened, however, with practical suggestions for electronic countermeasures that Dowding promptly endorsed. Churchill was relieved, but scarcely mollified, given the Air Ministry's failure to anticipate the problems posed by navigational beams. "All I get from the Air Ministry is files, files, files!" the prime minister lashed out. Around this time, Churchill began using a small, Cabinet Office staff under Lindemann to independently reassess critical air intelligence, including estimates of Luftwaffe bomber strength. Moreover, as the tempo of air operations accelerated during early summer the prime minister increasingly drew Dowding into his personal orbit.[40]

By the summer of 1940, Dowding had gone a long way toward establishing the personal rapport usually necessary for a senior officer to secure Churchill's confidence and support. As prime minister, Churchill habitually conducted business in the grand manner of the old aristocracy, mixing official meetings and conferences together with social occasions such as luncheons, dinners, and late-night entertainments, all well lubricated with champagne and brandy. The reputedly unsociable Dowding adapted to this Churchillian milieu, becoming a regular visitor to Chequers, the official country retreat of British premiers. Over dinner there one evening in July, he even shared something of his psychological state, according to Colville "telling the PM that the only thing that worried him in life was the ridiculous dreams he had every night." After Churchill extolled Fighter Command in a radio address the next night, the supposedly brusque and tactless Dowding's bread-and-butter note to his host included a quite exceptionally effusive expression of gratitude for the broadcast.[41]

Sinclair, oblivious, chose just this moment to matter-of-factly inform the prime minister, to Churchill's evident surprise, that Dowding was due to retire at the end of July. Was this simply another instance of the Air Ministry allowing bureaucratic processes to run on, regardless of context? Dowding had been slated for relief in July. Had the machine, in its typically "cumbersome" way, simply begun the process of replacing him automatically? Or had the Air Council decided to use Sinclair finally to rid themselves of Dowding? Whatever the case, Churchill immediately and firmly quashed the idea of removing Dowding from Fighter Command. An incautious aside in his response to Sinclair, about possibly moving Dowding "to a higher position," may actually have spurred the gathering of a "cabal," made up of the two Marshals of the Royal Air Force, Trenchard and Salmond, and several ambitious, active-duty air-rank officers, determined to empower a new generation of RAF leadership.[42]

Had Hugh Dowding retired from active duty in mid-1939 or early 1940, as scheduled, his professional accomplishments on the Air Council as air member for supply and research, and as the first air officer commanding-in-chief, Fighter Command, would have sufficed to earn him a modest but meaningful place in the history of the RAF, and perhaps a footnote in the world history of airpower. Much against the expectations of his professional colleagues, however, Dowding was fated to lead the command he had built into what came to be understood as one of history's great battles, and so burnished his substantive achievements with a measure of lasting fame.

Lieutenant Colonel Hugh Dowding, RFC (*right*), officer commanding, Ninth Wing, explains the use of an aerial camera to King Nikola I of Montenegro (*center*) and members of his suite; Fienvillers, France, 1916. *Imperial War Museum.*

Official photograph of Air Chief Marshal Sir Hugh Dowding as air officer commanding-in-chief, Fighter Command. *Imperial War Museum*.

The underground Operations Room at Fighter Command Headquarters, Bentley Priory. *Imperial War Museum.*

Chain Home radar installation at Poling, Sussex. *Imperial War Museum.*

A German Heinkel He 111 bomber flying over the Isle of Dogs in the East End of London at the start of the Luftwaffe's evening raids on September 7, 1940, the first day of the Blitz. *Imperial War Museum*.

A formation of Hawker Hurricanes from No. 1 Squadron RAF (*left*) and Supermarine Spitfires from No. 266 Squadron during a flying display for aircraft factory workers. *Imperial War Museum.*

Air Vice-Marshal Keith Park in flying gear. *Imperial War Museum.*

Dowding with some of his "chicks," after the Battle of Britain Day commemorative luncheon, September, 1942. *From left to right*: Sqn. Ldr. A. Bartley, DFC; Wg. Cdr. D. F. B. Sheen, DFC and Bar; Wg. Cdr. I. R. Gleed, DSO, DFC; Wg. Cdr. M. Aitken, DSO, DFC; Wg. Cdr. A. G. Malan, DSO, DFC; Sqn. Ldr. A. C. Deere; Dowding; Flt. Off. E. C. Henderson, MM (WAAF); Flt. Lt. R. H. Hillary; Wg. Cdr. J. A. Kent, DFC, AFC; Wg. Cdr. C. B. F. Kingcome, DFC; Sqn. Ldr D. H. Watkins, DFC; Wt. Off. R. H. Cretton. *Imperial War Museum*.

H. M. King George VI (*center*) and his wife Queen Elizabeth the Queen Consort received at Bentley Park by Sir Hugh Dowding. *Imperial War Museum.*

Air Chief Marshal (retired) Lord Dowding (*left*) with Air Marshal Sir Trafford Leigh-Mallory, AOC-in-C, Fighter Command, at Battle of Britain Day commemoration, Bentley Priory, September 1943. *Imperial War Museum.*

Air Chief Marshal (retired) Lord Dowding (*center left*) talking with Group Captain Douglas Bader (*center right*) before a Battle of Britain Day commemoration; RAF North Weald, September, 1945. *Imperial War Museum.*

"Study of Dowding" by artist William Rothstein, December 1939.
Imperial War Museum.

8
THE BATTLE OF BRITAIN

JULY–AUGUST 1940

Between mid-April and mid-June the Luftwaffe concentrated on the immense and fateful combined arms campaigns fought out across northwest Europe, from Denmark and Norway through the Low Countries, to the Channel coast and the Isle de France. Air operations against Britain were limited to high-altitude, high-speed daylight reconnaissance flights, and nighttime harassment raids by a few dozen bombers ranging widely across British airspace in *Staffeln* (flights of 6–12), in pairs, or even singly.

Nor did the Franco-German Armistice lead to an immediate increase in the tempo of Luftwaffe operations against Britain. For one thing, the Luftwaffe suffered significant attrition in its *Weserübung* and *Fall Gelb* operations, and like its British antagonist, needed recovery time. Moreover, until Hitler decided what do next, the German armed forces (Wehrmacht) could not begin serious planning for further operations.[1]

Although, beginning as early as the Sudetenland crisis of 1938, Luftwaffe and *Kriegsmarine* (navy) staff officers had studied the problems of air and naval operations against the United Kingdom, they had prepared no detailed contingency plans. In the absence of direction or guidance on the subject from Hitler,[2] the Armed Forces High Command (*Oberkommando der Wehrmacht*, or OKW) failed to produce even an outline strategic concept of operations against Britain until the end of June, when *Generalmajor* Alfred Jodl, OKW chief of operations, delivered an analysis of Germany's strategic options in the event that the British refused to concede defeat. As Jodl saw it, Germany could pursue a maritime strategy aimed at severing economic and strategic arteries of the British Empire; launch an all-out strategic air offensive against Britain itself; or, "as a last resort," invade the British Isles with ground forces. That same day, Göring issued to the Luftwaffe a directive concerning operations against Britain.[3]

Göring's initial campaign directive straddled Jodl's first two options and ignored the third, probably as a consequence of Hitler's unwillingness to choose. The Luftwaffe C in C not only failed to secure from his leader a decision on the fundamental, strategic choice, but shuffled off onto his air-fleet commanders and their staffs the task of working out detailed plans. As a natural consequence, *Luftflotte* (Air Fleet) 2 under Albert Kesselring and *Luftflotte* 3 under Hugo Sperrle developed different concepts of operations.[4]

Across the Channel, Dowding was standing by his 1937 assessment that the Luftwaffe had a choice of two concepts for air operations against Britain: either concentrate all their forces on a chosen point of attack in an attempt to win a decisive battle, or spread their attacks across a wide front, in hopes of wearing down British defenses by attrition. It appears, however, that in the first weeks after the French collapse, most British leaders feared an immediate invasion more than the prospect of a sustained, strategic air offensive by the Luftwaffe. Intelligence initially evaluated Luftwaffe attacks on ports as precursors to invasion, although a more accurate estimate of German intentions quickly emerged. Ironically, the offensive option most Britons feared most was the option least favored by the enemy; no one on the German side, neither army, navy, air force, nor the political leader, really wanted to force the issue with a Channel crossing.[5]

Making hasty logistical preparations for operations against Great Britain during the second half of June and the first half of July, the Luftwaffe also gradually expanded the scale of its night attacks. Even these initial, low-intensity night attacks were enough to unnerve some British leaders. In the prime minister's private office, Colville recorded, "the night-bombing is unexpectedly accurate and anti-aircraft fire extraordinarily ineffective." Major daylight operations did not begin until the second week in July. At that point, the principal Luftwaffe strike forces, Luftflotte 2 and Luftflotte 3, began steadily intensifying attacks aimed at gaining and exploiting air superiority over the Channel and probing British air defenses inland, while logistical preparations for an all-out, strategic air offensive (designated *Adlerangriff*, "Eagle Offensive") continued. It was this sudden, sharp upturn in the tempo of these operations from July 10 that Dowding and the Air Ministry later identified, fairly arbitrarily, as marking the commencement of the Battle of Britain.[6]

In the fighting that Luftwaffe airmen referred to as the *Kanalkampf* (Battle of the Channel), the Germans enjoyed considerable operational advantages. Over the channel, the Luftwaffe held the initiative at the strategic, operational, and tactical levels, and therefore could concentrate forces for attacks at times and places of their choosing. The geography of the theater of operations allowed them to assemble large formations outside the effective range of British radar, and then dash in to attack. Fighting mostly over water, at roughly equal distances from the relevant British and German bases, effectively neutralized two of Fighter Command's key advantages: radar warning time, and the chances of capturing German aircrew downed on British soil. Oddly, the Wehrmacht proved better prepared than the British armed forces for maritime combat search and rescue (CSAR).[7]

From Dowding's point of view the Channel fighting involved risks and costs disproportionately greater than what he perceived to be a strategically marginal issue. In fact, the Channel operations might well have been a German feint, designed to lure Fighter Command away from its carefully prepared battle space and divert defenders from more important targets inland. Moreover, at this time Dowding's relatively inexperienced sector controllers frequently underestimated both the numbers of aircraft in the German formations, and their altitudes. The latter was a serious failing: Fighter

Command expected to fight against the odds, but allowing enemy fighters to "bounce" British aircraft (dive on them from above) handed the enemy a lethal advantage. The key to survival and success in air combat was to structure the engagement as a hunt, not a duel, taking the enemy by surprise and at a positional disadvantage. In combat over the Channel, Fighter Command was not well positioned to control the structure of the engagements.[8]

Characteristically, Churchill's reaction to the sudden rise in the Luftwaffe tempo of operations was to head for Dover to observe the battle. Finding nothing to see there on July 11, next day the prime minister visited RAF Kenley to inspect a Hurricane squadron, then invited Dowding to visit him at Chequers on Saturday the thirteenth. Dowding briefed Churchill, who already was carefully following overall RAF losses and claims, regarding fighter aircraft performance (high on the Hurricane, down on the Defiant) and updated the prime minister on countermeasures against the enemy navigational beam Knickebein (British code-name "Headache"). Dowding also discussed his personal headache: the pending retirement the Air Ministry continued to hold over him. Presumably, he came away reassured by the same unqualified support that the prime minster had already communicated to Sinclair and the Air Ministry.

Despite demonstrably appreciating the importance of cultivating the prime minister's confidence, Dowding never hesitated to deliver bad news, when the news was bad. On July 16, Dowding reported personally—and negatively—on the prospects for quick answers to the night-bombing threat. The ever-observant Colville, highly sensitive to Churchill's moods, recorded that Dowding's report was "rather depressing." As the scale of Luftwaffe attacks ramped up during July, there was widespread concern, which Churchill and Dowding shared, about the growing strain on civilian morale. Moreover, direct protection of aircraft factories was thought necessary to sustain the output of fighter aircraft needed to win the battle for air superiority. Yet despite strong and recurring pressure from the Air Staff and even the prime minister, Dowding resisted redeploying fighters to provide point defense for factories, persuading Churchill that the technically correct solution was the development of radar-controlled AAA batteries.[9]

During the second half of July, the Luftwaffe repeatedly bombed historic and picturesque coastal towns including Falmouth, Plymouth, Portland, and Weymouth, as well as the important naval base at Dover. The outcomes of the resulting aerial combat fluctuated as sharply as the notoriously treacherous Channel currents. July 19 was a "disaster" for the British fighters, with ten lost against only four enemy planes downed. This unusually negative "score" was made worse for Fighter Command by the fact that seven of the ten losses were suffered by a single unit, 141 Squadron, which was operating the two-seat, gun-turret equipped, Boulton Paul Defiant as a "heavy" fighter. Twelve aircrew from 141 Squadron perished, and the squadron had to be temporarily withdrawn from combat. The Air Ministry had placed high hopes on the Defiant, but now was forced to recognize that, like the Luftwaffe's long-range Me 110 *Zerstörer*, it was incapable of daylight, air-to-air combat against single-seat, air-superiority fighters.

Fighter Command fared much better on July 20, however, successfully coordinating elements of four squadrons to repulse an attack by fighter-escorted *Stuka* dive bombers on Convoy "BOSOM." In this case, Park anticipated the German attack, and 11 Group controllers were able to preposition the British interceptors for maximum effect despite some rather eccentric maneuvers by a fifth squadron, the notoriously nonconformist 601 "City of London" Squadron, whose flight leader somehow gained the impression that controllers wanted his aircraft to orbit over a village pub some miles inland. As was becoming typical, the air-to-air "score" on the twentieth was roughly even. The circumstances surrounding the defense of Convoy "BOSOM" appear to have inspired British leaders to consider the possibility of manipulating convoy movements in an effort to turn the tables on the Luftwaffe, and secure for Fighter Command an element of tactical initiative in the air and sea Battle of the Channel.

On July 25, Luftflotte 2 combined with Kriegsmarine E-Boats to overwhelm the RAF fighters and Royal Navy destroyers attempting to protect Convoy CW 8, sinking five merchant vessels and damaging two destroyers. Next day, the Admiralty halted daylight merchant-ship movements through the Channel. The Luftwaffe's cumulative effect on Channel shipping during July was sufficiently serious to focus on the problem the attention of the prime minister and the Cabinet Defence Committee, who summoned

Dowding and Vice-Chief of Air Staff Peirse to a July 26 discussion. After another damaging attack on shipping and the port of Dover on July 27, the Defence Committee again considered the matter. Dover's importance as a base for a Royal Navy counterattack on a potential German invasion force inspired suggestions that Fighter Command should deploy more aircraft to stations near the southeast coast; there was even a proposal for an attack on the German bases in the Pas de Calais using Fighter Command assets.[10]

Once again under pressure from Whitehall, Dowding decided to order only limited redeployments. The Admiralty, however, like Dowding, was inclined to cut its losses, in order to preserve its rapidly dwindling destroyer force for use against the expected German amphibious invasion, which the navy believed would be the decisive battle in the defense of Great Britain. On July 29, therefore, the Royal Navy revised its position regarding Dover, redeploying its anti-invasion destroyer forces north to Harwich and Sheerness. The apparently deciding factor was intelligence that Dover would soon be within range of German siege artillery being mounted at Calais. Forcing the Royal Navy to abandon a principal operating base, its best base for close-in, counterinvasion operations, was a significant accomplishment for the Wehrmacht. The strategic gain in neutralizing Dover as a naval base was offset, however, by the tactical relief afforded Fighter Command, which made the Luftwaffe's task of gaining air superiority more difficult.[11]

The opposing, operational-level air commanders spent the first week of August tinkering with the postures of their forces and worrying about the weather. Dowding not only tracked the raw numbers of aircraft and pilots lost, but personally controlled deployment and redeployment of his squadrons, rotating tired or hard-hit units north to 12 Group, and replacing them with fresh—or at least, fresher—squadrons. Throughout, Dowding refused to increase the numbers in 11 Group at the expense of 12 Group. Indeed, less than 25 percent of Fighter Command's strength had been fully engaged in the fighting over the Channel at any one time. As a result of Dowding's insistence upon carefully conserving his forces, Fighter Command actually gained strength during July.[12]

The Luftwaffe was also attempting to learn from the fighting over the Channel, and ready itself for Adlerangriff. Göring's instructions defining Fighter

Command's radar and communications facilities as first-priority targets show that he had understood at least one key point. The Reichsmarschall's main concern, however, was the limited range and endurance of his high-performance, Messerschmidt (Me.) 109 fighters. His order to the fighters to refrain from chasing individual enemy interceptors was primarily intended to ensure efficient use of their limited time in the combat airspace; contrary to legend, Göring did not at this point order the fighters to confine themselves to close escort of the bomber formations. Copying the German army's well-known technique of war gaming a prospective operation, senior officers from the air fleets tested their operational concepts in early August, but the usefulness of the exercises probably was negated by the continued underestimation by Luftwaffe intelligence of both Fighter Command's strength and—astonishingly—the effectiveness of its IAD system.[13]

Before the Germans could begin Adlerangriff, a British attempt to sneak a convoy code-named "PEEWIT" through the Straits of Dover during the night of August 7 provoked intense fighting on the eighth. Churchill had been pressing since late July for a change in strategy, diverting important cargoes to safer routes and treating Channel convoys as "a tactical operation." Service advisers to the War Cabinet Defence Committee, Pound for the navy and Peirse for the air force, now decided that the coastal shipping losses were tolerable—although further destroyer losses were another matter. If the British goal was to lure the Germans, especially the vulnerable Junkers' Ju-87 Stuka dive bombers, into a trap, Fighter Command's first effort to spring it failed to produce a decisive concentration of force. Only the Hurricanes of No. 145 Squadron successfully intercepted the initial attack, ten Stukas escorted by twenty Me. 109s, that Sperrle's Luftflotte 3 launched against convoy PEEWIT.

Against a loss of two "Hurricanes" and pilots, No. 145 Squadron claimed to have downed six of the dive bombers and three enemy fighters, while preventing any loss to the convoy from air attack. Sperrle persisted, however, and at midday struck convoy PEEWIT with a force of thirty dive bombers escorted by more than sixty fighters. Fighter Command's controllers successfully positioned elements of five fighter squadrons to intercept, but the German fighters succeeded in drawing them away from the attacking Stukas, which were therefore free to sink four of the convoy and damage six or seven other vessels. A series of further attacks throughout the afternoon, in strengths ranging from fifteen to nearly a hundred, provoked intense air-to-air combat, but resulted in no further losses to the convoy. Still, combined with the losses inflicted the previous night in surface attacks by Kriegsmarine E-boats, Luftflotte 3 had practically destroyed convoy PEEWIT.

An Air Ministry narrative later praised the single-handed defense of convoy PEEWIT by No. 145 Squadron on the morning of August 8 as "a splendid example of . . . a determined squadron," and indeed the action seemed so singular that the prime minister, seconded by the secretary of state for air and by Air Vice-Marshal His Royal Highness the Duke of Gloucester, directed Dowding to commend No. 145 Squadron in the name of the War Cabinet. The prime minister's attitude toward the Battle of the Channel was oddly inconsistent. On the one hand, he was sentimental about the sinking of "those poor little ships" plying the coastal waters; on the other hand, convinced that Fighter Command was winning the air battles over the narrow seas by overwhelming margins, he was fully prepared to use convoys as bait. As he admitted to Colville, however, "the surviving bait are getting a bit fed up."[14]

The action over convoy PEEWIT climaxed the first phase of the campaign. It was also, in a number of ways, characteristic. British shipping losses had been substantial, but far from mortal. The same was true of their aircraft losses, although pilot losses gave more reason for concern. Fighter Command's overall "kill" ratio of roughly 1.5:1 was not as nearly as satisfactory as the 4:1 or 5:1 the British thought it was, but it was sufficient at least to put equal strain on the German aviators.[15] In light of the German objective for the first phase of their operations to gain local air superiority over the Channel, their operations achieved at best only partial success, at considerable cost. They did make it too expensive for the British to continue using some important ports and some coastal supply lines, but the Luftwaffe's ability to operate in the associated airspace continued to be bitterly contested.[16]

Hitler's Directive 17 called for the decisive air-superiority battle to begin on or after August 5. Luftwaffe planners expected to win this battle in four days. Unfavorable weather repeatedly postponed the start date, code-named *Adlertag* (Eagle Day). Adlertag finally fell on August 13, which seemed likely to begin a stretch of good weather. When a break in the weather two days earlier gave Kesselring and Sperrle the opportunity to resume large-scale operations, for some reason they decided to return to attacks on targets in the Channel and along the south coast of England. The resulting intense engagements proved costly in personnel to both sides, with Churchill "very excited" by the claims of Fighter Command's pilots. In fact, the thirty-eight kills they claimed was exactly double the losses they actually inflicted on the attackers. "Jock" Colville's diary and other first-person evidence make it clear, however, that at this stage even the inner circle of the Government was accepting RAF claims at face value.[17]

The final preliminary to Adlerangriff took place on August 12, when in accordance with Göring's operational concept, a well-planned series of attacks targeted Chain Home and Chain Low radar stations in key locations. The early morning strikes obtained surprise, and yielded excellent bombing accuracy. Despite heavy damage to several installations, however, every station was either back in service or replaced by temporary work-arounds within hours. Luftwaffe intelligence, while accurately identifying the radar stations and appreciating their importance, had incorrectly analyzed how the Fighter Command IAD system actually functioned, and therefore underestimated its flexibility and resiliency. Given the technological limitations of intelligence gathering and weaponry at the time, it was in any case up to almost random chance whether or not even sustained attacks would destroy the sector control rooms or interrupt the stations' electrical power and telephone communications, which were the critical elements of the system. Most importantly, the Luftwaffe leadership failed to comprehend the persistence in attack necessary to trigger system collapse.

On the morning of August 13, the Luftwaffe finally set out to deliver the so-long-awaited knockout blow, but the famous variability of the English weather combined with indecisive exercise of personal command by Göring to create a muddle. As Adlertag wore on, raids appeared in the skies of southern England one after the other, seemingly uncoordinated. Luftwaffe losses mounted, culminating in the "massacre" of an entire *Staffel* of Ju-87 Stukas. The overall result of the day's air-to-air combat was one of the most one-sided of the entire campaign: Fighter Command downed forty-seven German aircraft against a loss of thirteen. If the British pilots, out of the chaos of battle, distorted the after-action assessments by claiming seventy-eight kills, the Germans began an (ultimately) highly damaging spiral of delusion by adding dozens of imaginary shoot-downs to the admittedly large number of British aircraft destroyed on the ground, for a grossly exaggerated total of eighty-four.[18]

Despite the German airmen's gaudy claims, all ranks in the Luftwaffe were aware that Adlerangriff had proved—at best—an expensive sort of success, and at worst, a costly fiasco. The Luftwaffe leadership would have been depressed, rather than merely frustrated, had it known the reaction of their British opponents: "The question everyone is asking today," Colville wrote, "is what is the motive of these gigantic daylight raids, which cost so much and effect so little?" As the day's favorable kill rate demonstrated, massed, daylight attacks played into Dowding's hands. He was hoping that the Germans would impale themselves on his defenses. Even after he mentally discounted by 20–25 percent his pilot's claims from August 13, the results elated him. Characteristically, however, he reacted with redoubled attention to detail, devoting the fourteenth to carefully reshuffling his squadrons just in time to meet the Luftwaffe's greatest effort yet.[19]

The August 15 action began with relatively small-scale probing attacks on British defenses and air bases in Kent, apparently intended to distract attention from the first—and as things turned out, the last—major daylight attack on Britain by Luftflotte 5. Flying from Stavanger in southern Norway, seventy-plus He 111 medium bombers were escorted by twenty-plus Me. 110-D long-range fighters, and followed from Aalborg in northern Denmark by at least sixty of the fast Ju-88 strike aircraft, half configured as C-model heavy fighters; all targeted No. 12 Group bases in the north of England. Rested and alert squadrons from both 12 Group and 13 Group heavily attacked both strike forces, and in the absence of the Luftwaffe's air-superiority fighter, the short-range Me. 109, Luftflotte 5 lost twenty-four aircraft while inflicting only minor damage and no kills on the British interceptors. Unsurprisingly in the circumstances, Luftflotte 5's target identification and bombing accuracy were poor.

Churchill, "consumed with excitement" as the reports of enemy aircraft destroyed mounted, now drove to Fighter Command HQ to watch the battle continue to unfold on Dowding's own plotting table. Throughout the afternoon of August 15, Luftflotte 2 and Luftflotte 3 launched sustained attacks on the 11 Group sectors in southeastern England. These attacks, utilizing strike forces of different sizes, composed of different types of aircraft, employing different tactics, and engaging a wide variety of targets, nearly overwhelmed 11 Group's controllers with the sheer complexity of the defense problem. Despite some early afternoon successes for the Luftwaffe, however, the pendulum of battle swung back again in midafternoon, when No. 601 Squadron wiped out a *Staffel* of Ju-88s; in the late afternoon, three squadrons, Nos. 234, 213, and 87, downed 13 Me. 110s from the beleaguered heavy fighter wing ZG 76, whose I Group had been destroyed in the northern operation that morning.

Perhaps the worst blow to the Luftwaffe of an already historically bad day was the last. In the evening, No. 111 Squadron and No. 32 Squadron combined to decimate *Erprobungsgruppe* (Test Wing) 210, which during the preceding weeks had been the most effective of all the Luftwaffe strike forces in operations against Britain. Specializing in low-altitude, high-speed attacks by specially configured Me. 109 and Me. 110 fighter bombers, the missions flown by Erpro 210 were difficult to track, frequently achieved surprise, and had probably done more serious damage to Fighter Command's IAD system than all the rest of the Luftwaffe bombing combined. Moreover, Erpro 210's fighter-bombers came closer to realizing the airpower zealots' vision of a self-defending bomber formation than any other type then operational. Erpro 210's costly failure in its third raid on the fifteenth suggests that the combat effectiveness of the attacking Germans may have been wearing down faster than that of the defending Britons.[20]

Altogether, the Luftwaffe lost 75 aircraft on something over 2,000 sorties, its highest sortie total of any single day in the entire campaign. This amounted to a painful, but not necessarily unsustainable loss rate of almost 4 percent. The British lost 34 fighters, but with claims of 182 "kills," believed they had won a victory of monumental proportions. In his postwar account, Churchill implied that this action in the North had been, in at least a limited sense, strategically decisive. "Henceforth," he observed, "everything north of the Wash was safe by day." Why, therefore, did Dowding maintain the relative strengths of his groups essentially unchanged after the fifteenth? Numerous critics have alleged that stubborn inflexibility led him to over-insure against a threat that, never great, had now practically vanished. Shifting more squadrons to 11 Group sooner would have at least slightly improved odds that were to rise as high as 1:10 against the interceptors at points of attack.

Dowding's insistence on maintaining the balance of relative strengths that he had established among 13, 12, and 11 Groups rested on more, however, than simply the defense of Scotland and the north of England. His primary motive was to hold a strategic reserve of squadrons apart from the fighting in the southeast.[21] Throughout the 1940 campaign, the shadows of the Somme lay on him. His concept of operations was based on the Fabian strategy of endurance, fighting a protracted series of limited engagements; a middle course between gambling on winning an early, decisive battle of annihilation, on the one hand, or slogging through a campaign of annihilation by attrition, on the other. Dowding preferred to gamble that he could limit Fighter Command's attrition to losses that it could sustain indefinitely, and thereby frustrate Hitler's strategic purposes. Although this operational strategy has been adversely criticized as "conservative" and overly cautious, in fact it represented a daring exercise in calculated risk-taking.

Dowding deliberately left high-value targets such as airfields and aircraft factories exposed to potential attack in order to preclude catastrophic, short-term losses to the fighter force. The counterproductive effort to avoid all risk, the chimerical attempt to be strong everywhere, are hallmarks of mediocre generalship; the essence of Dowding's operational strategy was just the opposite. He traded the day-to-day, hour-by-hour tactical risks of engaging less than his maximum strength for the ultimate, strategic gain of denying the enemy a "decisive battle" for air superiority. The strength of will to adhere to this decision under almost unimaginable pressure truly was, as Churchill put it, "an example genius in the art of war."[22]

Accepting that Dowding's strategic judgment surpassed that of his critics, nevertheless the aftermath of the August 15 battles calls into question his practice of command. By some accounts Leigh-Mallory was "furious" at the limited role played by 12 Group's fighters. David Fisher has implied that Dowding was unable to focus his attention on the deteriorating command relationships because he was becoming emotionally overwrought by the slaughter of his fighter pilots. While it is clearly true that Dowding remained indefensibly, if not inexplicably, tolerant of Leigh-Mallory's behavior, Fisher's suggestion of emotional breakdown lacks credibility. During late August and early September the AOC-in-C carefully studied pilot readiness on a squadron-by-squadron basis, assessing the squadrons' condition in minute detail. Dowding's command focus on his pilots—not only their survival rates, but also their physical and psychological fitness—was altogether rational. Long before Churchill, Dowding had realized that the outcome of the campaign was in the hands of "the Few."[23]

9

THE BATTLE OF BRITAIN

AUGUST–SEPTEMBER 1940

Göring reacted to the losses on what his pilots termed "Black Thursday" by ordering a return to doctrinal fundamentals: specifically, a renewed concentration on airfield attacks. The Reichsmarschall's loss of faith in the apparently unproductive attacks on radar stations, however, yet again demonstrated the Luftwaffe leadership's failure to grasp the importance of persistence in the offensive employment of airpower: the need not only to knock out British installations, but keep them out of action. In an effort to reduce bomber losses, Göring decided to concentrate his Me. 109s in the Pas de Calais under Kesselring's Luftflotte 2. This forward basing would provide greater concentration of the fighter force, and extend the Me. 109s' reach deeper into the battle space. As such, it was a reverse or mirror image of Dowding's economy-of-force operational strategy. An unintended but fateful consequence of Göring's redeployment of the fighters was that Sperrle's Luftflotte 3, largely deprived of escorts, turned increasingly to night operations.[1]

Fighting on August 16 began with a series of midmorning attacks by Luftflotte 2 on 11 Group airfields in an arc from the east to the south and southwest of London. Perhaps due to initial misevaluation of German strength and intentions, losses were relatively steep among the defending fighters. That afternoon, attacks by Luftflotte 3 evidencing sound staff planning (including a willingness to ignore Göring's operational directions) set out to tear a gap in the British radar chain, and then exploit it with strikes on Fighter Command stations timed to catch 11 Group's fighters refueling and rearming after the morning's engagements with Luftflotte 2. These strikes disabled the Chain Home radar station at Ventnor for a week, and RAF Tangmere, among other installations, was heavily damaged. No. 11 Group's Tangmere Wing and No. 10 Group's fighters were alert and ready to scramble, however, and as a result No. 43 Squadron brought down 7 Ju-87s from 1 Group, 2nd *Stukageschwader.* (A Luftwaffe *Geschwader* was actually more like an RAF wing; a Luftwaffe group was roughly equivalent to an RAF squadron.)

The day's most physically destructive attack was small and stealthy, a diminutive raid by a pair of Ju-88s that destroyed 46 trainers and bombers, and damaged 11 Hurricanes packed into hangers at RAF Brize Norton. Once again, however, the Luftwaffe's weak intelligence analysis led to a waste of excellent tactical performance by the operational forces, since much of the weight of the August 16 attacks fell on what should have been low-priority targets, either peripheral or irrelevant to Fighter Command operations. Luftwaffe intelligence still apparently had failed to identify the vital role played by the sector stations, the vital nodes in Fighter Command's C^3 system in the RAF's Integrated Air Defense system, much less devise a plan to attack them effectively. Overall, Fighter Command lost 18 fighters and 9 pilots; the Germans lost 21 bombers and had 27 fighters destroyed. Although the British kill-to-loss ratio was satisfactory (particularly with respect to fighters) the absolute numbers of fighters and pilots lost was steadily rising.[2]

Churchill watched the afternoon's engagements from 11 Group's operations room, and was greatly impressed by the odds Park had to cope with. Major General Hastings Ismay, an army officer serving as chief of staff to Churchill in his capacity as minister of defence, later described feeling "sick with fear" as the indicator lights showed all of 11 Group's fighters airborne, apparently leaving no reserves to deal with any further German strike forces that might appear on the plot. Ismay's reaction suggests that, despite Churchill's efforts going back to the prewar period to master the air-defense issue, the prime ministerial inner circle still did not fully understand the "Dowding system." No. 11 Group's "reserves" were the squadrons carefully based in the 13, 12, and 10 Group areas, outside the hot zone of southeastern England. The tactical problem was not lack of reserves, but bringing the reserves to bear where and when they were most needed.[3]

After a recovery day on the seventeenth, the Luftwaffe struck again on the eighteenth, with the bombers enjoying fighter escorts amounting to a maximum effort by the Me. 109s. The concentration on airfields continued, as well as the innovative tactics: objectives were attacked by multiple, closely timed waves of bombers at different altitudes. Moreover, for once the main effort was directed at remunerative targets such as RAF Kenley and RAF Biggin Hill. The results of all this operational and tactical virtuosity were mixed, however. Kenley was rendered inoperative for a week, but poor bombing accuracy left Biggin Hill only slightly damaged. The air-to-air fighting was costly to both sides, in roughly equal proportion. When the Germans again launched late afternoon dive-bomber raids, however, they met with disaster. In return for serious but reparable damage to the Chain Home radar network, British fighters "wiped out" yet another entire group of Ju-87 Stukas, forcing withdrawal of the Stukageschwader from cross-Channel operations.[4]

The fighting on August 18 represented a new climax of the air campaign. The one-day toll of aircraft destroyed and damaged, and aircrew killed, wounded, or captured on both sides would remain unexceeded, and the eighteenth became known as "the Hardest Day." In a slightly longer perspective, the first week of Adlerangriff had been a worryingly costly proposition for both sides, and the five days of thick weather that followed ushered in a reduced operational tempo that was welcome to both. While aircrew sought physical and mental recovery from the strain of battle, leadership scrambled to apply lessons learned. On the German side, in addition to implementing the decisions regarding fighter redeployment and the (non)employment of dive bombers, Göring began replacing senior fighter commanders with younger and more active pilots boasting proven combat records as high-scoring aces, the "*Experten*." Meanwhile, Park issued to his sector controllers a meticulously detailed directive specifying changes to 11 Group's tactics, techniques, and procedures.[5]

Park's "Instruction No. 4" directed the group to avoid fighting over water in order to minimize pilot losses. Fighters were to be deployed in pairs to provide combat air patrols over airfields, but if "heavy attacks" were directed toward the critical sectors stations, these were to be protected in squadron strength, "or even [by] sector training flight[s]" if necessary. Controllers received a mandate to call on 12 Group to cover airfields north of London. The instruction also reinforced previous guidance that the enemy fighter escorts should be engaged by "minimum" interception forces; the main interception effort should be directed against the enemy bomber forces. Instruction No. 4 reflected the very real concerns on the part of the 11 Group AOC regarding rising pilot losses and damage to airfields. Designed to blunt the airfield attacks while improving Fighter Command's kill ratio, with Luftflotte 2 massing ever-larger fighter escorts around the bombers, Park's operational strategy would prove difficult to implement.[6]

While Park was parrying the thrusts of Kesselring and Sperrle, Dowding was coping with the ever-shifting concerns of the British political leadership. As the German attacks proliferated, concerns mounted that air-raid warnings were, in themselves, producing major disruption of the British war effort. As AOC-in-C, Fighter Command, Dowding was deeply involved in the Churchill Government's extended debate about how to balance potential saving of life through early warning of attack against the maximizing of industrial production by encouraging workers to remain at their tasks unless an attack was actually imminent. Beaverbrook in particular was worried by increasingly effective and persistent attacks on "his" aircraft factories. At this point, however, despite statistical evidence that the late-August aircraft loss rate was unsustainable in the long run, Dowding's critical and immediate problem was not aircraft losses, which for at least another few weeks could be made good from the combination reserve stocks and new production, but rather, pilot losses.[7]

The heart of Dowding's difficulty was that while the training units known as OTUs might, at a stretch, keep up with the numbers killed, incapacitated by wounds, or missing, they could not replicate the combat effectiveness of the lost men. Sending inexperienced pilots into the inferno of aerial combat over southeastern England soon appeared to be something like a death sentence. A characteristic anecdote from this period describes two new arrivals at No. 111 Squadron shot down (one dead, one hospitalized) before their luggage was unpacked. For reasons of morale and efficiency, Dowding deployed squadrons intact, rotating entire units in and out of combat while integrating individual replacements into the squadrons. But as the fighting wore on, Fighter Command ran out of squadrons that were both fresh and experienced. And with the casualty rate of inexperienced pilots five or six times that of veterans, the prospect of committing to battle whole squadrons of novices was appalling.[8]

Searching for replacement pilots who were, if not experienced in fighter combat, at least practiced fliers, Dowding asked the Air Staff to direct the retraining of light bomber pilots for fighter service. The urgency of the request did not impress itself upon the Air Ministry, which took a month to agree to the proposal. The Air Ministry's attitude substantiates Churchill's conviction that one reason for the looming shortage of fighter pilots was bureaucratic reluctance to upset established organizational structures and standard operating procedures. Reflecting his continuing lack of trust in the Air Ministry, for some weeks Churchill had been making a point of personally mastering the details of the pilot-training problems. The prime minister's inquiries on the subject touched off a long-running debate with the ministry regarding "the method . . . employed for expanding operational strength." This debate, in turn, became entangled in the venomous, political battle between Beaverbrook and Sinclair.[9]

In view of the desperate need for trained pilots, it is surprising that both the Air Ministry and Dowding himself initially under-appreciated an obvious source of trained manpower. As the Wehrmacht had overrun one continental state after another, thousands of airmen (ground crew as well as aviators) from the armed forces of the defeated states had fled, in many cases first to France, then to Britain. The largest contingent, which was to have the greatest impact on the Battle of Britain, came from the Polish Air Force. Dowding seems to have shared a common attitude of cultural as well as professional condescension—amounting in some cases to prejudice—toward the Poles in particular; his first, semi-public encounter with refugee Polish airmen joining the RAF did not go all that well. The RAF subsequently put a lot of mostly misplaced effort put into trying to Anglicize the Polish airmen.[10]

In the aftermath the French débâcle, however, the eagerness of thousands of Poles who had escaped to Britain to continue the fight against Germany began to change British attitudes. Apparently, a partial exception was Dowding himself, who ironically swung from opposing formation of separate, Polish squadrons to "very strongly" supporting them, supposedly because he was unhappy with the effect on British squadrons of integrating individual Polish pilots. The reconstitution of the Polish Air Force under RAF administrative and operational control therefore began with the formation of No. 302 Poznań Squadron in July (operational August 14) and No. 303 Kościuszko Squadron in early August. The latter famously earned operational status on August 31 after an unauthorized—but successful—interception of a German bomber formation during a training flight. These two Polish fighter squadrons proved to be, by at least one measure, vastly more combat-effective than their British counterparts, posting an overall kill-to-loss ratio of 10.5:1.[11]

Under enormous pressure to obtain effective pilots wherever they might be found, Fighter Command became in some respects a truly international force. In addition to substantial contributions from the Commonwealth (No. 1 Canadian Squadron becoming operational on August 26), the Poles, for example, provided more pilots than any of the British Dominions; the Czechs, almost three times as many as Australia; Belgium, more than South Africa. The numbers involved ranged from single digits to just over a hundred. Churchill best captured the sense of wonder that a military campaign of world-historical importance could turn on such margins when he told the House of Commons on August 20, "Never in the field of human conflict have so many owed so much to so few."

By the last week in August, the fighting had developed into a protracted, attritional campaign fought out in the confined airspace over southeastern England. Beginning with repeated attacks on the vital sector stations at Biggin Hill and Kenley, as well as the satellite airfields at Manston, Hawkinge, and Lymphe, Kesselring finally displayed the persistence necessary to keep key facilities out of operation. After flattening Manston and crippling Hawkinge and Lymphe, Kesselring's attacks surged north of London, striking sector stations at Hornchurch, Debden, and North Weald. Carefully limiting the exposure of his vulnerable bombers and massing the largest possible fighter escorts, Kesselring also succeeded in increasing the ratio of British to German losses. All this inspired a bitter dispute between Park and Leigh-Mallory. The core issue was how to protect the 11 Group airfields exposed to attack while Park's squadrons sought to intercept the enemy formations as far forward as possible.

The friction between the 11 and 12 Group AOCs, which became Dowding's most fateful leadership challenge, intensified after 12 Group failed to satisfy 11 Group's requests for cover on August 24 and 26. Park came to believe that Leigh-Mallory was deliberately shirking urgent requests for immediate fighter support, instead taking the time to assemble multiple squadrons into large, counterstrike forces of a type that came to be known as the "Big Wing." Leigh-Mallory, advised by—among others—Squadron Leader Douglas Bader, was indeed convinced that the proper way to meet the Luftwaffe's massed attack forces was with mass formations of fighters. In 12 Group, Big Wing advocates argued that this was the only way to destroy enough German aircraft to secure a decisive victory. Unfortunately, initial efforts to implement the concept failed to bring 12 Group's fighters into action against the Germans.

Leigh-Mallory either rejected, or failed to comprehend, why and how Dowding and Park were applying the principle of economy of force. Park's mission was to protect the targets of the German air raids; 11 Group's application of the Dowding-Park concept of operations involved dispersing the Luftwaffe formations before they could bomb. The obvious disadvantage of this concept was that many of the bombers thus repulsed would return for another try next day, or some later day. Its great advantage was that it minimized British exposure to losses both in the air and on the ground, making it a rational, operational concept for the quantitatively weaker combatant. Underlying the operational concept was the strategic premise, dating back nearly a decade, that Britain would win a protracted contest if the Germans failed to force a quick decision through decisive battle. Dowding and Park were therefore as determined to avoid an all-or-nothing throw of the dice, as Göring and Kesselring were to force one.[12]

Taking advantage of another weather-imposed slowdown of operations, on August 27 Park issued his "Instruction No. 7," directing sector controllers to route requests for assistance from 12 Group through Fighter Command Headquarters. The instruction included a gratuitous explanation of why this new procedure was necessary that should have rung alarm bells for Dowding:

> Thanks to the friendly co-operation offered by No. 10 Group, they are always prepared to detail two to four squadrons to engage from the west. . . . Up to date No. 12 Group . . . have not shown the same desire to cooperate by dispatching their squadrons to the places requested.

Park then went on explicitly to blame the drubbing 11 Group's airfields were receiving on 12 Group's lack of cooperation:

> The result of this attitude has been that on two occasions recently when 12 Group . . . were requested to patrol our aerodromes, their squadrons did not in fact patrol over our aerodromes. On both these occasions our aerodromes were heavily bombed.

Given the wide circulation such a document must necessarily receive within RAF command and staff echelons, Park's comments constituted an extraordinary, semipublic rebuke from one senior operational commander to another, in the midst of an ongoing campaign. Yet Instruction No. 7 provoked no corrective action by Dowding, who not only allowed a potentially dangerous divergence in concepts of operations to go on unresolved, but also permitted a legitimate difference of professional judgment to escalate into a disruptive personal and political schism between his two most important subordinates. Dowding's senior air staff officer, the memorably named air vice-marshal D. C. S. Evill, blandly directed the command controllers to handle Park's requests, without addressing Park's claims regarding noncooperation by 12 Group.[13]

Kesselring's skillful combination of mass and maneuver in his handling of Luftflotte 2 meant 11 Group's success would depend on the group controllers' and flight leaders' ability to recognize the Germans' elaborate deception tactics, place the British fighters in advantageous interception positions, and secure the prompt arrival of reinforcements from 10 and 12 Groups at the

Germans' points of attack. High-intensity operations resumed on August 28, signaled by further catastrophic losses of the two-seat, turret-gun Defiant "heavy" fighters, this time from No. 264 Squadron, which was hastily pulled back to 12 Group. By now, Kesselring was straightforwardly using relatively small bomber formations as bait, attempting to lure 11 Group into engagements with much larger fighter formations, as on the twenty-ninth when he deployed nearly the entire Luftflotte 2 fighter force to escort a single bombing mission. For his part, Park continued to insist that 11 Group minimize fighter engagements and concentrate on shooting down bombers.[14]

Meanwhile the Luftwaffe had also been expanding and intensifying its night attacks by Knickebein beam-guided bombers. Concern about mounting civilian casualties led the prime minister to undertake a tour of the southeast on August 28, inspecting damage to the ports and gauging morale. Much worse was in store for the civilian population; the week's casualty totals prompted Churchill to visit 11 Group's HQ on the thirty-first. This turned out to be Fighter Command's worst day, in terms of total losses. Observing the action from Park's command post, "The P.M. was deeply moved," according to Colville; "he said that what he saw there brought the war home to him." Dowding, accompanying Churchill to Chequers that evening, made no attempt to downplay the gravity of the situation, but when the prime minister again returned to Uxbridge the next day, the operations he observed were reassuring. As he put it to Colville, "The air is all right."[15]

For the most part, Park successfully evaded Kesselring's fighter traps, so the Luftflotte 2 commander returned to attacking in successive waves, timed to catch the defenders out of position, or worse, on the ground refueling and rearming. Dowding thought this a mistake, telling Colville, "he could not understand why the Germans kept on coming in waves instead of concentrating on one mass raid a day which could not be effectively parried." In fact, Kesselring's "wave" attacks did have some success, as on September 4, in confusing the controllers in Fighter Command's plotting rooms. Several times "a lucky hit" took down a key element of the British IAD system, on one day severing a line feeding electric power to multiple radar stations, on another day, cutting important telephone connections. Unfortunately for the Germans, the Luftwaffe's bombing damage assessment was too weak to recognize such successes before the British made repairs, and consequently successful strikes were not systematically exploited.[16]

The fortnight overlapping the end of August and the beginning of September is generally understood to have been a crisis period for 11 Group's infrastructure. In August, Park had expressed confidence (presumably based on the fluctuations in the Luftwaffe sortie rate) "that the Germans must already have developed their maximum [air] attack and could not stand the strain much longer." Yet the Luftwaffe maintained its pressure, and cumulative damage to 11 Group's ground facilities mounted. Symbolically, at Biggin Hill on September 1 Luftflotte 2 at last (albeit unknowingly) scored a direct hit on a sector station operations room. As with the pilots, the physical and mental strain on Fighter Command's support personnel was immense, and could not have been borne indefinitely. At some point in the indefinite future, the slow but measurable decline in Fighter Command's efficiency must have culminated in organizational failure, unless its squadrons were withdrawn from the effective range of daylight bombing—or the Luftwaffe cracked first.[17]

Then there was the problem of aircraft losses. By early September, the production of fighters was no longer keeping pace with attrition, and the gap had to be closed by drawing down reserve stocks, an expedient that could only continue for a few weeks. Fortunately for Fighter Command, this was one problem the Air Ministry had well foreseen, and acted energetically to solve with the creation of civilian repair units to supplement the RAF's internal repair capabilities. As a result, more than a third of the aircraft reaching the operational fighter squadrons between June and October came from repair rather than new production. Notwithstanding this very seasonable accomplishment, on September 5 Dowding acted to anticipate a potential aircraft supply crisis, ordering—despite his longstanding aversion to point defense—"maximum fighter cover" for aircraft factories in southeastern England. It was not the last significant reversal of policy forced on Dowding by the German onslaught.

Pilot attrition—not only in numbers of pilots but also in leadership and combat effectiveness—was still the most immediately critical problem that Dowding urgently needed to solve. Everyone in Fighter Command was tired, from the air chief marshal down to the aircraftsmen laboring to fill bomb craters with shovelfuls of earth. Many were beginning to show signs of what at a later stage of the war would be termed combat fatigue, or in a much later generation, post-traumatic stress disorder. Dowding was conscious that stress and exhaustion were leading to mistakes, not only in combat but also in routine air and ground operations, resulting in unnecessary damage to equipment and injury to personnel. But the heart of the matter remained Fighter Command's ability to fill its fighter cockpits with pilots capable of meeting and defeating the Luftwaffe's seemingly inexhaustible supply of veterans.[18]

In a dramatic confrontation at Bentley Priory on September 7, Dowding, Evill, and Park jointly sought to bludgeon the Air Ministry, represented in the person of Deputy Chief of Air Staff Sholto Douglas, into agreeing to Dowding's request for the reassignment of light bomber pilots to fighters. Dowding eventually got his way, but as often in the past, his methods further envenomed personal and official relations between the Air Ministry, on the one hand, and the senior leadership of Fighter Command, on the other. Douglas openly expressed resentment at the way the Fighter Command staff minutes portrayed his part in the meeting. Douglas and his Air Ministry colleagues were, of course, well practiced in this sort of bureaucratic power play, and it was not long before Dowding and Park found the political score being run up against themselves. For the moment, though, what mattered was extracting the promise of a few more pilots.[19]

Pilot conversions, however, at best would yield modest results some weeks in the future. Continuing heavy casualties demanded an immediate, large-scale response, and Dowding was compelled to fundamentally change his squadron-rotation policy. On September 8, the day after meeting with Douglas, Dowding adopted the so-called Stabilization Scheme. All Fighter Command squadrons were to be graded A, B, or C, according to combat effectiveness. Class A squadrons would deploy in the hot sectors most vulnerable to attack; class B squadrons would be stationed in less-active sectors of 12 Group and 10 Group, where they would serve as the immediate, operational reserve. The class C squadrons would be, effectively, withdrawn from combat and exploited as a source of individual replacements for the A and B squadrons. Class C squadrons would be replenished by drafts of new pilots from the training units, who would be worked up to combat effectiveness by the surviving handful of experienced though weary veterans left in each unit.[20]

The Stabilization Scheme was an evidently fragile expedient, depending on the ability of the class C squadrons to supply enough rested veterans and adequately trained newcomers to enable the hard-pressed A and B squadrons to maintain control of the battle space. Dowding's decision to adopt the Stabilization Scheme was an uncharacteristic leap in the dark, reflecting perhaps the courage of desperation. Certainly it took considerable moral courage to violate the squadron ethos so carefully nurtured by the Royal Air Force during its short history, based as it was on deeply rooted beliefs concerning the essential character of a fighting service borrowed from the ancient, warship-centered culture of the Royal Navy and, more directly, from the regimental culture of the British army.[21] While fully sharing these beliefs and values, Dowding dared to take responsibility for this novel measure, because he could no longer afford the status quo.

The salient feature of the situation at the beginning of September was that the Luftwaffe's loss rate had come down since Adlerangriff, mostly thanks to the withdrawal of the highly vulnerable Ju-87 Stukas, while Fighter Command's loss rate had risen, partly due to the steep losses among its increasing proportion of inexperienced pilots, and partly due to Kesselring's ability to concentrate overwhelming numerical superiority in fighters at his chosen points of attack. Fighter Command was still shooting down more aircraft than it was losing, but the gap was gradually closing as Kesselring, his staff and subordinate commanders, slowly figured out how to attack the "Dowding system." Had these trends continued for more than another month or so, Dowding would have been forced to adopt still more drastic measures to reduce his rate of attrition. That the adverse trends did not continue, most analyses of the campaign have attributed to an abrupt shift in Luftwaffe operational strategy.[22]

10
THE BATTLE OF BRITAIN

SEPTEMBER–OCTOBER 1940

On September 7 the Luftwaffe began the massive bombing attacks on London popularly known as the Blitz. This abrupt change of operational strategy is generally considered the most important turning point in the Battle of Britain. In this view the Germans, having through trial and error hit upon a course of action that was, however slowly, loosening Fighter Command's grip on the battle space over southeastern England, now abandoned it for an alternative course of action that proved both more costly, and ultimately, strategically futile for the attackers. Strangely enough, Dowding himself had anticipated this turn of events before the campaign began, when he counterintuitively predicted after the Wehrmacht occupied northern France: "The nearness of London to German airfields will lose them the war."[1]

At his August 16 conference with Kesselring and Sperrle, Göring had relaxed the reins on his bombers. By late August, significant attacks on Britain's urban centers had been underway for some time. Daylight attacks on airfields and oil-storage facilities continued, together with widespread night attacks on scores of urban area targets. Night attacks on military, industrial and transportation targets around the periphery of Greater London on August 24 predictably, if not intentionally, produced widely scattered damage and started fires, not only in the suburbs but also in London boroughs and the City itself. Once again the most serious damage was caused by the smallest raids, as when a single aircraft bombed an oil storage depot that burned for days afterward. Much the same thing had happened on August 15, but this time the Churchill Government reacted forcefully, ordering Bomber Command to attack Berlin the following night. All concerned fully expected British retaliation to provoke large-scale German attacks on London.[2]

Churchill was under pressure from public and parliament to "give it 'em back," as was shouted at him during a tour of bomb-damaged areas. Contrary to his reputation for frequent "interference" in operational matters, to this point the prime minister had largely kept his distance from RAF Bomber Command's targeting process.[3] Now, however, with the scope of death and destruction from German bombing steadily increasing, and with no end to it in prospect, his political intuition unleashed his native pugnacity. "I want you to hit them hard," he told his airmen, "and Berlin is the place to hit them." Bomber Command proved unable to find, much less hit Berlin on its first try, but a few dozen RAF medium bombers did succeed in striking the German capital on three out of four nights starting August 28, ostensibly targeting military objectives. On August 30 a predictably enraged Adolf Hitler removed the last restrictions on Luftwaffe bombing.[4]

The first political reward for Churchill's intuition arrived on September 4, when Hitler publicly rose to the bait. In a speech broadcast from the Berlin Sportpalast, the Führer promised a suitably hysterical audience, "If they attack our cities, we shall simply rub theirs out!" Both Churchill and Hitler were playing to their respective populations, based on their respective assessments of the two home fronts' Achilles' heels. Military strategy was being made to serve political ends, but in this case political and military motives were fully congruent. Dowding's Fabian strategy, based on economy of force, had frustrated the Luftwaffe beyond endurance, all but defeating the Wehrmacht's short-war strategic concept. When Göring arrived at Calais to supervise the rubbing-out of London, he finally granted Kesselring the opportunity the field marshal had long sought: to force Fighter Command into a decisive battle. The pivotal assault on London was code-named Loge after the giant in Norse mythology, "the personification of fire."[5]

British and American historians, almost unanimously, have disparaged this decision—along with others such as providing close escorts for the bombers—mainly because the decisions were Göring's. Yet close escort in fact accomplished its purpose, making it harder for British fighters to attack the German bombers. Notably, most of the infrequent occasions when the Germans downed more British aircraft than they themselves lost occurred during this period. Contrary to legend, Göring continued to allow Kesselring some tactical flexibility, which the latter employed creatively to close the gap between British and German aircraft losses. The subsequently much-retailed complaints of Adolf Galland and other German fighter Experten were identical in substance to those of their British counterparts like Bader. Fighter pilots—especially the best ones—wanted to roam the skies as hunters, catching their prey at a disadvantage, using speed and agility to elude the hunters on the other side. The hunters argued, all that mattered was the kill.

On September 6, Dowding received the King and Queen at his Bentley Priory headquarters. While engaged in this royal ritual, his decision to establish fighter patrols over at least some key aircraft factories was paying dividends. In an important success for the Dowding-Park emphasis on preventing bombing, a fighter patrol disrupted an attack on Brooklands, which turned out half of the RAF's supply of Hurricanes. Significantly, experience was confirming that fighter opposition interfered with Luftwaffe bombing accuracy far more seriously than antiaircraft artillery fire. German bomber formations frequently were reported as breaking up under fighter attack. Clearly, not all bomber pilots pressed through to their targets; many jettisoned their bombs at random. The result generally seems to have been a toss-up: bomb damage on the ground often was diffuse and militarily inconsequential, but the bombers mostly escaped the fighters' guns. On this day, however, Luftwaffe losses overall were roughly 50 percent higher than Fighter Command's.

Fighter Command optimistically interpreted the Germans' relatively limited attacks on the night of September 6 as evidence that the tempo of operations was wearing down foe as well as friend, but other data supported a more alarming conclusion. Air reconnaissance and other intelligence indicated hundreds of barges the Wehrmacht had been collecting to serve as troop transports and amphibious landing craft were moving into attack positions. The withdrawal of the Stukageschwader from "strategic" bombing operations could be interpreted as releasing the dive bombers for their doctrinally correct role as "tactical," close-support aircraft. Finally, the combination of the phase of the moon and the state of the Channel tides was favorable for amphibious operations along the southeast coast of England from the eighth to the tenth of September. Meeting on the afternoon of the seventh, the Chiefs of Staff endorsed an assessment that an invasion attempt could be "imminent," and directed Home Forces Command to "stand by at immediate notice." General Headquarters Home Forces famously overreacted to the warning, issuing the invasion code word CROMWELL, which meant immediate action, and set bells ringing across the southeast before the alert could be canceled.[6]

As the chiefs deliberated in the Central War Room just a short walk from No. 10 Downing Street, the greatest single force yet employed in the short history of aerial warfare was thunderously arriving over London. With Dowding struggling to find means of protecting the aircraft factories while keeping half an eye on the invasion scare, and with Park preoccupied by the tactical dilemmas of protecting his own airfields, the sudden appearance of Luftflotte 2 concentrated in two massive waves converging on London caught Fighter Command by surprise. Few British fighters managed to intercept before the German bombers reached London. Extricating these bombers from the battle space proved another matter, however, as Kesselring unaccountably chose not to reserve a fighter force for rendezvous with the bombers on their return flight. No. 12 Group, summoned this time to defend the capital itself, again assembled a Big Wing that joined the bulk of 11 Group's squadrons in attacking the retreating German bomber stream.

The RAF and the Luftwaffe each lost 23 fighters in the day's fighting, but the Germans also lost 16 bombers and 3 reconnaissance aircraft, along with many more pilots than the British. More apparent at the time, however, was that an escort of some 600 German fighters had enabled more than 350 bombers to accurately target the great arsenals and dockyards in the East End of the metropolis. Nor did darkness bring respite; Sperrle's Luftflotte 3 sent further streams of bombers toward target areas illuminated by widespread, out-of-control fires, to intensify the destruction in the East End. It was the beginning of eight months of fear, fire, and destruction from the air for the citizens of London, and the poorest—densely packed into slums in close proximity to "legitimate" industrial and transportation targets directly related to the British war effort—suffered the most.[7]

In the morning, Dowding conferred with Park for the second time in twenty-four hours, to assess what both men quickly sensed was a significant turn of events. They decided to downgrade two more of Park's squadrons to class C, although Dowding could find only one squadron to replace the pair. Operations during the next week fell into a pattern of alternating moderate- and low-intensity days, partly imposed by unstable weather, partly resulting from the Luftwaffe's need for recovery time between launching its mass strikes. Night attacks continued, however, as Göring made the round-the-clock bombing of London official policy on the ninth. That day both 11 Group and Bader's Big Wing from 12 Group engaged German bombers attacking airfields, aircraft factories, and other targets in the London area. Deteriorating weather on the tenth did not preclude further night attacks, and improving weather on the afternoon of the eleventh permitted Luftflotte 2 and Luftflotte 3 to coordinate strikes on London. In an interesting twist, the long-endurance Me. 110 Zerstörers were dispatched to rendezvous with the bombers on their return flights. Once again, Fighter Command was unable to intercept the bombers before they reached the target area, but nine British squadrons struck the Germans as they withdrew, downing 7 of the Me. 110s.[8]

The overall results of the September 11 fighting were unsatisfactory for Fighter Command, however, as it lost more aircraft than it shot down. The loss ratio in single-seat fighters was particularly bad for the British, with 21 Spitfires and Hurricanes destroyed, as against just 3 Me. 109s. A forty-eight-hour easing in the intensity of the German attacks during September 12 and 13 was then followed by renewed strikes against Fighter Command's radar installations, by this point the Luftwaffe's standard prelude to a maximum-effort attack. The attempt to "blind" Fighter Command now included electronic countermeasures known as "jamming," which quickly proved far more consistently effective than bombing. Exploiting a break in the weather, Göring and Kesselring determined to launch another maximum effort in the apparently sincere belief that the British defense was near collapse. The reassurance given to hard-pressed frontline aircrew, to the effect that Fighter Command was "down to its last 50 fighters," may have been hyperbole to shore up sagging morale, but apparently Luftwaffe leaders did believe that, at long last, a decisive battle truly was in prospect.[9]

Park apparently thought so, too. Taking advantage of a request from Dowding's senior air staff officer for a situation report, he made abundantly clear his profound concern that while, as he claimed, 11 Group had been winning its fight in the air, the RAF had come close to losing the battle on the ground. Weeks of concentrated attacks on his fighter stations had had "a serious effect on the fighting efficiency of the fighter squadrons." Incensed by what he thought was official complacency, Park asserted that, "the Air Ministry's arrangements for labour and equipment quickly to repair aerodrome surfaces were absolutely inadequate." Such plain speaking can have done him no good in the higher circles of RAF leadership, but Park enjoyed some protection from immediate repercussions, not least because the prime minister had already communicated the same message to the Air Ministry after a post-air-raid visit to RAF Manston.[10]

Appropriately for an AOC-in-C, Dowding took a more detached, although by no means a complacent, view of the situation. In forwarding Park's report to the Air Ministry, Dowding chose to emphasize the overriding importance of the fact that, despite "the extent and determination of the enemy air offensive in the South-East . . . Air Vice-Marshal Park and his Staff have dealt most successfully with the rapidly changing phases of the tactical situation." Recognizing that the attacks on 11 Group bases during the three weeks up to September 10 had been "beginning . . . to effect materially the efficiency of our fighter operations," he pointed out that, even so, only two of 11 Group's thirteen fighter stations had been knocked out of action for more than "a few hours." While acknowledging the need for continuous improvement in repair and reconstruction capacity, Dowding in effect disavowed Park's main complaint: "I do not wish to express any dissatisfaction with the measures taken."[11]

Dowding's gloss on Park's mid-September report provides unique insight into his style of command at a moment that both sides in the air campaign expected to be decisive. Poised between the exigencies of his key operational commander and a service bureaucracy struggling to identify, much less respond effectively to critical needs, Dowding in effect was telling both—in the words of the legendary poster—"Keep calm and carry on." In still broader perspective, it was a profoundly ironical role reversal for Dowding, the "Dismal Jimmy" who, a quarter century earlier at the height of the Somme campaign, had so exasperated Trenchard with his exclusive focus on the operational problems of his wing. Unlike Trenchard, however, Dowding quietly corrected what he saw as his subordinate's loss of perspective, while continuing to hold the ring for him, preserving the operational autonomy Park needed. It was not so much Dowding's finest hour as, in a sense, his finest moment as AOC-in-C.[12]

Sunday, September 15, dawned what the English call a "fine" summer day, meaning that the morning mist was expected to burn off, as in due course it did. The clearing weather, plus the slow, systematic massing of German formations all across his front, caused Park to alert his entire force, and warn his neighboring group AOCs, Brand and Leigh-Mallory. Kesselring's initial strike crossed the English coastline around 11:30, to be met by successive pairs of squadrons from 11 Group. As usual, the German escort fighters sought to tie up the interceptors, but this time Park had decided to blue the lot, positioning three additional pairs of squadrons for a free run at the now-unescorted bombers. These six squadrons and a pair from Brand's 10 Group assailed the bomber stream as it reached London; then, just as the Germans released their bombs on the East End and turned for home, Bader's Big Wing of five squadrons from 12 Group joined the fight.[13]

This most concentrated British fighter reaction to date was engaging only Kesselring's holding force; his main thrust, designed to catch a depleted Fighter Command on the ground—refueling, rearming, and regrouping—appeared on British radar screens even as the first wave of attackers escaped eastward toward waiting fighter cover. The new German strike force consisted of some 114 bombers in three columns, escorted by more than 350 fighters flying high above, in position to intercept the interceptors. Once again, Park dispatched his paired squadrons to try to fight through the German escorts, while calling on 10 Group and 12 Group to attack the bomber stream as it neared London. Reversing roles with Kesselring, Park now hoped to achieve his own battle of annihilation. Taken together, these aerial combats of September 15, 1940, made for one of the most dramatic, set-piece battles of Britain's war, and in the history of air warfare.

It was one of those events that metamorphose into myth even before it can be recorded as history. Literally hundreds of Hurricanes and Spitfires attacked the German bomber formations again and again in squadron-strength waves, with much of the action taking place directly over London. The emotional impact on the British still echoes in the narratives. Usually prosaic historians like Richard Hough and Denis Richards compare a column of German bombers to the British light cavalry at Balaclava, charging "into the jaws of death." The highly analytical and quietly skeptical Stephen Bungay refers to Park's pairing of No. 602 Squadron and No. 303 Squadron as his "Praetorian Guard," and subtly compares Park to Wellington at Waterloo by remarking, "They seemed to be coming on in the same old way, so he would throw them back in the same old way." Afterward, it was of course Churchill who immortalized the myth with an arresting word picture in his history and memoir, *The Second World War*.[14]

The prime minister was again observing the action from 11 Group's operations room. By his account, when at the peak of the fighting the indicator lights showed all of 11 Group's squadrons engaged, he asked Park, "What other reserves have we?" According to Churchill, the air vice-marshal replied, "There are none." More than one historian has noted the similarity of this exchange to Churchill's description of a colloquy with the French generalissimo, Maurice Gamelin, during the Battle of France.[15] Churchill wrote that upon hearing Park's reply he "looked grave, as well I might" (given the Gamelin precedent) but claimed that, as in Paris four months earlier, he remained uncharacteristically silent. Again, more than one historian[16] has suspected that, if Churchill was quoting Park aright, then the latter was playing service politics. If asked why he had no reserves, he could have replied truthfully that Brand, and—more to the point—Leigh-Mallory, were responsible for providing them.

That evening, the Air Ministry triumphantly reported 183 German aircraft shot down; published British losses were 30 fighters and 20 pilots. As the Luftwaffe had flown approximately 650 sorties, this would have amounted to a "kill" rate of nearly 30 percent. Had these claims been anything like accurate, Fighter Command would have been well on its way to making good on Churchill's (private) boast that Hitler would "break his air weapon" in attacking Britain. Actually, total German losses were 56 aircraft, against a final tally of 28 British. Losses in the fighter engagements were nearly "dead" even, 13 to 12. "'Twas a famous victory," but it was not the annihilating victory Park had sought. Can seventy-five years of analysis and validation of statistical evidence give us the history of "what actually happened" over the Home Counties on that Sunday?[17]

Fighter Command's top operational priority continued to be intercepting, and repulsing or dispersing incoming enemy bomber formations before they could accurately bomb important targets, rather than maximizing the fighters' opportunities for individual kills. In his September 12 report, Park had patiently explained how the Luftwaffe, possessing the strategic initiative, set the conditions for operational strategy. Recognizing that the penetrations by the German bombers into the Home Counties as far as London, and even beyond, created opportunities for his fighters to inflict heavy losses on those formations both coming and going, he also explicitly recognized the desirability of employing paired squadrons, or even larger wing formations, for that purpose. The operational objective should be to maintain a high interception rate, while exploiting opportunities to destroy more German bombers. It was the same argument he had laid out as Dowding's SASO two years earlier. Dowding had backed Park then, and the AOC-in-C backed him still.[18]

After the September 15 battles, Leigh-Mallory submitted to Dowding a report of his own, which centered on the kills claimed by his Big Wing pilots. He reported that in five engagements overall the Big Wing tactic produced 163 victories (105 destroyed, 40 probable, 18 damaged), against 14 fighters and 11 pilots lost. Park apparently confined his reaction to these flamboyant claims to a laconic notation on his copy: "Did these Wings engage before the targets were bombed?" Dowding's reaction, conveyed directly to the 12 Group AOC, was dismissive: "I think I am beginning to pick out those [reports] which can be relied on and those which throw in claims at the end for good measure." Significantly, rather than personally endorse Leigh-Mallory's report as he had Park's, Dowding allowed his SASO, Air Vice-Marshal Evill, to forward it to the Air Ministry. The politically smooth Evill sought to side-step any controversy about claims, referring in his cover letter to approximations of enemy losses.[19]

The same day that Leigh-Mallory signed out his provocative report, on the other side of the Channel Hitler's military headquarters issued a more consequential official communication. A Führer Order addressed to the three armed service commands indefinitely postponed the decision date for executing *Seelöwe* (Sea Lion), the Wehrmacht plan for the invasion of Great Britain. Hitler had previously designated September 21 as the date for a go/no-go decision; given the expected fall and winter weather conditions in the North Sea and the English Channel, postponement amounted to a tacit decision not to attempt an invasion before the spring of 1941. If Fighter Command's overall, strategic objective in the summer 1940 campaign was to deny the Wehrmacht the theater air superiority necessary for an invasion attempt, then it may be reasonably asserted that September 17 was the day that Fighter Command won that campaign: the day Hitler registered the failure of the Luftwaffe's fight for theater air superiority over Britain in 1940.[20]

However, with no knowledge of the decisive Führer Order, Dowding had to maintain Fighter Command in readiness to deal with the contingency of a German invasion attempt, in addition to the ongoing, defensive counter-air operations. Although Bomber and Coastal Command attacks forced noticeable dispersal of the barges and landing craft being collected by the Wehrmacht along the Channel coast, as late as mid-October "ultra-secret" intercepts of German radio transmissions continued to reflect invasion preparations. Anti-invasion operations projected in the 11 Group area included: interception of Luftwaffe troop-carrying aircraft, provision of fighter escort for Bomber and Coastal Command counterattacks, and fighter cover for counterattacking British naval and ground forces, as well as direct assaults by Fighter Command aircraft on German landing craft. In addition, moreover, Fighter Command's ground echelon would have to be prepared to defend their airfields against ground attack and, in extremis, conduct demolitions to ensure that they did not fall into enemy hands in usable condition.

Keeping in view all the requirements of counterinvasion operations, while continuing defensive counter-air operations in a major campaign whose outcome apparently remained in doubt, required staff work of the highest order. It is to Dowding's credit that the organization he built did not buckle under the stress—although it was probably just as well that after mid-September the operational pauses between the Luftwaffe's large-scale strikes grew longer. Fighter Command used the relative decline in the tempo of operations to provide some respite for its pilots, and to replace inadequate or exhausted squadron-level leaders. Dowding's personnel options continued to be straitjacketed, however, by the tardiness of the prewar expansion of the RAF pilot force. Although the Air Ministry finally promised to reassign some pilots from light-attack squadrons, as well as provide more new pilots from the training establishments, despite its heavier losses the Luftwaffe still possessed a much larger personnel base of experienced pilots.[21]

Meanwhile, even the resourceful Albert Kesselring seemed to be reaching the bottom of his bag of tricks. After scattered, apparently pointless sorties in the aftermath of the climactic battle on September 15, his bombers met a stinging defeat on the eighteenth, when the Big Wing operating from RAF Duxford finally made a big impact, mauling III Group, *Kampfgeschwader* 77, and killing the group commander. Once again resorting to offensive fighter sweeps, Kesselring tried to entice 11 Group into fighter duels without putting bombers at risk, but as before, Park refused to be drawn. More profitably, the Luftflotte 2 commander reemphasized high-speed, low-altitude fighter-bomber attacks on high value targets, particularly factories producing fighter aircraft. Fighter-bomber attacks had proved the Luftwaffe's most cost-effective tactic and, had they been more intensively employed earlier, might have significantly affected the overall outcome. By late September, however, the British aircraft industry was sufficiently dispersed and resilient to absorb these precise but relatively light blows.

Maintaining and increasing aircraft production rates was obviously of critical importance, to both short-term survival and to victory in the long run. In his early weeks at the Ministry of Aircraft Production, Beaverbrook identified constant air raid warnings as a major impediment, insisting the disruptions "must stop." As AOC-in-C of Fighter Command, Dowding found himself caught up in protracted debates and negotiations among business and union leaders as well as members of Government all the way up to the War Cabinet and the prime minister, regarding how best to balance risks and rewards. All concerned eventually accepted the idea that essential workers should ignore the public air-raid warnings, seeking shelter when rooftop spotters identified imminent attacks on the factories. The apparent agreement nearly collapsed, however, when the Air Ministry flatly refused to provide RAF personnel to serve as spotters, and agreed to provide only limited training for civilians with whom to fill the gap.[22]

The long-simmering dispute over "roof spotters" boiled over just as the daylight air battles reached their climax. Dowding, for once, concurred with the Air Ministry view: from the standpoint of rational allocation of scarce manpower, at this critical juncture trained RAF personnel should not be employed as "roof spotters" for factories, however important. This assessment was consistent with his long-held position, shared by nearly all airmen, that point defense was the wrong way to employ airpower. Having himself finally yielded to MAP's demands for combat air patrols over (some) aircraft factories, however, Dowding now advised the secretary of state for air to do the same regarding Beaverbrook's demand for spotters. Acknowledging that the MAP's specific arguments were "preposterous," he nevertheless suggested compromise; a remarkable instance of a military commander urging political sensitivity on a cabinet minister. Sinclair may not have appreciated receiving essentially political advice from Dowding, but clearly, Dowding fully appreciated Beaverbrook's commanding position in the Government.[23]

The penultimate round of the long, drawn-out daylight air campaign was fought from the twenty-seventh to the thirtieth of September. The twenty-seventh was a particularly costly day for the Luftwaffe, which lost 57 aircraft (against 29 British) while failing to fight through to any of its targets. Next day, however, one of Kesselring's traps finally worked, as Luftflotte 2 shot down 16 British fighters for a loss of only 4 Me. 109s. Yet follow-up attacks the next day only emphasized the Luftwaffe's failure to crack the British defenses. Kesselring reverted to his "wave" attacks of 100- to 200-plus, and met with shattering losses: 14 bombers and no fewer than 28 Me. 109s in exchange for 19 British fighters. The overall loss ratio in the three days' fighting was roughly 5:3 in Fighter Command's favor, but more importantly, one Luftwaffe bomber unit after another was being destroyed as an effective combat organization without achieving commensurate results on the ground.

The September 27–30 battles constituted the sharpest tactical defeat of the German fighter force in entire campaign. It is curiously fitting that the thirtieth was the day the King conferred on Dowding the highest military honor in Britain's orders of chivalry, the Grand Cross of the Bath.[24] At the time, however, the climactic nature of the late September battles was not apparent, as the Luftwaffe's daylight raids did not abruptly cease, but rather petered out during October. In retrospect, moreover, the much larger battles on September 15, later memorialized as "Battle of Britain Day," seemed to render the late September fighting anti-climactic. Yet, as the last two weeks' fighting in September demonstrate, it was not weather—the end of the summer "campaigning season" alone that temporarily relieved the threat of an invasion attempt.

Between mid-August and mid-September, Sperrle and Kesselring's air fleets nearly neutralized the operational advantages created by Fighter Command's integrated air-defense system; by the end of September, the operational momentum clearly had shifted back in favor of Fighter Command, which regained the advantage in kill-to-loss ratio it held in early August, during Adlerangriff. It had become evident to the German high command that, at least in the short run, the Luftwaffe fighter force could not destroy enough British fighters to prevent them from, in turn, destroying the German bomber force. If checkmate was nowhere in sight, this was, at least, the first great check the Wehrmacht received in its "march of conquest."

11

THE BLITZ

OCTOBER–NOVEMBER 1940

On October 5, Churchill's principal private secretary, Eric Seal, warned him that the "menace of night bombing" required urgent countermeasures. Rising alarm among civilians both in and out of government provoked this unusual foray into military affairs by the senior civil servant in the prime minister's office. The diary of one of Seal's assistants, "Jock" Colville, illustrates how worrisome even the modest beginnings of night area attacks during July and August had been. As direct impacts on the civil population, as well as on war production and transportation, steadily mounted in late summer, Churchill devoted much personal attention to such matters as delayed-action bombs and parachute mines. The devastating, overnight attack on London of September 7, followed by nightly, mass attacks on the capital and other cities, indicated Hitler had set out to make good on his Sportpalast speech with, it seemed to many of the best-informed Britons, reasonable prospects of success.[1]

The port cities of southeastern England had taken a horrific beating during July and August; London came under almost nightly bombardment beginning in September; the Luftwaffe subsequently destroyed the city center of Coventry and any night might do the same to any other medium-sized urban area in the industrial Midlands. As usual, Churchill himself best captured the intensity of the moment:

> [O]ften night after night ten or twenty thousand people were made homeless, and when nothing but the ceaseless vigil of the citizens as fire guards on the roofs prevented uncontrollable conflagrations; when hospitals filled with mutilated men and women were themselves struck by the enemy's bombs; when hundreds of thousands of weary people crowded together in safe and unsanitary shelters; when communications by road and rail were ceaselessly broken down; when drains were smashed and light, power, and gas paralyzed; and when, nevertheless, the whole fighting , toiling life of London had to go forward. . . . We did not know how long it would last. We had no reason to suppose it would not go on getting worse.[2]

Longstanding fears regarding a probable, "moral" collapse of urban populations under bombardment arose from the potentially catastrophic scale of destruction. Envisioning the knockout blow, British policy makers and strategists imagined overwhelming numbers of dead and wounded, as well as the interruption of vital services to the survivors, all compressed into a few days, perhaps even a few hours. Although the actual, material damage, and particularly the human casualties, were far less than the worst-case scenarios, the protracted ordeal of the Blitz caught home-front agencies off guard. As short-war assumptions collided with the differing demands of a protracted campaign, to the public, and to elements of the political class, it appeared that "someone had blundered." With neither professional allies among the senior military commanders and senior civil servants, nor personal followers among the military or civilian staffers, therefore, and entirely aside from the lingering Big Wing controversy, Dowding offered a convenient scapegoat.[3]

Motivated by fears for civilian morale but guided by Lindemann, Seal implicitly blamed Dowding for Fighter Command's apparent impotence in the face of the nightly bombardment of London and other British cities. Urging the prime minister to summon both Dowding and his Antiaircraft Artillery commander, Major General Frederick Pile, for cross-examination on the issue, he claimed that "Dowding has the reputation of being very conservative, and of not being receptive to new ideas." Both these assertions were, if not outright falsehoods, certainly misleading. Dowding had the reputation of being aloof and stubborn; certainly he was unreceptive to attempts by the Air Staff and the Air Ministry to impose on Fighter Command decisions he considered properly belonged to him as AOC-in-C. In technical matters Dowding remained, as always, committed to "science thoughtfully applied to operational requirements."[4]

Certainly receptive to Tizard's concerns, as early as 1936 when he first began organizing Fighter Command to take over from the old Air Defence of Great Britain organization, the problem of countering the menace of night attacks became an agenda item for Dowding. Together, Tizard and Dowding identified airborne radar as the correct, technical solution to the problem. Their support for the development team led by Dr. E. G. Bowen ensured that by the summer of 1939, the RAF possessed the world's first working prototype of an airborne radar. During the first months of the war, amid all his other responsibilities Dowding encouraged, guided, and closely monitored the application of airborne radar technology for use by night fighters. Both Churchill and Lindemann were well aware of all this, not least because in June 1939, Dowding had made a point of inviting the them to observe a demonstration of an aircraft interception guided by airborne radar.[5]

Churchill, having squeezed into the crowded cockpit of a radar-equipped Battle and observed a radar interception from the grounded aircraft, had been impressed. "The Prof," as Churchill affectionately called Lindemann, observed a subsequent demonstration, and declined to be impressed. Bowen later pointedly contrasted Dowding's well-informed, thorough, and above all professional debriefing of the test pilots on an earlier visit to the station, with Lindemann's almost contemptuous dismissal of the exercise he saw. Admittedly not a disinterested or dispassionate commentator, Bowen years afterward implied that Lindemann, infected with the not-invented-by-me virus, actually tried to derail the whole concept of radar-guided night interception. It is difficult to avoid the conclusion that Dowding's particular crime, in Lindemann's eyes was, as a mere air marshal, to have bested "the Prof" over radar—a matter of applied science and technological development. Worse still, he had done the deed in collusion with Lindemann's academic and political archrival, Tizard.[6]

At the outbreak of war, the airborne-radar development facility at Martlesham was busy adapting thirty of Bristol Aircraft's twin-engine Blenheims to carry airborne intercept (AI) radar. Acquired toward the end of Dowding's tenure as Air Council member for research and development as a "light" bomber, the Blenheim had been fast for its day, and enjoyed a highly adaptable airframe. The AI radar development team had scarcely begun, however, to overcome the myriad technical obstacles involved in handcrafting thirty radar sets, installing them in aircraft, and training Fighter Command personnel to maintain and operate the equipment, when the Air Ministry decided to disperse the Martlesham activities among sites less vulnerable to German bombing. This perhaps overcautious dispersion, which engineer and historian Ian White described as, "an unmitigated disaster to the radar research programme," certainly interrupted the progress of Bowen's team."[7]

Nevertheless, Dowding lost no time converting Blenheim squadrons to the night-fighter role, starting with No. 25 Squadron. By October 1939, the Air Ministry had authorized manufacture of three hundred Mark II AI radar sets, and Fighter Command had begun equipping and training five more night-fighter squadrons. Unfortunately, the early AI radars proved unable to meet the technical standards Dowding demanded for combat operations. Moreover, Dowding initially underestimated the amount of training required to form a pilot and a radar operator into an effective night-fighter crew. The experience of No. 25 Squadron soon revealed a multitude of additional troubles, including radar reliability and maintenance, aircraft performance, and ground control, which had to be worked out step-by-step. Although the early AI radar sets provided necessary tools for developing radar-guided interception tactics, and for training combat aircrew, producing an operationally reliable AI radar and marrying it to an effective night-fighter would take much longer.[8]

The fact that coordination of training and operational requirements had to run back and forth between the Air Staff and Fighter Command HQ did not help matters. The Air Ministry addressed this coordination issue with the standard, Whitehall response: creating a new committee, initially styled the Night Interception Committee and chaired by the then deputy chief of Air Staff, Sir Richard Peirse. With the Air Ministry Research Establishment (AMRE) speeding through the development cycles of AI radars at an astonishing rate—the debut of the Mark III was followed by that of the Mark IV within less than six months—this committee amounted to little more than a cheerleading squad. Whatever its successes in expediting AI radar development, however, they certainly did not quell the open expression of misgivings by the Air Staff's director of signals regarding the dangers of prematurely deploying unreliable systems. Even Tizard remarked that, "service personnel were trying to run before they could walk."

The rapid technical improvement in, and operational employment of, advanced radar technologies during the spring and summer of 1940 was a real factor in Churchill's strategic optimism after the collapse of French military power in June. In mid-June, Lindemann—perhaps based on faulty statistical data[9]—actually encouraged optimism regarding AI radar, which the prime ministerial "secret circle" referred to under the code name "Smeller." By this time, seventy Blenheims had been equipped with the AI Mark III radar set. A month later, the Prof asked the prime minister to accord priority to development work on radar-controlled searchlights (SLC, or "Elsie") "which Dowding is so anxious to press forward." But continuing doubts among those closest to the problem regarding actual operational performance were fully justified by experience, as the enemy's relatively agile night bombers repeatedly escaped from the obsolescent would-be interceptors, even when one of the latter managed to achieve a favorable attack position.[10]

Hopes at the highest levels of government regarding the prospective impact of "the war of science" on the shooting war continued to flourish during August, apparently based on expectations that airborne radar and radar-controlled searchlights very soon would become fully combat-effective. On August 30, the prime minister discussed with the Joint Planning Committee future offensive operations based, in part, on the presumed effectiveness of Smeller and Elsie. Yet the first confirmed kill by AI radar-guided interception had only been recorded on the night of July 22; just two more confirmed kills followed in August, and none in September. At this pace, the Luftwaffe bomber force would be a long time dying; a fact that ludicrously optimistic reports of up to 75 percent interception rates could not conceal from seasoned professionals like Dowding and Tizard. (A part of the problem with the statistics may have been a failure to distinguish properly between a "contact" and an "interception.") Along with efforts to improve night interception by better ground control, Dowding was counting on delivery in quantity of Beaufighters and Mark IV AI radars.[11]

The realities of the situation hit home with a vengeance as a consequence of the switch by Luftflotte 3 to primarily night operations, steadily becoming heavier and more geographically concentrated during the last week in August and the first week in September. The immediate, military impact of the Luftwaffe's change of tactics was to reduce the strain on Fighter Command's infrastructure; the political impact was to erode the confidence of Dowding's military colleagues and political superiors in his methodical approach to operations. On August 19, Göring issued orders specifically emphasizing "attacks on the enemy aircraft industry," and Beaverbrook was soon complaining about the mounting damage. The accompanying, sharp rise in civilian casualties sent waves of anxiety through officialdom, evidenced by a remarkably agitated War Cabinet meeting on October 15. At the Air Ministry, Deputy Chief of Air Staff Douglas minuted to Newall, "We must tackle" night interception "rather more vigorously than at present."[12]

Having filled key Air Staff positions continuously since January 1936, Douglas naturally was concerned to deflect criticism, and the leadership of Fighter Command obviously represented the likeliest, alternative lightning rod. Significantly, in his minutes for the CAS on the September 12 situation report from 11 Group, Douglas decried a lack of emphasis by Park on night fighting.[13] Douglas's comments could be interpreted as merely a somewhat heavy-handed way of advocating a change in operational priorities. Given that the report was written at a point in time when high-intensity night attacks were just beginning, and covered the period of time when the daylight air battles were at peak intensity, Douglas's comments could also be interpreted as a cheap shot at both Park, the report's signatory, and Dowding, its endorser. The suspicion arises that Douglas was concocting a paper trail of Air Staff concern and Fighter Command fecklessness regarding night air defense.[14]

Douglas advanced several ideas for "more vigorously" conducting night operations, including technical modifications to the Defiants, and converting some Hurricane squadrons to night operations. Dowding concentrated his available night-fighter squadrons (including two squadrons of Defiants) for the defense of London, but questioned the soundness of Douglas's technical ideas, and stoutly of resisted demands for conversion of Hurricane or Spitfire squadrons to night fighting. This was partly because, with the daylight air-superiority battle still very much in doubt, Dowding had no Hurricanes or Spitfires to spare for night action; but also because he had concluded, on the basis of study and experience, that the limited resources available for night-fighter development should be concentrated on the only feasible solution: the Beaufighter married to the Mark IV AI radar. Resources devoted to hasty improvisations involving obsolescent airframes like the Defiant would be wasted; lacking radar, Hurricanes or Spitfires would be as useless as Blenheims in night fighting.[15]

By mid-September, public concern already was beginning to focus on the intensifying night bombardment, and the steadily diminishing, daytime threat already beginning to recede in prominence. The prime minister himself, in a radio broadcast to the nation on September 11, distinguished between the "effort of the Germans to secure daylight mastery of the air over England . . . the crux of the whole war . . . [which] so far . . . has failed conspicuously," and "These cruel, wanton, indiscriminate bombings of London . . . [which Hitler] hopes . . . will terrorise [*sic*] and cow the people." Against this background Beaverbrook, spurred by Salmond, instigated an Air Ministry/MAP study of night air defense by a group of senior officers and officials chaired by the former CAS, which met from September 14–18. Beaverbrook's move was not necessarily conspiratorial; he was genuinely worried about the impact of the Blitz on production, and genuinely discounted the Air Ministry's competence to act on its own.[16]

The "conclusions" hastily orchestrated by Beaverbrook's departmental subordinate implicated both Newall and Dowding.[17] The latter responded to the committee's conclusions with a reasoned, moderate, and judicious reply, which revealed no substantive disagreement on several of the committee's points, most important among them the critical need for Beaufighters equipped with the latest AI radar; the importance of further development of the ground control intercept (GCI) radar system; the need for better air-ground communications generally; and the pivotal role of training in bringing together all the elements of a functioning system. The most important points of disagreement involved the old arguments, now recycled, regarding decentralizing "filtering" to the group level, to which was now added decentralization of night-fighter control from the groups to the sector stations; and the new dispute over employment of Hurricanes and Spitfires as night fighters. Initially, the Air Council backed Dowding's refusal to redeploy air-superiority fighters from the day to the night battles.[18]

Much has been made of the famous tick marks on Dowding's copy of the Salmond committee report, which appeared to show summary rejection of most of the report's recommendations. The markings were seized upon by Dowding's critics to explain, if not altogether justify, Air Ministry frustration with Dowding's alleged "obstruction." J. E. G. Dixon's close reading of Dowding's files, however, fully justifies the AOC-in-C's own frustration, with Salmond's essay in counterproductive and provocative micromanagement. It is easy to understand, for example, Dowding's "obstruction" of the seemingly reactionary demand that night-fighter aircrew training be reorganized to ensure that officer pilots teamed only with officer radar operators, and only NCOs with NCOs.

Implementing this proposal would not only have disrupted current training but also retarded the pace of future training by introducing a new and, as the combat experience of Bomber Command was to demonstrate, entirely unnecessary element of organizational rigidity. Proposals such as this suggest that the Salmond committee "conclusions" constitute an Air Ministry/Air Staff wish list of institutional preferences and individual pet projects, rather than a systematic effort to, as Clausewitz put it, "trace effects back to causes" and identify corresponding courses of action. Despite understandable annoyance with the whole exercise, however, Dowding nevertheless patiently sifted the wheat from the chaff in the committee report, "cordially" approving its recommendations, when sensible.

Most of what was sensible in the report—such as accelerating deployment of Beaufighters equipped with the Mark IV AI radar—was either obvious and long under way as a matter of highest priority, or else—like establishing a dedicated Night Fighter Section within Fighter Command HQ—clearly a direct responsibility of the AOC-in-C. If the functioning, or malfunctioning, of Fighter Command actually demonstrated that Dowding needed Air Staff advice on such matters of internal administration, then he was by definition incompetent to serve as an AOC-in-C, and should have been removed from his post, forthwith. The predictable response of any proper commander in chief, of almost any service, nation, or era, to such gratuitous interference by a hastily assembled miscellany of retired flag officers and mid-level bureaucrats would be to demand of his Government, "Back me or sack me." That Dowding restrained himself may be interpreted as an indication that he considered the operational situation too serious for histrionics.

In addition to reasoning with the Air Council, Dowding also took the precaution of making his detailed case directly to the prime minster in the manner most effective with Churchill: in person, and immediately afterward, briefly, in writing. Dowding was back at Chequers on the evening of the twenty-first, and among the papers the prime minister read over that weekend was an analysis of the night-interception problem by Dowding, which Churchill considered "masterly." Lindemann, entirely unsurprisingly, was dismissive, suggesting to Colville that Dowding was only belatedly coming to grips with facts others had been emphasizing for some time. Colville's opportunities of observing "war at the top" were beginning to ripen an independent judgment of men and measures. After describing a talk with Lindemann during which the Prof was "rather gloomy about the initial lack of success won by the A.I., G.L., *etc.*," the younger man commented, "He alternates between startling optimism and querulous pessimism."[19]

Lindemann's and Seal's disparagement of Dowding's handling of night air defense was reinforced by a letter from Jack Salmond, who also met with Churchill, to insist that his committee's findings warranted the ouster of Fighter Command's AOC-in-C. On October 7 the prime minister convened an emergency meeting to consider the night-defense problem—or crisis. The attendance list for this meeting, ostensibly focused on the specific issue of nighttime air defense, gave mute testimony to the breadth and depth of Dowding's opposition. In addition to Lindemann, Sinclair, Newall, and Salmond, also present (among others) were his longtime Air Staff sparring partners, Air Marshals Joubert de la Ferté and Douglas. With Beaverbrook's attitude ambiguous, only Dowding's AAA commander "Tim" Pile represented a likely source of support. The upshot, however, was merely the translation of the meeting into yet another standing committee on Night Air Defence, this time at the prime ministerial and War Cabinet level.[20]

That evening, Dowding, Pile, and the prime minister dined together in Downing Street, before setting off for an overnight tour of some London-area defense posts, including AAA batteries in Richmond Park, and the operations room at Biggin Hill. Dowding was particularly eager for the prime minister to get the overall perspective from Biggin Hill, before handing him off to Pile for a close-up look at Elsie in action. Churchill spent several hours outdoors with Pile and Lt. Col. George Harvie-Watt, Conservative MP and CO of the 31st AA Battalion, one of the units newly fitted with radar controls. In his memoirs, Pile provided a comic account of their misadventures, involving lost guides, sodden half-frozen fields, malfunctioning weapons systems and "neat whisky," but the increasingly grumpy prime minister was on a deadly earnest mission. Whenever possible, Churchill headed for the operational frontline, to see things for himself and to look the warfighters in the eye.[21]

Three days later, the prime minister gave the AAA batteries another opportunity to show off, with visits to Richmond and Kenley, and invited Pile and Dowding to join the next weekend house party at Chequers. Significantly, Portal, whose appointment as CAS would take effect on October 25th, also joined the party. In the ensuing discussions Dowding, perhaps unwisely, characterized the German night attacks as "lacking in purpose" because they did "not concentrate on one target, or on a small area." At the same time, however, Dowding seemed to Colville "depressed" by the apparent, technical superiority of German night bombers as compared to British night fighters: the Germans could fly in weather that grounded British warplanes. In fact, the Luftwaffe had not merely changed tactics, but fundamentally altered its concept of operations, in a way that—as Dowding later admitted—posed the most difficult challenge of all. Having failed to land the knockout blow, the German airmen would attempt an aerial siege.[22]

Meager results issued from the prime minister's Night Defence Committee during October.[23] Churchill ordered a report from the MAP on production of 1,000,000 aerial mines, and the meeting of October 21 overruled Dowding on the issue of converting some of the precious air-superiority fighters to night operations. The subsequent performance of the three so-called cat's eye squadrons Dowding assigned helped to promote the Hurricane's reputation as a versatile fighting platform, but they did not become combat-effective until the spring of 1941, when the GCI system Dowding had been pressing forward finally matured. Fighter Command's attempts to exploit the German electronic-guidance systems to intercept the bomber streams failed; this was another creative, new idea hamstrung by the lack of adequate numbers of Beaufighters. The battle of memoranda continued throughout October and into November (even the assistant chief of Naval Staff, the ill-fated Admiral Tom Phillips, registered an opinion), but the realities of the battle space changed not a whit.[24]

By contrast with Fighter Command's struggle to operate effectively at night, by October the Luftwaffe had achieved an operational tempo that was both effective, and sustainable. While the Blitz posed no direct threat to British military capabilities, and little immediate threat to the industrial output necessary to sustain those capabilities, the continuous strain on the civil population posed the question: How long would the British people have to wait for countermeasures, either offensive or defensive, offering credible promise of relief? This question, posed most starkly by the terrible November 15 attack on Coventry, was by then no longer Dowding's to answer. Two days earlier, the secretary of state for air had informed him that he was to be relieved as air officer commanding-in-chief, Fighter Command. The Blitz had handed to the cabal of active and retired air-rank officers an opportunity, which they skillfully exploited, finally to bring down both Newall and Dowding.[25]

At least up until June, criticism of the RAF circulating in political circles consisted mainly of generalized allegations, including lack of efficiency, urgency, and imagination at the Air Ministry. Toward the end of June and early in July, however, at least one well-connected critic began to name names. Wing Commander E. G. Kingston-McCloughry, a disgruntled, Air Staff officer who for months had been feeding Beaverbrook insider gossip, began critiquing the qualifications and performance of key air-rank officers in a series of anonymous memoranda. The first two specific targets were Beaverbrook's leading, bureaucratic antagonists, Newall and Freeman. Then, around the time of the Air Council's unsuccessful attempt to retire Dowding at the end of July, Kingston-McCloughry escalated his rhetoric. Two additional memoranda, composed in a style long associated with Beaverbrook's newspapers, leveled brutal, ad hominem attacks on nearly a dozen senior air-rank officers, now pairing the CAS with Dowding, rather than Freeman, as particular objects of vituperation.[26]

In mid-August, the most scathing of these Kingston-McCloughry diatribes reached the prime minister's office, under cover of a letter from Conservative MP Irene Ward. The Tory MP claimed that the unnamed writer's criticisms of senior air-rank officers, most prominently Newall, Dowding, and the Fighter Command senior staff, were representative of opinion at the working staff and flying levels of the service. A claim, from such a source, that active-duty officers favored removing both their service chief and their service's most senior, operational commander, would be startling under any circumstances; at the crisis of a desperate battle for national survival, it was positively alarming. Ward's letter is intriguing as well as startling, because it went beyond what Kingston-McCloughry had written. Ward not only called for Newall's removal as CAS, but also nominated Portal to replace him, and further asserted, "the RAF would consider it a disaster if the Commander in Chief of Fighter Command were given the supreme office."

This last assertion had the merit of being, insofar as senior RAF officers are now known to have held opinions on the point at the time, undoubtedly correct. But what gave Ward the notion that Churchill needed warning against replacing Newall with Dowding? How did Ward, who disclaimed any knowledge of the personalities discussed in the memo, arrive at Portal's name? The most plausible source from which the notion could have reached her is Sinclair, either directly or indirectly; the most plausible source for the name, again either direct or indirect, is Salmond. Ward's advocacy of Portal for CAS, surprising in several ways, suggests a convergence between the goals of the RAF establishment's external opponents, like Beaverbrook, and the insider cabal led by Salmond and Trenchard.[27] Beaverbrook's involvement in drafting Kingston-McCloughry's July and August memos provides circumstantial evidence that Salmond helped contrive the de-targeting of Freeman and the emphasis on Dowding.

Freeman's air of disillusioned innocence regarding the intrigues of Kingston-McCloughry and the Beaverbrook clique does not carry credibility. Freeman served as Trenchard and Salmond's go-between with Portal, at the same time Salmond and Kingston-McCloughery were colluding with Beaverbrook. In orchestrating the cabal, Trenchard directly consulted Freeman, his contact with the Air Council. It is worth recalling that Arthur Tedder, one of Dowding's longest-standing service enemies, at the time was Freeman's right-hand man.[28] The odd man out in these convoluted maneuvers was the incumbent CAS, who had already angered Trenchard by refusing to launch Bomber Command on a Trenchardist "continuous offensive" against Germany, and worse, allowing Bomber Command's resources to be diverted to other uses. Actually, as all concerned must have known, it was Churchill himself who had repeatedly warned the Air Ministry not to risk losses on a scale that would handicap future expansion of the bomber force. During July, Portal had pushed back against the Air Ministry's interpretation of the prime minister's guidance, which did not, however, mark him as "uncooperative" in his colleagues' eyes.[29]

A September 25 Air Council meeting apparently was the last straw for Trenchard and Salmond. Sinclair and Newall temporized regarding Dowding, aware of the prime minister's strong support for the AOC-in-C, which the dramatic events in the daylight air campaign during the previous ten days could only have strengthened. This "incomprehensible" vacillation sent Salmond over the top, issuing threats of an appeal to the King. The Air Council's unwillingness, or inability, to sack Dowding ironically became the decisive argument for dismissing Newall, and within a week, the CAS was done for. The shift in emphasis by Salmond and Trenchard is palpable: by early October, they were taking Newall's exit for granted, and concentrating on generating external, political pressure on the Government to make sure that Dowding followed. Churchill's towering, historical stature makes it easy to underappreciate his Government's political vulnerability during its first six months in office; the prime minister had many reasons to settle the Dowding imbroglio quickly and quietly.[30]

On October 2, Colville recorded an impending change in the Chiefs of Staff Committee in parallel with a War Cabinet shakeup: "Newall goes to New Zealand as Governor General and will be succeeded as Chief of the Air Staff by Portal." Replacing the fifty-four-year-old Newall with the forty-four-year-old Portal represented a climax in the ongoing, generational change of RAF senior leadership. The revamped Air Council included Freeman, a four-star equivalent air chief marshal, replacing Peirse, a three-star equivalent air marshal, as vice-chief of Air Staff. Peirse in turn, replaced Portal as AOC-in-C of Bomber Command. Air Marshal Sir Christopher Courtney, having for reasons still unexplained missed his chance at the Fighter Command in 1938, continued as air member for supply and organization. Philip Babington, replacing Leslie Gossage as air member for personnel, and A. G. R. Garrod, taking a new portfolio, air member for training, were both two-star equivalent air vice-marshals with the acting rank of air marshal.[31]

The resulting Air Council was notable for Freeman's relative seniority among the air members. Freeman had been senior to Portal prior to the latter's appointment as CAS, which carried with it permanent promotion to air chief marshal, just as Dowding had been senior to Newall. Unlike Dowding, Freeman appears to have actively pushed forward his junior for the top job. With Dowding's removal, Portal (ex officio) and Freeman would be "the two most senior serving officers in the RAF." The two were close friends, and would work together in double harness, almost as dual chiefs, dividing the CAS responsibilities, with the former handing the internal administration of the service, and the latter handling the Chiefs of Staff Committee and the defence minister (the Rt. Hon. Winston S. Churchill). Energized by Portal and Freeman, the Air Council acquired the resolve, and the political leverage, to complete the generational revolution in RAF leadership by securing Dowding's replacement as AOC-in-C, Fighter Command.[32]

Viewed in this light, the much-ballyhooed Big Wing controversy, which gradually intensified from August through early November, does not appear to have been the main ingredient in Dowding's professional demise. It was Portal's apparently unrelated appointment as chief of air staff that finally made Dowding's position truly untenable. The Big Wing controversy did further weaken Dowding's overall professional standing, however, by adhering a Duxford contingent to the already formidable array of anti-Dowding factions, in addition to toxic working relationships with his secretary of state, his service chief, and his ministry, as well as—above all—his inability to deliver an effective night air defense. During October, yet another Tory MP, Flight Lieutenant Peter MacDonald, then serving in Bader's 242 Squadron, visited both the parliamentary under secretary of state for air, Harold Balfour, and the prime minister, arguing vehemently that Dowding was mishandling his forces, underutilizing 12 Group, and missing opportunities to crush the Luftwaffe's bomber force.

At the infamous Air Ministry meeting on October 17 that followed, Dowding and Park were ambushed by a crowd of Air Staff officers and 12 Group representatives including Bader. The set-up was more than simply Sholto Douglas's revenge for his scolding by Dowding and Park at Bentley Priory on September 7.[33] Rather, the meeting was carefully contrived to frame the Big Wing controversy as a dispute between Park as 11 Group AOC, and Leigh-Mallory as 12 Group AOC, which Dowding had failed to resolve. This failure remains a salient criticism of Dowding's leadership, but at the time what mattered more was whether the service determined Park, or Leigh-Mallory, to be correct on the substance of the Big Wing issue. In effect, Douglas and Leigh-Mallory, with the participation of other next-generation RAF senior leaders including Portal and "Jack" Slessor, staged the October 17 meeting to begin shaping a post-Dowding regime at Fighter Command. Removing Dowding was already a foregone conclusion.[34]

Decades later, Wing Commander (by then, Air Chief Marshal Sir) Kenneth Cross, who was Leigh-Mallory's group controller in August of 1940 recalled, "coupled with all I heard in the various telephone conversations, I believe this meeting was just part of a move to discredit the two principal figures with a view to the takeover later . . . it was altogether a disgraceful episode and highly discreditable to Douglas and Leigh-Mallory."[35] Neither Dowding nor Park had ever opposed, in principle, meeting large bomber attacks with massed fighters in wings made up of multiple squadrons. Both regarded the issue as a matter of selecting the correct force employment for a given set of circumstances—the art of the operational commander.

So long, however, as Park remained at 11 Group as a demonstrably successful AOC, it would have been difficult for a new AOC-in-C, with no relevant experience comparable to Park's, to dictate the latter's force employment. It was not enough, therefore, to convict Dowding of failure to resolve the issue; it was necessary for Park to be wrong, and Leigh-Mallory to be right. Balfour, a former Royal Flying Corps pilot who had served in Douglas's fighter squadron during the last year of the First World War, visited Duxford early in November, and then produced the so-called Duxford Memorandum, which amounted to a charge sheet against 11 Group based on complaints he collected from 12 Group.[36]

The Air Ministry having thus established, at least to its own satisfaction, justification not only for a change of AOC-in-C, but also for dispensing with the Dowding-Park regime at Fighter Command, the government chose to reopen the question of Dowding's future. The Air Ministry's last word to Dowding on the subject had been that he could expect no further, active-duty employment when he finally relinquished his current post. Given that by November 1940 he was within eighteen months of the RAF's mandatory retirement age of sixty, and notwithstanding that in wartime, especially, governments frequently make exceptions to such regulations for uniquely qualified senior officers, Dowding might have shuffled quietly onto the retired list in a warm shower of insincere, official praise. At this point, however, Beaverbrook intervened to contrive a special assignment for Dowding, representing the Ministry of Aircraft Production on a mission to Canada and the United States.[37]

Sinclair met with Dowding on November 13 to convey the news. Dowding did not protest his relief from command, but did ask to discuss the new assignment with the prime minister, to which Sinclair agreed. Then, on November 17, Sinclair informed Dowding that he was to relinquish command "immediately." Dowding's later recollection of an abrupt dismissal over the telephone, omitting any mention of a face-to-face interview, would become a main count in his supporters' indictment of the Air Ministry's conduct. The reason for an "immediate" change of command appears to have been an Air Ministry press release announcing a major "reorganization," which included news that Deputy Chief of Air Staff Douglas was replacing Dowding.

In the midst of the ensuing press hullabaloo, Portal wrote asking the outgoing AOC-in-C to remain at his post until his successor could take over on November 25, to which Dowding assented in gracious terms. Portal's note represented the only written notice of his termination as AOC-in-C that Dowding ever received from the Air Council. The usual, highly ceremonious, written thanks normally accorded a successful—to say nothing of a victorious—commander in chief upon relinquishing appointment were notably absent. It was only in later years, after a backlash against Dowding's treatment became discernable, that the Air Council and the secretary of state thought it necessary to indicate official appreciation for his accomplishments. As Churchill famously remarked to Portal, "In war you don't have to be nice. You only have to be right."

On November 24, Dowding sent his squadrons a final signal:

> My Dear Fighter Boys,
>
> In sending you this last message, I wish I could say all that is in my heart. I cannot hope to surpass the simple eloquence of the Prime Minister's words. "Never before has so much been owed by so many to so few." The debt remains and will increase. In saying goodbye to you, I want you to know how continually you have been in my thoughts, and that, though our direct connection may be severed, I may yet be able to help you in your gallant fight. Goodbye to you and God bless you all.[38]

12 LAYING DOWN THE SWORD

1941–1942

Churchill was conspicuously inconspicuous in the process of retiring Dowding from command. Legions of researchers, combing archive after archive, decade after decade, have noted Churchill's intimate involvement in the hiring and firing of Britain's wartime high commanders. Given the exhaustive documentation of his words and deeds in this regard, the very scarcity of direct evidence regarding what happened to Dowding in November of 1940 calls attention to itself. An explanation for this unusual gap in the Churchillian record may be found in his—to later generations, surprisingly—precarious hold on power at the time.

In the second half of 1940, Dowding became entangled in the prime minister's conflicted relationship with the Conservative Party that dominated the House of Commons. By 1939, Churchill had successfully positioned himself to fill the national leadership vacuum created by the undeniable failure of

Chamberlain's foreign and defense policies. Tory politicians realized, and in some cases hoped, that similar failures might well see Churchill similarly supplanted by a new, popular idol. As summer gave way to fall, frustrations and misfortunes accumulated, and the balance of political-military success and failure was delicate indeed. The most important of the former was, of course, the perceived victories in the daytime air battles over southeastern England; the most significant of the latter was the undeniable failure to defeat, or even seriously hamper, German night bombing of British cities.[1]

Lesser but cumulative frustrations and misfortunes included a "fiasco" at Dakar on September 25, when a British naval expedition supporting a planned coup by DeGaulle's Free French movement suffered an embarrassing repulse. Operation Menace evoked unsettling memories both of Churchill's role in the serial fiascoes in Norway that precipitated Chamberlain's downfall, as well as earlier, Churchill-sponsored amphibious failures at the Dardanelles and Antwerp. On the home front, a financial scandal erupted that forced the resignation of a junior minister, Robert Boothby—a longtime Churchill ally, or as many would have it, "crony." With the political morals as well as the strategic judgment of his Government in question, among the political and military elite if not yet the public at large, Churchill decided to accept the resignation from the War Cabinet of the mortally ill Neville Chamberlain, and begin the treacherous task of Cabinet reconstruction, as well as the extremely sensitive maneuver of succeeding Chamberlain as Conservative Party Leader.[2]

The prime minister had been developing a standard procedure for dealing with politically inconvenient (or simply annoying) statesmen and commanders. The previous month Newall had found himself catapulted even farther away, and shortly after Dowding's expatriation, Lord Halifax, the foreign secretary Churchill inherited from Chamberlain, like Dowding found himself unable to gainsay the prime minister's insistence that his unique talents were required at the British embassy in Washington. Numerous others would be eased onto similar voyages in the years to come.[3] Dowding considered that his active, professional employment ended on November 25, 1940. Yet the final twenty months of his forty-two-year military career had a few twists and turns left in store for him.

The fact that almost to the end of 1941, Churchill kept coming back to Dowding as a possible AOC-in-C—long after he clearly was no longer current regarding operational conditions—suggests that, in the early stages of the war, Dowding really was one of his favorite high commanders. Certainly, along with Wavell in the Middle East, and Cunningham in the Mediterranean, he was among the handful of British officers in high command to record anything like a victory during the first three years of the war. It is also, incidentally, evidence that Churchill, who had so much personal interaction with Dowding, did not think him either physically or mentally exhausted. Yet the prime minister found himself having to reassure both Sinclair, and Dowding himself, that the latter was right for the American job.

Dowding's mission to Washington had first been publicly aired by the Air Ministry press release of November 18, which stated that the assignment was at the special request of the minister of aircraft production. Beaverbrook probably actually did value Dowding's potential contribution on the issues relating to aircraft production and allocation that constituted a major arena of contention in UK-US relations at the time. Contention spiked when Brigadier General George V. Strong, chief of the US Army's War Plans Division, delivered a highly influential report on his summer tour of observation in Britain. In his memoirs, Slessor frankly recalled the "consternation not unmixed with resentment" with which the Air Staff learned that an American infantry officer had delivered an adverse judgment on the RAF's aircraft requests, without consulting the "Expansion and Re-equipment Policy Committee . . . [or] anyone who was in a position to know" the rationale for the requests. From the Air Staff point of view, the minister of aircraft production was not one of those "in a position to know"; the new CAS hastily launched Slessor across the Atlantic "to explain to the US administration the Air Staff plans for expansion and replacement of wastage." Naturally, Beaverbrook saw this as another manifestation of the Air Ministry's determination to bypass the MAP, and deprive him of his proper, ministerial role.[4]

Dowding's new assignment therefore represented a clever solution to multiple political problems. It provided a respectable explanation for Dowding's abrupt replacement, nipping in the bud any speculation that the AOC-in-C of the RAF's (and indeed, the British armed services') most successful, operational force and the Churchill government might have found it impossible to work with each other. That is, if Dowding could be persuaded to act the part of the victorious commander on tour—keeping fresh the American perception of a stirring British triumph in the daylight air campaign against the might of the Luftwaffe. As historian Anthony J. Cumming has rightly emphasized, the strategic narrative of the Battle of Britain as a heroic victory won by Fighter Command against all odds was becoming a central pillar in Churchill's larger political-military strategy for securing maximum American support.[5] Finally, Beaverbrook could well expect that, as his representative in Washington, Air Chief Marshal Dowding would easily overshadow Slessor, a mere air commodore.

Such expectations, if indeed cherished by Churchill and Beaverbrook, were not altogether without foundation. Dowding had already begun to receive an international press buildup as a significant, historical figure. A *New York Times* special report published at the end of September had excited widespread comment for its almost rapturous characterization of Dowding and his achievements. "'Stuffy' Dowding, Savior of Britain," blared the headline of a column next to a full-length photo. The report speculated, "it may be that . . . [future historians] will decide the man who saved Great Britain was not . . . [Field Marshal Lord] Gort or even Winston Churchill, but . . . 'Stuffy' Dowding." Accurate on some points, wildly inaccurate on others, the main thrust of the column was that Dowding, "Idolized by Junior Officers," had put the RAF's fighter pilots in position to fly, fight, and win by relentlessly battering down opposition from the "British Air Council," which finally "gave in" to his prewar "reforms."[6]

Just seven weeks after this sustained peal of herald trumpets, however, the *New York Times* tamely reported the Air Ministry announcement that, following "changes . . . in the organization" of the RAF, Dowding would be coming to America. The *Times* reporter "hinted" that Dowding's assignment would involve "efforts here to standardize British and United States fighting planes." On its face, this job might have seemed more appropriate for a committee of mid-level, uniformed bureaucrats than one of history's Great Captains. It was left to *New York Times'* ace reporter James B. "Scotty" Reston to clear up the contradiction, with a remarkably well-informed profile.

Dowding's mission appeared "important . . . for both Britain and America," Reston judged; "Sir Hugh . . . can probably help us a lot if we understand his record and point of view." In addition to supplying Americans an accurate timeline of the main assignments in Dowding's service career, Reston also uncovered at least part of the inside story.[7]

Reston directly addressed the until-then mostly unspoken question: why transfer the RAF's most senior, operational commander, at the climax of a victorious campaign, to duty representing a civilian ministry in a neutral capital? Acknowledging that "a lot of people . . . [in London] believe he is the savior of his country," Reston claimed the service was divided, between "those who think he is the greatest fellow in the world and those who think he is inhumanly tough." Reston then revealed the view of Dowding long propagated by Tedder, and recently twisted by Salmond, of all people, into a shocking blood libel on Dowding's operational leadership: his alleged lack of "any humanity toward his men." The *New York Times* reporter went on to assert, "there is reason to believe that this is one of the reasons he is allowed to leave the Fighter Command." Surprisingly bluntly, Reston reported that, "as soon as Sir Charles Portal became head of the R.A.F. it was rumored that 'Stuffy' might be replaced."[8] Carefully avoiding mention of the name Churchill, Reston commented slyly, "evidently . . . the British Cabinet, believe Dowding to be more valuable in the United States than anywhere else."

Attempting to put Dowding's professional achievements into an organizational context, Reston downplayed the story of Air Council opposition to Dowding's initiatives when he was air member for supply and research, observing correctly that "Other people on the Air Staff had the same idea" for the eight-gun fighter, but incorrectly crediting the Air Council with the specification that ultimately led to acquisition of the Spitfire and Hurricane. Implying that the Luftwaffe failed in the daylight battles as much because of the shortcomings of its own striking force, composed largely of twin-engine, medium bombers, as because of the excellence of the British fighter force, Reston offered a key insight most historians have missed. "Dowding," he wrote, "was not nearly so successful with the bombers that were designed when he was in the research department."[9]

Predicting that Dowding would recommend weighting US aircraft production in favor of large numbers of heavily armed and armored, very long-range bombers, Reston argued ironically that the former fighter commander's most important contribution in the Unites States might be providing a syllabus of mistakes to be avoided in bomber design and production. A further irony is that, were this analysis valid, Dowding would be placing the persuasive value of both his prewar development experience, and as his wartime operational experience, behind precisely the sort of bomber program the USAAC had advocated since its inception on the strength of little more than its own assumptions regarding the nature of war and theories of airpower.[10]

On arrival in Ottawa, his first official stop in North America, Dowding made another wave of world headlines with a press statement disclosing a "new device" to counter German night-bombing operations, and expressing confidence in terms very similar to his August, 1939 broadcast. Readers encouraged by word of yet another technological advance on the order of (the still semisecret) radar, may have failed to appreciate fully the implications of Dowding's careful assessment that the new countermeasures against the night Blitz would bring the threat under control "by the spring." This remarkably accurate forecast of future developments in night-fighter interception, which he repeated in Washington for the benefit of the US media, meant that British cities would have to endure another three-to-six months of pounding. Despite making big news at the outset, however, further press coverage of Dowding in the United States was curiously limited in scope and muted in tone, especially in light of the buildup he had received.

There is no evidence that Americans reacted strongly to Dowding one way or another. The United Press wire service distributed a much terser version of Reston's analysis, omitting the personal characterization and the RAF service politics, and placing greater emphasis on Anglo-American "standardization." Coverage of Dowding's first US press conference was anodyne. There do not appear to have been complaints—public or private—about Dowding of the sort to be expected had he rubbed Americans the wrong way, as did not a few of his countrymen.[11] The only serious hint of controversy was dropped by another legendary *New York Times* staffer, military affairs correspondent Hanson Baldwin, who reported that, "some British observers and most of our own do not agree" with Dowding's public statements to the effect that

Germany had generated its maximum air effort in the summer 1940 air campaign, and "cannot ever dominate the air over Britain."

Baldwin's new analysis correctly identified a difference of opinion regarding the Luftwaffe's aircraft end-strength, and the industrial production capacity upon which that strength rested. Dowding would have been well aware that British estimates, including those produced for Churchill by Lindemann's statistical section in the Cabinet Office, had been trending downward for months. In the course of his talks in Washington, he could scarcely avoid learning that the US War Department General Staff believed, based on its analysis of American intelligence reports, that the British government and armed services were far too optimistic, particularly regarding the security of what Dowding liked to call "the base," the British Isles. That Dowding, certainly optimistic regarding prospects for defense of the base in the spring of 1941, was by no means complacent, is attested by the record of a War Cabinet Defence Committee meeting he attended before leaving London.[12]

Dowding had warned the prime minster and the chiefs of staff that, "although we had been successful in defeating the German air attacks by day, we had only done so with a narrow margin and it would be dangerous to assume that we could repeat this success in the face of sustained and determined German air attacks unless the fighter force, and training organization behind it, were both expanded." Significantly, Portal is recorded as agreeing "that in the formation of new squadrons, preference would be given during the next few months to fighter squadrons in order that we should be ready to meet a renewal of the German onslaught in the Spring." Although Portal gave notice that he intended to shift emphasis to "New bomber squadrons" in time to support an offensive air campaign in the fall, Dowding in early 1941 had every reason to regard near-term emphasis on fighters as settled policy.[13]

Dowding's performance of his new duties was very much in character with the whole tenor of his career—and so was the reaction to Dowding of the senior officers (especially RAF) and officials in the various branches of the British mission in Washington. "Character is destiny," and in this instance the artful contrivance of those two masters of the political arts, Churchill and Beaverbrook, was confounded by it. Slessor immediately set to work undermining Dowding, exploiting three advantages: he had been first on the ground, some two months ahead of Dowding; he had already established friendly relations with key USAAF officers during their observation tours of Britain the previous summer; and the incumbent MAP representative in Washington, Sir Henry Self, was a former Air Ministry official and potential bureaucratic ally for Slessor. Moreover, other British civilian officials in Washington, such as Australian high commissioner R. G. Casey, also had absorbed the critiques of Dowding that had been circulating in political circles at Westminster.[14]

Under any circumstances, it could only be awkward for officers new to flag, general officer, or air rank (especially holders of acting ranks) to work collegially with a newly retired commander in chief, ten years or more their senior in age as well. Dowding of course was notoriously un-collegial in style, and had been the source of years of bureaucratic friction and frustration for many of these same "Whitehall warriors," who could scarcely be expected to welcome their Dowding problem following them to Washington. For his part, Dowding carried out the classic routine of a high-ranking Washington visitor, seemingly oblivious to political machinations of his juniors. He met with the president; with the cabinet secretaries, Henry Morgenthau at the Treasury and Henry Stimson at the War Department, primarily concerned with material assistance to Britain; and with Air Corps chief "Hap" Arnold, presenting a formal, military briefing to key members of Arnold's inner circle.[15]

Exercising his penchant for firsthand observation of empirical testing, he asked Dr. E. G. Bowen, now working on advanced airborne radars at one of the largest American research laboratories, to arrange for him a demonstration flight in a USAAF B-18. The demonstration was important because an effective air-to-surface radar mounted in long-range aircraft would be an essential component of Allied success in the next great campaign of the war, the Battle of the Atlantic. Clearly, Dowding was keeping abreast of technical developments, and staying ahead of the curve in the application of new technology to critical, operational requirements. He seems to have remained remarkably disengaged, however, from the main current—the flood—of decision making from January through March 1941 that was transforming US national policy, and creating an Anglo-American coalition grand strategy.

These were weeks of historical high drama, and but Dowding was not one of the historical actors to make an impression.[16]

That Dowding did not participate in the January-to-March, American-British Staff conversations can be explained partly by the protocols of military rank: Dowding was a four-star equivalent; his participation would have required the Americans to match him with their own four-star chiefs: General George C. Marshall and Admiral Harold R. Stark. Four-star participation would have raised the conversations above the "staff" organizational level, and the Roosevelt administration insisted on keeping the profile of the talks as low as possible. Given the nature of his assignment, the fact that Dowding left no trace of his presence, let alone influence, on the planning and enactment of Lend-Lease during these same, busy months is harder to explain. The prejudices which Slessor and others in the British mission entertained regarding Dowding clearly mattered; so did Dowding's disdain for the club-like atmosphere of the committee system within which the British government and armed services planned and directed policy and strategy.[17]

Embarking on a cross-country inspection tour, on the East Coast Dowding visited the US Army Air Forces Air Defense Headquarters (the American equivalent of Bentley Priory) and briefed the staff there. On the West Coast, he toured aircraft factories, carefully dispensing praise of American aircraft types. In between, he found time for skiing. It was all a bit like a stratospheric-level reprise of the work-and-play regimen he followed decades earlier, as a thirty-year-old lieutenant. Ever the stern critic of himself and others, he considered that he was accomplishing little, and made no secret that he thought the same of numerous other senior officers swelling the ever-multiplying British missions in Washington. Dowding still invested himself in work for which his expertise, experience, and temperament made him a good fit, but it is difficult to refute Vincent Orange's conclusion that Dowding was simply not interested in the governmental-political process of making coalition grand strategy. As a consequence, when Slessor's malicious report of purported comments on the hypersensitive bombers versus fighters issue, and an equally hostile message from Ambassador Lord Halifax, resulted in Dowding's recall, the outcome was unlamented; least of all, by himself.[18]

On his return journey, Dowding chose to put himself in harm's way as he had done on the final test flight of the airship R-101 eleven years earlier, in order to inform himself by direct observation regarding a critically important aircraft performance issue. The only practical way of maintaining the necessary flow of heavy bombers from North American factories to operational bases in Britain was to fly them there, but in 1941 mass transatlantic flight was still a hypothetical proposition full of unquantified risks. Dowding made the flight himself, in the belly of a B-24 Liberator, and while personally assessing the challenges, nearly fell victim to a worst-case scenario. The bomber suffered multiple system failures to landing gear, heating system, and electronics. Fortunately, the pilot was an expert in long-distance flight, the dead-reckoning navigation proved exceptionally accurate, and the fifty-nine-year-old air chief marshal arrived home in one miserably frozen piece.[19]

When Dowding returned to Britain he was less than a year short of the mandatory retirement age. If, however, the Air Ministry was expecting finally to retire him without further perturbation, it was seriously misgauging the depth of Churchill's genuine regard for Dowding's professional merits. Already that spring the prime minister had erupted with scorn over publication of an Air Ministry pamphlet presenting a brief, official narrative of the Battle of Britain air campaign that mentioned Göring, but not Dowding.[20] It soon became apparent that Churchill's attitude was not merely one of proper appreciation for past services to the State. In June, the prime minister sought to reemploy him as an AOC-in-C, proposing to send to the Atlantic Ferry Command Acting Air Marshal Sir Arthur Barratt, AOC-in-C of the six-month-old Army Cooperation Command, and replace him with Dowding. Churchill's rationale was that Dowding "will give confidence to the Army that they will have their interests fully represented."[21]

In other words, Dowding was an air officer so senior, and so notoriously impervious to RAF service opinion and Air Ministry pressure, that he could be relied upon to fight for every inch of whatever area of responsibility he might be given. The only result of this particular prime ministerial brainwave was an angry exchange with his old friend Sinclair ("Dear Archie"), but when Churchill reluctantly concluded that another old friend, Sir Arthur Longmore, had lost the make-do spirit needed for the increasingly crucial Middle East Air Forces command, Dowding's was one of the names he considered in his search for a replacement. Persuaded by the RAF leadership to give Longmore's deputy Arthur Tedder a chance, Churchill remained unimpressed with the Middle East Air Forces' attitude and capacity for generating fighting power. During the second week in September, Churchill made a final bid for Dowding's active services with a proposal that, from an Air Ministry perspective, almost defied belief.[22]

The prime minister actually floated the idea of stepping back half a generation, replacing Tedder with Dowding as AOC-in-C, Middle East Air Forces. The very thought must have shaken Adastral House to its foundations. The "representations" Sinclair and Portal made to the prime minister in this connection are not specified in the prime ministerial minutes, but opposition to replacing Tedder with anyone—Freeman himself refused consideration—after only three or four months in command was so intense that Portal and Freeman privately agreed they would resign rather than submit. The strength of the RAF leadership's reaction to these close encounters of the Dowding kind may explain why, in October, the Air Ministry actually went so far as to publish a retirement order for Dowding "By Authority" in the official *London Gazette*, without prior notice to the prime minister. A furious Churchill forced the ministry to cancel and retract the retirement order.[23]

Retracting the retirement order ought to have been a severe, public embarrassment for the Air Ministry, and probably was Churchill's way of punishing Sinclair for ignoring repeated warnings that the prime minister must be consulted on all personnel actions affecting the most senior military officers. Certainly, the press was both mystified and suspicious when Dowding was first, retired without the sort of eulogistic, public farewell customarily accorded so senior and prominent an officer, and then in a matter of days, unretired, also without official comment. The Air Council was then put to the further, internal, embarrassment of offering Dowding another station of assignment. Churchill himself settled on the thankless task of proposing economies in RAF ground establishments, which cannot have been a welcome prospect either to Dowding or the Air Staff.[24]

Reduction in the services' logistical "tail" was, however, no make-work project to Churchill's mind. The belief that the services' administration of combat support—especially that of the RAF—was grossly inefficient and insupportably wasteful in manpower, long had been one of the prime minster's idées fixes; a source of recurring friction with senior military officers who thought Churchill, the old light-cavalry subaltern, failed to comprehend the logistical requirements of "modern" warfare. Dowding's—as it turned out—truly final, active duty assignment thus appears in the light of a minor-key reprise of the notion of placing him in charge of Army Co-Operation Command.

If anyone knew where to look for waste and inefficiency in the RAF ground establishment, and could be trusted to report the facts as he uncovered them, without fear or favor, it was Dowding. Yet the nature of this assignment was such that the Air Council could scarcely object to it; they could only prime the Air Staff for the inevitable rebuttal phase. In the event, Dowding eventually proposed a modest reduction in the scale of motor transport (a special bugbear of Churchill's) provided to RAF home stations, but provoked one last, swinging series of exchanges with Freeman and Sinclair, for daring to suggest that the Air Staff was oversupplied with officers of prime fighting age whose staff duties could be performed by WAAFs and even—civilians![25]

Returning Dowding to the active list, with a pending assignment, also served to delay publication of a potentially embarrassing book. Upon his return home from North America, he had written the customary, formal "Dispatch," providing the commander in chief's personal campaign narrative, which the Air Ministry withheld from publication until 1946. Privately, Dowding also wrote short monograph, entitled *Twelve Legions of Angels*. At his reassignment interview with the prime minister, Dowding told Churchill about the latter book, and asked for a couple of weeks to complete it. Trying head off another round of Dowding versus RAF, Churchill wrote to both Sinclair and Portal, "I have undertaken to read the book myself, at the week-end. I cannot think it will affect technical matters in any way." The Air Ministry had no desire to see Dowding's book appear in print, and Churchill sent him a personal note asking him to defer publication.[26]

A week later, the prime minister invited Dowding to "dine and sleep" at Chequers, and they discussed the book. It would be pleasant to imagine Dowding addressing Churchill, "We authors, Prime Minister, We authors," in the manner of Disraeli to Queen Victoria, but the image does not really fit the situation. Dowding always maintained that he had carefully excised from his book any hard data, or other statements that might be useful to the enemy. He also insisted that it contained no criticism of the Air Ministry. Nonetheless, an impartial reading of *Twelve Legions of Angels* discloses numerous statements of at least some utility for purposes of hostile propaganda, if nothing else, although no more so than innumerable wartime statements and publications by other British public figures. The Air Ministry did have reason to fear the sting of implied criticism. Dowding suspected, however, that Churchill's actual objection was political: the airman's expression of his views on postwar, international order.[27]

Dowding went on briskly to complete the "Review of RAF Establishments in the UK," and then accept translation to the retired list for good, as of 1 July 1942.[28] Already in the previous year, the inconsequent, if not absurd, way Dowding's name kept appearing, disappearing, and reappearing in RAF announcements of senior-officer retirements and postings had begun to attract public comment. His final retirement provoked a few indignant, newspaper counterblasts including one headlined, "Britain's 'Savior' Is Too Old at 60," as well as some outright ridicule, such as in a survey of senior military officers discarded since 1939, which appeared under the headline "War Is Unkind. To the Brass Hats." No parliamentary questions were tabled, however, which there certainly would have been, had the public attitude toward Dowding, as reflected in sections of the press, been widely shared in the houses of Parliament.[29]

A few months later, however, Dowding managed to attract parliamentary attention by engaging in a newspaper spat with another retired senior officer, Admiral Sir Herbert Richmond. Fully as controversial among his brother admirals as Dowding amongst his fellow air marshals, Richmond was more distinguished as a naval historian and theorist than as an operational commander. A habitual controversialist, ahead of the Government's presentation of its naval estimates for 1943, Richmond chose to argue the case for the navy's needs in part by blaming Air Ministry mismanagement of aircraft development for perceived, wartime deficiencies in naval aviation. Perhaps feeling that his personal stewardship as member of the Air Council for Supply and Research during the crucial prewar period had been besmirched, Dowding rose to Richmond's bait, publishing an article in the *Sunday Chronicle* that placed squarely on the Admiralty responsibility for any deficiencies in naval aircraft procurement.[30]

The judgment of two such distinguished and visible military figures in thus reopening a generation-long, bureaucratic battle royal that supposedly had been concluded six years earlier with the transfer of sole responsibility to the Admiralty, is open to question. With the outcome of the global war still uncertain in the winter of 1942–43, and with Britain straining to maintain her place in the Allied battle lines, it was no time for a historical debate that, however significant for long-term defense organization, was irrelevant to immediate budget choices, and potentially disruptive of interservice cooperation. That said, it may also be said that in the exchange, Dowding more than held his own. Describing his opposite numbers on the Board of Admiralty at the time as friendly but inflexible, he claimed that because of their unwillingness to be guided by the expertise of his department, he was compelled to give the navy "precisely the [aircraft] types they specified and demanded."[31]

Dowding's succinct framing of the issue has stuck. Even Anthony J. Cumming, perhaps Dowding's severest critic among historians, in this case conceded his main point—the Admiralty's insistence on writing its own, overly complex, specifications for multi-role aircraft—while concluding that the Air Ministry and the Admiralty share overall responsibility for the outcome. In the January 27, 1943, House of Lords debate on the Fleet Air Arm, the Lord Winter used Dowding's statement as one of the ample supply of sticks with which he belabored the Government. It was left to Beaverbrook, of all people, to intervene; for once to tamp down, rather than to incite, political mischief. While paying tribute to "That most splendid figure Sir Hugh Dowding [who] always had plans and schemes for developing aircraft," and emphasizing that "there was always something to be gained by listening to him," he nevertheless artfully suggested that their lordships might more profitably direct the debate along other paths.[32]

When Dowding's latest retirement proved to be the actual conclusion of his active service, the King upon recommendation of the Government (i.e., Churchill), raised him to the peerage. Churchill secured a barony for Dowding after the RAF denied him promotion to Marshal of the Royal Air Force, citing precedent reserving that rank for former chiefs of Air Staff. (The King himself was among many who thought Dowding should receive the promotion, and twice inquired about it, only to be rebuffed by "his" air force.) As soon as the war was over, the RAF promptly—and more than once—broke the "precedent" regarding MRAF rank that it refused to break for Dowding, beginning with the ineffable Sholto Douglas. It says much about the service elite's scale of values that Douglas ended with both MRAF rank and a peerage.

Despite his failure to become a MRAF, the new Lord Dowding of Bentley Priory was "delighted" to be only the second RAF officer ennobled, after the great Trenchard himself. No doubt relieved to put behind him yet a further, increasingly querulous series of round-robin exchanges with the Air Ministry and the prime minister concerning current fighter development and the internal circulation of his "Dispatch" for the information of RAF senior officers, Dowding claimed to be "completely happy as my own master for the first time in my life," and settled down to write and to speak his mind. As he had put it in *Twelve Legions of Angels*, "Now, therefore, as I lay down my sword, I take up my pen and testify."[33]

13

TAKING UP THE PEN

1942–1951

The twenty-eight years following the conclusion of Dowding's military service, from 1942 until his death in 1970, may be thought of as falling into two phases. From 1942 until the early 1950s, Dowding maintained a degree of intellectual engagement with military affairs and airpower, and played the conventional, public role of a retired senior officer, albeit on a rapidly diminishing scale as his intellectual and emotional engagement with Spiritualism took hold. There followed a closing phase of nearly two decades, during which he concentrated his remaining energies primarily on matters relating to his Spiritualist and Theosophical beliefs.

The phase of Dowding's public life from the later years of World War Two through the early 1950s presents a curious, at times confusing, duality of thought and action. Even before his final retirement was "gazetted," Dowding gave an interview in 1942 to the *Birmingham Daily Post* in which he disclosed his belief that in the 1940 air campaign, "The hand of God [was] on our side . . . without whose intervention victory would have been impossible." Dowding's remarks were noticed by commentators, who explained the airman's words in the context of orthodox expressions of patriotic religion by famous British war leaders, from Cromwell to Churchill. Dowding's initial foray into the spiritual meaning of the war thus slipped comfortably into the gathering press buildup for September commemorations of the third anniversary of outbreak of war with a National Day of Prayer on the third, and of the Battle of Britain on the fifteenth.[1]

The latter commemoration, marking the second anniversary of the great air battles, began the fixing of September 15 in the public mind as Battle of Britain Day. Dowding's attendance at subsequent commemorations of Battle of Britain Day, and perhaps more importantly, at eventual reunions of Battle of Britain pilots, played a crucial role in confirming his transformation from "Stuffy" Dowding, military manager, into "Stuffy" Dowding, "the Leader of the Few." Emblematic is the black-and-white photograph taken after the second-anniversary luncheon. A lanky, solemn-faced Dowding, in black suit with bowler hat and umbrella, is posed with a WAAF officer on his arm; the two are flanked by eleven laughing young men in RAF uniform, including some of the most famous Battle of Britain pilots. Dowding's remarks at the luncheon, as reported by British Official Wireless, were utterly conventional, and in themselves, wholly unmemorable. The photograph would become iconic.[2]

British political and military leaders from the prime minister down were acutely conscious of a vital need to manage the both the domestic and the wider, international perceptions of events. Political leaders actively sought, in twenty-first century jargon, to "control the narrative" absorbed by multiple, internal and external audiences.[3] Service leaders were sensitive, after the events of 1939–40, of the potential for political blowback; the sorting of military leaders into heroes and scapegoats could be swift, and professional autonomy could be at risk, especially with "Winston" in the center chair at the Cabinet table. Managing the problem on behalf of the RAF was Air Vice-Marshal Richard Peck, an assistant chief of Air Staff and a member of the Trenchardist inner circle.[4]

Peck's actions in publishing the best-selling, first Battle of Britain pamphlet, and establishing the tradition of Battle of Britain Day commemorations, led to a continuous flow of print, radio, and film stories, which coalesced into a British narrative that ultimately influenced the international mythology of the Second World War. That Dowding did not "fade away" into obscurity, as his erstwhile colleagues probably expected, but was swept up into the narrative and the myth creation, was a deeply ironic, unintended consequence of what today would be termed Peck's strategic communications strategy.[5]

The limited but generally adulatory wartime press treatment of Dowding's tenure as AOC-in-C of Fighter Command continued between hard covers. As early as 1941, A. B. Austin, a journalist who in 1939–40 served under Dowding as a public information officer, published a friendly work entitled *Fighter Command*, which Dowding later used in the preparation of his official "Dispatch" reporting on the air campaign of 1940. Less friendly was a book by J. M. Spaight, a longtime Air Ministry civil servant and prolific author on airpower. Probably the first in the endless stream of books to bear the title *Battle of Britain*, and adorned with a warm forward by Lord Trenchard, Spaight's book adopted the Air Ministry strategy of disparaging Dowding by implication through omission. In 227 pages, Spaight mentions Dowding just once, and only to note that on the epic fifteenth of September 1940, "Fighter Command [was] then still commanded by Air Chief Marshal Sir Hugh Dowding." That Churchill received nineteen mentions requires no comment.[6]

By contrast, Lord Londonderry, a former secretary of state for air scapegoated by the political Establishment for his role in the inadequate rearmament and failed appeasement policies of the thirties, made a point of highly praising Dowding in his self-exculpatory *Wings of Destiny*. Sharing credit for aircraft acquisition in the mid-thirties between Sir Edward Ellington, the Air Staff, and Dowding, Londonderry wrote, "The masterly administration of Fighter Command, with its outstanding system of intelligence . . . was the work of Sir Hugh Dowding." Regarding the 1940 air campaign, the former secretary of state claimed that "Fighter Command, under the splendid leadership of Air Chief Marshal Sir Hugh Dowding in general and of Air Vice-Marshal Keith Park who commanded No. 11 Group, in particular . . .

gained a decisive victory in the Battle of Britain, saved the country from the threat of invasion and laid the foundations of victory." Already during the war, then, a Dowding subplot to the larger Battle of Britain narrative had emerged.[7]

By the time of the next cycle of public remembrance, in September 1943, Dowding had undergone an internal transformation more rapid than that of his public reputation.[8] In May and June, he published what he believed to be messages transmitted through the medium of a Mrs. Hill, mostly from Allied soldiers, sailors, and airmen killed in action, who wished to signal the survival of their spirits to their loved ones. As a consequence, he was inundated with letters from the public, which he referred to wryly as "A somewhat mixed postbag." In true Dowding fashion, he decided to make his point unmistakably clear. Speaking at Christ Church, in the fashionable London section of Mayfair on September 1, 1943, Dowding said: "I want to tell people who have lost dear ones that I have received a very large number of messages from men who have passed over in this war, and the tone of those messages is that 'We are OK.'"[9]

Press reports of the Christ Church address varied widely, but accounts of his remarks at the third anniversary Battle of Britain commemoration on September 17 resolutely conformed to the framework of patriotic religion. Dowding was quoted as saying the battle had been won by men and women at the stations, not the headquarters. But then he went on, "These series of events had been planned for years, nay, for centuries. . . . It was all part of a plan for the part Britain was to take in the regeneration of the world." Group Captain "Sailor" Malan, one of the most respected fighter-squadron commanders of the campaign, was represented in the press as ignoring Dowding's historical idealism, but returning his compliment to the fighting men, modestly averring that the "pilots . . . received too much a share of the glamour. Much also was due to the intricate linking up of the whole fighter organization, including the executives and the ground crews."[10]

In effect, Dowding was delivering to the public the main point he had sought to make in *Twelve Legions of Angels*, utilizing forums less readily censored and harder to ignore. His conclusion in the still-unpublished book that future peace and security must be achieved gradually, beginning with the forcible disarmament and political reformation of Germany, followed by creation of a broader, international order backed by effective military force, was not very different from ideas secretly under discussion at the time among representatives of the US State, War, and Navy Departments. Dowding's views at this stage were thus still largely consonant with evolving Anglo-American ideas of liberal internationalism; or at least, remained within the utopian end of the liberal-internationalist spectrum of opinion.

Even Dowding's spiritual vision of a world evolution, eventually culminating with secular nationalism dissolving into a transcendent, spiritual unity, bore some resemblance to views being formulated at the same time by the then vice president of the United States, Henry Agard Wallace. Notwithstanding vast differences between the two men in temperament, intellectual orientation, and experience, each in his own way represented responsible leaders of the world's great democracies striving to invest the horrific, global conflict with greater meaning than a mere sordid contest for material power.

Two months later, Dowding's second (but first published) book appeared under the title *Many Mansions*, to cautious reviews. Like commentators on Dowding's public statements and addresses, reviewers treated the theme of the book as an extension of conventional, British religious belief—which of course it was, in its own way. Dowding adopted an attitude toward the Church of England strikingly similar to his attitude toward the Royal Air Force: he appeared to regard archbishops of Canterbury and chiefs of Air Staff alike, with the weary reproof of a patient headmaster toward the incorrigible heir to a great lineage. His rebuke of the Church's suppression of its own committee's investigation of Spiritualism is redolent of his comments on the report of Salmond's night interception committee: "The irresistible implication at present is that the Church appointed a committee to discover the truth, discovered it, didn't like it, and is now trying to cover it up again."[11]

Dowding's remarks about the archbishop and the committee are significant, because they help locate his thinking about Spiritualism in its broader social and cultural context. In 1937, Cosmo Lang, as archbishop of Canterbury—and the senior cleric of the Church of England—had appointed a committee to investigate the Church's loss of communicants to Spiritualism. The committee split over its conclusions, the majority holding that Spiritualism, so long as it did not challenge "fundamental Christian obligations or values," could provide "those who have the assurance that they have been in touch with their departed friends" a harmless "sense of enlargement and of unbroken fellowship." A minority of committee members, however, decried the lack of "evidence that would convince a scientist or an open-minded layman that Spiritualists do communicate with discarnate spirits," and denounced "alleged communications [that] may not only be valueless but . . . also misleading and . . . dangerous."[12]

Members of the archbishop's committee agreed, however, that one reason for the defections to Spiritualism was that the Church of England was failing to bring the comfort of religious faith to the grieving. The committee criticized the Church's excessive caution in seeking to avoid theological controversy even at the expense of ministering to the needs of its flock, and urged "much more freedom in our recognition of the living unity of the whole church, in this world and in that which lies beyond death." At this time the Roman Catholic Church was, by contrast, both clear regarding the unity of the "mystical Body of Christ," and unbending in its position that such mysteries were the business of the hierarchy, and not to be trifled with by lay people. With centuries of experience in containing challenges to the magisterium, the Catholic Church was better positioned for such a contest than the Church of England, which rested on uneasy compromise between its High Church Catholic tradition and its Low Church Protestantism.[13]

Dowding's straightforward exposition of the Spiritualist position in the opening chapters of *Many Mansions* effectively pinpointed this theological weak spot in the position of the mainstream Christian churches in the modern era. In a strictly empirical, "scientific" sense, there wasn't much difference between the official positions of the Christian churches regarding the existence of the spiritual realm, the possibility of spiritual intervention in the material world, and even the desirability of appeal to the spiritual for practical aid and comfort, and the beliefs of the Spiritualists. The debate between Christianity and Spiritualism thus was in danger of resolving itself into a contest over who possessed legitimate powers of intermediation.[14]

Although *Many Mansions* was very much a work in the popular tradition of British religious Spiritualism, one author cited by Dowding serves as a connecting link to secular and elite Spiritualist thought. Sir Oliver Lodge, a storybook Victorian character and in the early years of the twentieth century one of Britain's most honored physicists, sought to "reconcile science and religion" in a stream of lectures, articles, and books from about 1910 up to the early 1930s. Lodge was perhaps the most academically prominent among the minority of British scientists who opposed the increasingly exclusive empiricism of modern, scientific inquiry, and upheld the "essential continuity between the phenomena of this world and the unseen realm beyond it." Although Dowding specifically disclaimed engagement with the secular-scientific debates pursued by Lodge and others, nevertheless some of the lines of reasoning popularized by secular Spiritualists interestingly parallel those of better-known and more influential thinkers, such as the Swiss psychiatrist Carl Gustav Jung.[15]

Jung questioned the arrogant assurance with which empirical scientists dismissed spiritualistic claims as not just unproven, but "impossible." Heavily influenced by Immanuel Kant's distinction between objects of knowledge (the perceptions of the human senses) and objects of belief (things-in-themselves) that are inaccessible to the senses, and by Arthur Schopenhauer's suggestion that the latter might influence the phenomena perceived by human beings, Jung concluded that "this would make it exceedingly difficult to separate the living from the dead." Such speculation provoked the scientific elite (Jung's sometime mentor, Sigmund Freud, parted ways with him on the issue), but over the course of his career Jung elaborated the hypothesis in highly sophisticated forms that moved far beyond the "naïve Spiritualism" of the late nineteenth century and that later would be popularized by many other twentieth-century writers. Simple and arguably naïve though Dowding's exposition may have been, some of the concepts embodied in it were by no means simplistic.[16]

At odds with his contemporaries in experimental psychology, Jung claimed that "*a priori*, inborn forms of 'intuition' determined all psychic processes," and developed a theory of psychological "complexes," which were autonomous, "and therefore psychologically real." Stressing the thinking/feeling duality of human understanding, Jung concluded that "from the point of view of feelings and subliminal perceptions, the independent existence of spirits may be an object of belief," and not pathological. In plain words, beliefs like those such as Dowding came to hold by the 1940s did not, at least for Jung, constitute evidence of mental illness. Further, while in 1919 Jung acknowledged that he knew of no proof of "real spirits," by 1948, he "doubt[ed] whether an exclusively psychological approach can do justice to the phenomena in question." Jung's scientific paradigm had been rattled, if not broken, by the theory of relativity, which he admitted, "opens up the whole question of transpsychic reality immediately underlying the psyche."[17]

In December 1943, Dowding supported the Spiritualists' National Union petition to Home Secretary Herbert Morison, requesting an inquiry "into the position of mediums under the Vagrancy Act [of 1824]." The Spiritualists were reacting to a small number of highly publicized cases that they considered were intended to have a chilling effect on their public activities. The Spiritualists' National Union demanded that any "future prosecutions . . . [be] under common law to ensure a trial by jury." The refusal by Morison, one of the more politically hard-edged Labour Party ministers in the Churchill Coalition Government, was blunt enough to give offense. The rough manner was Morison's, but the policy reflected the Government's continuing preoccupation with wartime social control. Just as some religious leaders perceived in Spiritualism a threat to traditional Christianity, some secular leaders considered it a potential threat to social "morale," both in the armed forces and among the general public.[18]

Dowding's public activity on behalf of Spiritualism did not, however, preclude him from working with the political and religious Establishment; as he defiantly proclaimed in print, "the letters C. of E. are stamped upon my identity disc."[19] He was even willing to collaborate with his professional incubus, Trenchard. The same month as the Spiritualists'—in some eyes, humiliating—rebuff from the home secretary, Dowding joined a very different group that included Trenchard, a member of Parliament, and the dean of Westminster in announcing plans for the bomb-damaged Henry VIII Chapel of Westminster Abbey to be restored as the RAF Chapel. This undertaking, of the sort normally graced by very senior and highly respected retired officers, was crowned with success. Today, the ashes of both Trenchard and Dowding rest beneath the Chapel, near the stained glass Battle of Britain

Memorial Window, with its greatly admired blending of patriotic and religious themes.[20]

In the spring of 1944, while much of the world, including all of the Anglo-American political-military elite, focused on the approach of D-Day for the Allied invasion of northwest Europe, Dowding was conducting a crusade of his own, carrying on an intensive round of platform addresses, not only to publicize Spiritualist ideas but also to bear personal testimony in the form of messages he believed came from people who had departed their earthly life. In May 1944, for example, a reporter described "Lord Dowding read[ing] from a platform '*letters*' he said he had received supernaturally from James Little, commander of a night fighter squadron during the Battle of Britain, but dead a year." Despite the competition from war news, such events drew him renewed attention from the press. The persistent lecturer noted, "An unkind journalist has called me a 'peripatetic evangelist,'" adding with the unexpected glint of engagingly self-deprecatory humor that runs through his writings, "I shouldn't mind so much if it wasn't true."[21]

Dowding still occasionally rendered unto Caesar. During the war he sometimes reviewed airpower-related books, and he wrote an article for the Beaverbrook press on Government-business relations in the aircraft industry. Shortly after V-E Day marked the end of the European War, he publicly championed Beaverbrook's claim to a large share of the credit for the outcome of the Battle of Britain air campaign. (Although in a later, "restricted" address to a War College audience, he admitted that Beaverbrook's methods probably would not have worked "except for a comparatively short period.") Dowding's surprisingly warm personal esteem for a man of a character so different from his own may be explained by his having incorporated Beaverbrook into his increasingly miraculous, personal mythology of the battle. Still, it may not be excessively cynical to point out that any credit Dowding could deflect toward Beaverbrook was credit denied Wilfrid Freeman, Arthur Tedder, and the Air Ministry in general.[22]

In the fall of 1945, there appeared the first of Dowding's books that could not be disguised by friendly or embarrassed commentators as mere patriotic religion. In *Lychgate*, Dowding chronicled his transformation from "objective" student of Spiritualist phenomena to active participant in the intercourse between the spiritual realm the earthly realms, to which he had already "testified" in his public appearances during the previous three years. *Lychgate* is a work of personal testimony in the tradition of Sir Oliver Lodge's most famous book, *Raymond*, which recounts the Lodge family's posthumous contacts with the son and brother killed in action on the western front in 1916. Dowding's book is populated with a multitude of sons and brothers, "lads who have made the ultimate sacrifice for us," but the most striking figure in his book, as in Lodge's, is a loved one. Dowding describes his late wife, Clarice, functioning as a kind of intercessor with, and guide through, the seemingly endless complexities of the spiritual realms.

Following *Lychgate* came the delayed publication of Dowding's wartime extended essay, *Twelve Legions of Angels*. The first three-quarters of the eighty-page work present an admirably clear and concise overview of the main problems in generating airpower, although—no doubt because of the constraints imposed by wartime discretion—this analysis was not substantially different from what might have been expected from a thoroughly well-briefed, journalistic pundit on military affairs. Parts of it are surprisingly funny, in an understated manner some people refer to as "dry." There is, for instance, an imagined discussion between Göring and Luftwaffe general Ernst Udet on the subject of bomber design that would do justice to a 1930s highbrow comic novel. The last quarter of the book, belatedly, summarized the first stage of the exploration that was to occupy the last three decades of Dowding's life. It describes, in simple terms, the beginning of Dowding's intellectual and spiritual journey toward understanding the experience of war, and the implications for the future that he drew from that experience.

The delayed appearance in early 1946 of *Twelve Legions of Angels*, which Dowding considered "a resounding flop," was followed by the similarly delayed publication of Dowding's official "Dispatch," shortly before the sixth anniversary of Battle of Britain Day. The "Dispatch" had a considerable impact on shaping subsequent historical narratives of the 1940 campaign, not least because, for whatever reasons, the official campaign narrative prepared by the Air Ministry's Air Historical Branch was not published until the year 2000. Ironically, Dowding himself used Air Staff papers, including the controversial Battle of Britain pamphlet—which he termed "admirable"—in preparing his "Dispatch." Notwithstanding some technical quibbles, such as the speed of the Hurricane fighter under operational conditions, no great differences emerged between the official line and Dowding's views regarding the actual course of the campaign, although he did take strong exception to the Air Ministry's triumphalist assertion that Fighter Command was stronger at the end of the campaign than at the beginning.[23]

The most important single influence on the grand narrative of, at any rate, the European phase of the 1939–45 war was the sequential publication, beginning in 1948, of the six volumes of Churchill's *The Second World War*. Dowding makes a cameo appearance in the first volume, entitled *The Gathering Storm*, constructing the communications network that would become Fighter Command's central nervous system, but is not mentioned in Churchill's fairly detailed explanation of how radar interception was developed to revolutionize air defense. His visit to RAF Martlesham to see airborne radar demonstrated is presented as by invitation of Sir Kingsley Wood, the secretary of state for air at the time, not Dowding. The main thrust of the account is to place in the best light the role played by Churchill himself, and to defend his friend Lindemann from "jealous" scientific colleagues. Historian David Reynolds, going further, asserts that "the radar row is a good illustration" of how Churchill massaged the record to exaggerate his own prescience.[24]

In *Their Finest Hour*, the second and the most compelling of the six volumes, Churchill was extremely circumspect in his handling of Dowding and Dowding's role in the turbulent events of 1940. Dowding himself believed that this was because the once and future prime minister had much to hide. In his account of "the French agony" of May–June 1940, Churchill's version of the protracted debate inside his Government over reinforcing the RAF air component in France is scattered, relatively brief, somewhat misleading, and in at least one respect, literally incredible. "Air Chief Marshal Dowding," he wrote, "had declared to me that with twenty-five squadrons of fighters he could defend the island against the whole might of the German Air Force." Privately, Dowding strenuously denied he ever said anything of the sort; it would have made nonsense of the fifty-two-squadron strength he had been demanding for months. Skillfully, Churchill disguised his own frequent changes of mind during the crisis.[25]

Altogether uncharacteristically, in this singular instance Churchill consistently presented himself as acting on professional advice—Dowding's—not only on the technical question of fighter requirements, but on the grand strategic question of where the "decisive point" of the campaign and the war lay. Regarding operational strategy, he quite properly put Park the battle manager in the foreground, with his well-told tale of the drama in the 11 Group control room. Dowding the strategist received his due, in Churchill's account of the repulse of Luftflotte 5's attack in the North. Most readers, not pausing to parse the narrative, probably carried away the simple impression that Churchill had called Dowding a military genius. And with that, Dowding disappears from Churchill's version of *The Second World War*. There is no hint of internal, RAF controversy over fighter operations, and nothing about Dowding's departure from Fighter Command. He goes unmentioned in two entire chapters devoted to the Blitz.[26]

It was nearly otherwise. David Reynolds' diligent research uncovered a draft of *Their Finest Hour* in which Churchill "explained that he had reluctantly yielded to Air Ministry pressure" to acquiesce in Dowding's departure from Fighter Command, and included the extraordinary admission, "I was wrong not to insist on my view." There is no reason to doubt that these words, dictated by Churchill in 1948, represented his feelings in retrospect, if not necessarily in 1940. Why did he decide not to publish them? The answer must be speculative. Probably, in part, he sought to avoid drawing attention to a "political intrigue" that was most discreditable both the current generation of RAF leaders, and to elements of the Conservative Party, which he still led. Perhaps more importantly, however, Churchill probably was loath to smudge or tarnish or distract from—even a little—the mythology of national deliverance, of the Few, of the united, lionhearted "race," he was intent upon nurturing.[27]

Ironically in light of Dowding's own beliefs, the resolutely historicist, if not agnostic Churchill presented Dowding as an oddly disembodied hero, a sort of essence of air officer commanding, rather than as a human being. At the same time, an army officer, General Sir Frederick "Tim" Pile, who served throughout the war as general officer commanding, Antiaircraft Command, published a memoir that, in sharp contrast, provided credible insights into

Dowding the man. As GOC of an integral, army component of Fighter Command, Pile worked as closely with Dowding as any senior RAF officer, including Park, but presumably holding a more detached perspective.[28]

While professing great admiration and even affection for Dowding, he proved a somewhat double-edged witness for the defense. On the one hand, Pile's rating Dowding "the outstanding airman I met in the War" is a carefully limited tribute, coming from a senior general officer who throughout the war circulated in the most rarefied spheres of interservice and Allied high command. On the other hand, the specific accomplishments he credits to Dowding, the eight-gun fighter concept, acquiring Hurricanes and Spitfires, "the technique of night-fighting" and "the conduct of the great aerial combats of the Battle of Britain," are if anything somewhat too unqualified. At the same time, Pile acknowledged Dowding's well-known faults: "A difficult man, a self-opinionated man," and added a fault unmentioned by anyone else.[29]

Contrary to the legend of his taciturnity, Pile claimed that on his own turf, Dowding would "lecture"—at great length—rather than discuss or converse. On one occasion after Dowding's retirement, when the airman boasted that "The only two men in different Services who ever got on together are Pile and myself," the general "longed to tell him that was largely because . . . I never got a word in edgeways." Like everyone else, Pile gives examples of razor-sharp memoranda from Dowding that, however right in substance, can only have wounded the self-importance not only of RAF colleagues, but even the Chiefs of Staff. The picture that emerged from Pile's account, therefore, was of a man who only too obviously shared Pile's opinion that he "knew more than anybody about all aspects of aerial warfare." Upon close reading, Pile seems to hint that he deplored the timing and the manner, rather than the fact, of Dowding's relinquishing command.[30]

The 1950s saw the peak of Dowding's nonpartisan, political activities as a member of the House of Lords, as well as the last of his commentaries on defense policy and military affairs. He remained intellectually sharp and physically fit throughout the decade—until he was nearly eighty. The last, great watershed of Dowding's life was the year 1951, an extraordinarily active and eventful year for a sixty-nine-year-old retiree.

14

HISTORY AND MYTH

1951–1970

Whether because the frightening implications of the war in Korea prompted a renewed interest in the victorious leaders of World War Two, or because the Korean conflict reenergized Dowding's professional interests, February 1951 found him deep in the heart of the American South, lecturing to the War College of the newly independent US Air Force at Maxwell Air Force Base in Montgomery, Alabama. His lecture was of sufficient interest, at least to the leadership of the War College and its parent Air University, to result in another invitation, which Dowding accepted, to repeat the presentation for the next year's class. The lecture remains significant, because, speaking in a "restricted" setting to American professional officers and airmen, Dowding was candid, analytical, and introspective, generously sharing the fruits of ten years' reflection on the historic climax of his professional life.

Much of what Dowding had to say may have seemed disappointingly elementary to the veteran combat pilots—former squadron and group commanders—who dominated the US Air War College Class of 1951. Some of his comments were exceptionally self-revealing, however, and well worth pondering by any future general officers among them. At the very outset, he cautioned the officers against becoming too enmeshed in details, including the details of his own great campaign. "You've got to get down to . . . basic fundamentals," he exhorted them. He then proceeded to give them "a human picture of the difficulties of a commander-in-chief," which he hoped would be of use to his audience when they rose to positions of high command, and had to decide when to accept, and when to resist, service and governmental decisions.[1]

Dowding reviewed at length a supreme example of such an issue: his protracted struggle with Churchill (whom he did not mention by name) and the War Cabinet over the deployment of fighters to France in May 1940. He urged his listeners to find the middle ground between the "yes man" and the obstructionist, to "fight for your principles," while bearing in mind that "extremes are wrong. The fellow who will never accept any decision that doesn't tally with his own ideas . . . Well, that man's no good." Few in the audience could have appreciated just how hard-earned that particular piece of senior officer wisdom was.[2]

The other "fundamental" Dowding highlighted was what later generations of airmen would refer to as "decentralized execution," stressing that "I devolved all tactical responsibility to [the] groups and sectors." Beyond that, he staked out clear-cut positions on most of the key, operational issues that veterans and historians would debate in the coming decades. He declined to criticize Luftwaffe operational strategy, implying that the rapid changes had kept Fighter Command on the hop, and admitting that the attacks on air bases by fighters and fighter-bombers had been "very difficult to counter." Dowding insisted, however, that even during the ten days of the Luftwaffe's most concentrated and sustained attacks on his bases, the damage had been tolerable, that he did not believe their continuation would have put Fighter Command out of action, and that the enemy "couldn't have done [*sic*] indefinitely along that road."[3]

Dowding did criticize "loose thinking" regarding German objectives in the air campaign. In his view, the Luftwaffe had shifted targets, not objectives. Whether attacking Channel shipping, ports, radar stations, or airfields, the operational objective had always been "to get Fighter Command into large-scale combat." Had the Air War College Classes of 1951 and 1952 internalized this implied warning not to conflate targets with objectives, or targeting with strategy, it might have helped save the USAF much institutional pain during the next twenty years. Dowding observed that his own "limiting factor" had been command and control; the danger of reaching a "saturation point" constrained the employment of forces in 11 Group. This constraint, however, had enabled him to resist pressure to overcommit his forces, allowing him to frustrate the enemy's quest for decisive battle. Tying daylight air superiority to the invasion threat, he discounted the navy's ability to operate "in the narrow waters" if the Luftwaffe had secured "complete" command of the air. Finally, Dowding reemphasized that his role as AOC-in-C was primarily to set favorable conditions for battle; during the campaign he had directed much of his personal attention to the technical problems delaying effective night-fighter operations.[4]

Back home in Britain, one of Dowding's last major efforts in the field of military affairs was a series of newspaper articles, which made for yet another Battle of Britain narrative, appearing in the fall of 1951. Following the formula he employed a decade earlier with *Twelve Legions of Angels*, Dowding began with an extended, military-historical analysis, before ending the series with an exposition of his personal experience with spirit communications. The final installment may have provided the motive for the whole enterprise. *The Dark Star*, his third book on the subject of Spiritualism, was published around the same time as the newspaper series. What Dowding wrote in the concluding article was similar in content to his books, and the newspaper series may have been a sophisticated communications strategy, designed to secure a wider readership for *The Dark Star*. At a minimum, the Battle of Britain articles served to remind the public of Dowding's professional achievements, and undiminished powers of analysis.[5]

Dowding was by this point a leader, not so much of hopeless causes, as of causes perched precariously on the outer edge of utopian, but respectable, idealism—as for example, when he spoke in opposition to capital punishment.[6] And despite protests of his own unsuitability, he seemed comfortable mixing unconventional religion and nonpartisan politics. He joined the Spiritualist deputation petitioning James Chuter Ede, home secretary in the postwar Labour Government, renewing opposition to prosecutions for witchcraft, which was an issue raised by continuing prosecution of Spiritualist mediums under the Witchcraft Act of 1735. The deputation began the last stage of a decades-long effort by Spiritualists to repeal the Witchcraft Act, and amend the Vagrancy Act of 1824, both of which, they believed, had been abused to constrain their free exercise of religion. He was willing to exploit his status as an unelected legislator to promote his causes, having taken the loyal oath before the peers of the realm assembled, so that he might speak "in your Lordships' House."[7]

In May, Dowding had the satisfaction of rising in the House of Lords to take charge of a Fraudulent Mediums Bill, designed to correct abuses of antiquated statutes, which had been sent up from the House of Commons. Dowding guided it through to final passage with a smooth, parliamentary performance. He began by pointing out that, for a so-called Private Member's Bill, the proposed legislation had received a remarkable level of helpful attention from the Government, including assistance from civil servants in the Home Office and the parliamentary draftsmen, friendly amendments by the under secretary of state for the Home Department, and a supportive intervention in the House of Commons by the home secretary. Altogether, it was a complete reversal of the dismissive, even hostile, wartime attitude the Spiritualists had encountered less than a decade earlier. The change was underlined when Viscount Simon, as a former solicitor general, attorney general, and lord chancellor, a lawyer of some prominence if not exactly distinction, rose immediately after Dowding to offer his characteristically oily congratulations.[8]

In September, Dowding married for the second time. When his engagement to Muriel Whiting, widow of a wartime pilot officer killed in action with 5 Group, Bomber Command, became public, one newspaper was rude enough to head the announcement, "69 to wed 43." Mrs. Whiting was one of the many bereaved whom Dowding met through shared interest in the spiritual survival of deceased loved ones; the two decided that their late spouses wished them to continue their earthly progress as a couple. As Lady Dowding, Muriel became an author and a movement organizer in her own right. She helped pioneer the idea of marketing "Beauty without Cruelty," synthetic furs and cosmetics manufactured without harming animals, as well as supporting her husband's expansion of his political activities in the House of Lords beyond the defense of Spiritualists' free exercise of religion, to include animal cruelty legislation, conceived in terms that prefigured the animal rights movement of a half century later.[9]

After 1951, Dowding largely confined his interventions in the House of Lords to debates on animal cruelty legislation, concerning which he was a respected, if not necessarily persuasive, speaker. Indeed, allowing for the discursive, if not disjointed, rhetorical style that traditionally characterized the old upper chamber, Dowding's non-rhetorical style was positively crisp. In nearly two decades of attendance, he rose only some half-dozen times to join debates on defense and military affairs, including twice to encourage the RAF to equip its forces in the Middle East with helicopters, and twice on his old specialty, aircraft development and acquisition. In April 1952 he spoke in the debate on air defense and supply,[10] and in February 1953, made his only controversial intervention on a professional subject, in a debate on supply of aircraft.[11]

The issue that reawakened the redoubtable air chief marshal slumbering within the gentle Spiritualist was the same issue that had provoked him in 1942 to cross swords with Sir Herbert Richmond: what he regarded as an attempt to propagate a false historical narrative of RAF responsibility for the deficiencies of the Fleet Air Arm. Once again, Dowding let fly at the Royal Navy; past seventy now, but still demonstrating his capacity for reasoned, empirical—and wounding—argument. In a parliamentary performance the more impressive for being, apparently, an extemporary reply to remarks by an earlier speaker, Dowding reviewed in some detail the technical difficulties created by the Admiralty's approach to aircraft acquisition in the 1930s, using homely analogies and specific examples to hammer in the point that the combination of size restrictions and multiple roles was bound to result in less-than-optimal performance.

Closing in for the rhetorical kill, he then attributed what he considered the

Admiralty's mistakes to "the basic reason . . . that they had not at the Admiralty in the high positions where the orders were placed, where the specifications were made out, people with practical experience" in aviation. He then went on, in an example of the sort of argumentative overkill that contributed so much to his professional difficulties during his active career, "It has always been difficult to introduce any startling new development to the Navy. The development of steamships was fiercely rejected; the supply of breech-loading guns was delayed for ten or fifteen years after it was due." Dowding rested his case after allowing generously, "I hope that now that a new generation has grown up, the people at the Admiralty have the necessary practical experience to avoid the kind of mistake about which I have been speaking."

Dowding's intervention in the aircraft-supply debate may seem little more than a case of a tetchy old gentleman relitigating the controversies of his days in power—a phenomenon thoroughly familiar to the pre-reform House of Lords. Alternatively, it might be seen as Dowding displaying an unsuspected streak of light-blue partisanship, and closing ranks as Trenchard had enjoined him to do when he became the second RAF peer. It may be argued, however, that Dowding's persistence regarding this issue provides an important clue to his thoughts and feelings as he reflected during his retirement on his life and career. Dowding came to believe that his life and career formed part of a grand historical narrative, a myth in the profound sense of the word—a story of explanatory power and moral significance. For Dowding the obligation of defending the integrity of that mythic narrative paralleled, in the empirical domain of history, his burden of testifying to the immanence of the spiritual realms.

Also in 1953, four years after the appearance of *Their Finest Hour*, with its mythic narrative of the Battle of Britain, Denis Richards, a senior member of the Air Ministry Air Historical Branch, published the first of three volumes on the RAF in the Second World War. Richards' difficult task was to produce a "popular," rather than an "official" history, which was nevertheless based on scholarly analysis of official sources. The skill with which Richards squared the circle is exemplified by his treatment of the running bureaucratic struggle over resource allocation during 1939–40 that so envenomed relations between Dowding, on the one hand, and the Air Ministry, the Chiefs of Staff, and the Chamberlain Government, on the other. In his *The Fight at Odds*, Richards gives a fair assessment of the complex web of strategic dilemmas confronting Whitehall, before concluding that events proved Dowding right in his insistence upon priority for the security of the home island, and crediting Newall with supporting him.[12]

Richards also pairs Newall and Dowding in opposing "the demands of the French" in May of 1940, and carefully ties Dowding's achievements at Fighter to those of his fellow major command AOC-in-Cs, writing, "Fortunately Portal [Bomber Command], Dowding and Bowhill [Coastal Command] were all men who recognized a crisis when they met one, and the organization, though cumbrous, somehow worked." Analyzing the role of 11 Group in the "miracle" of Dunkirk, Richards shrewdly identifies the beginning of political concerns regarding the Dowding-Park concept of fighter operations. Churchill and his War Cabinet were exposed to Air Staff frustration and the Navy's rage at Fighter Command's apparent caution, and although Dowding's refusal to allow meddling with Park proved wise, seeds of future political trouble for them both were sown. Once again, Richards gives a fair hearing to the Air Staff view that, "a greater initial commitment" of forces might have reduced overall British losses, before gently leaning in favour of the Dowding-Park decision to minimize the exposure of an already battered fighter force.[13]

Richards thus, without engaging in apologia, puts into a broader context both the political-bureaucratic frustration with Dowding, and the readiness to hear later criticism of the Dowding-Park concept of operations instigated by Leigh-Mallory and Bader. He then suggested, reasonably and at least for most students of military organizations, persuasively, that there were good reasons for reassigning Dowding and Park once the tempo of daylight operations had wound down, but that the matter was (some would say, appallingly) ill handled. In general, Richards' position is that Dowding's narrow focus and caution as AOC-in-C were vindicated by events. In this case, it was better to be right than bold.[14]

Having privileged historical analysis over mythmaking, Richards (with a nod to what some would begin to call "the many") chose to conclude by reinforcing the myth of the Few: "The public verdict, though it was has done much less than justice to others, has thus rightly acclaimed Dowding's pilots as the foremost artisans of victory; and when the details of the fighting grow dim, and the names of its heroes are forgotten, men will still remember that in the summer of 1940 civilization was saved by a thousand British boys." This conclusion might be seen as a kind of mandatory bow to popular opinion; but may also stand for a genuinely scholarly recognition that the mythology of 1940, and indeed, the mythology of the Good War as a whole, was and is neither truth nor falsehood, but—to paraphrase C. G. Jung—a psychological reality.[15]

Four years further on, Dowding himself became a late and indirect, but successful entrant into the memoir battles fought out after the war among the surviving World War Two high commanders. In 1957, the professional military historian Basil Collier published an authorized biography, *Leader of the Few*. Collier's book, benefiting from an eighty-page personal narrative provided by Dowding, fit together well with prominent, historical studies including not only Richards's work, but also other relevant volumes in the official United Kingdom Military Series, *History of the Second World War*, under the general editorship of Sir James R. M. Butler, and helped to fix for at least two generations what may be termed the Dowding-Park interpretation of the air campaign at the heart of the Battle of Britain. Dissenters there were, such as Dowding's old antagonists Grennell-Milne and Joubert de la Ferté, but determined critics were few, isolated, and overborne by the strength and breadth of favorable opinion.

Popular interest in the battle and its heroes spiked toward the end of the 1960s, as the young men and women of 1940 reached midlife and struggled with a generation gap of their own in the Swinging Sixties. The star-studded 1969 film *Battle of Britain* reflected both a retrospective romanticization of their defining moment, and Dowding's status with the generation of 1940 as an iconic leader. While the film was in production, Robert Wright, one of his personal assistants in 1940, published a second authorized biography, *Dowding and the Battle of Britain*,[16] which ripped the last veil of discretion from the bitter disputes between Dowding and his fellow air officers. This revival of the old controversies struck a jarring note that many thought gratuitous, given Stuffy's reputational ascendancy over his rivals.[17]

By the time of Dowding's death in February 1970, his mythologization as a visionary and victorious leader, discarded in the moment of triumph by an ungrateful Establishment, was deeply imbedded in the British narrative of the Second World War. The Establishment of 1970 honored him with a splendid memorial service at Westminster Abbey, and the placing of his ashes in the RAF Memorial Chapel near the remains of Lord Trenchard. The address at the memorial service delivered by Denis Healey, the secretary of state for defence, raised a profound question about the meaning of Dowding's life and service, calling him, "One of those great men whom this country miraculously produces in times of peril." It is unlikely that Healey intended the word "miraculously" to be taken literally, but there is little doubt that Dowding, while denying that he was a "great man," would have reiterated his oft-expressed belief that the events of the summer of 1940, and his part in them, were literally miraculous: the results of a cosmic plan unbounded by earthly time and space. History—and myth.

CODA

When the veterans entitled to wear the Battle of Britain clasp on the ribbons of their 1939–45 Star service medals formed the Battle of Britain Fighter Association, they asked Lord Dowding to serve as president. When Dowding died in 1970, the members elected Sir Keith Park to succeed him. After Park died in 1977, the presidency of the association was left vacant. "The Few" would have no other leaders.[1]

NOTES

1 THE MAKING OF A SOLDIER 1882–1914

1. Basil Collier, *Leader of the Few* (London: Jarrolds, 1957), 27–33, 38–39; Paul Kennedy, *The Rise and Fall of the Great Powers* (New York: Random House, 1987), 151–58, 224–32.

2. Lord Vansittart [Robert Vansittart], *Bones of Contention* (London: Hutchinson & Co., 1945), 43.

3. Collier, *Leader of the Few*, 41–50; Tim Travers, *The Killing Ground: The British Army, the Western Front and the Emergence of Modern Warfare, 1900–1918* (London: Allen & Unwin, 1978), 4–6, 26–27; Tami Davis Biddle, *Rhetoric and Reality in Air Warfare* (Princeton, NJ, and Oxford: Princeton University Press, 2002), 15–16. See also, Arno J. Mayer, *The Persistence of the Old Regime* (New York: Pantheon Books, 1981), 179, 257–61.

4. Collier, *Leader of the Few*, 50; *Encyclopædia Britannica*, 1947, 23:736.

5. Collier, *Leader of the Few*, 50–52; Richard Holmes, ed., *The Oxford Companion to Military History* (Oxford and New York: Oxford University Press, 2001), 137–40.

For the impact of the Boer War on the British army, see, for example, Michael Howard, "Men against Fire: The Doctrine of the Offensive in 1914," in *Makers of Modern Strategy from Machiavelli to the Nuclear Age*, ed. Peter Paret (Princeton, NJ: Princeton University Press, 1986), 515–21; Jay Stone and Erwin A. Schmidl, *The Boer War and Military Reforms* (New York: University Press of America, 1988), 11–13, 17–25, 36, 38–49, 55–57, 79, 101.

6. Collier, *Leader of the Few*, 54–55, 65–66; Vincent Orange, *Dowding of Fighter Command: Victor of the Battle of Britain* (London: Grub Street, 2008), 13. Cf., "Extract from the Report of Lieutenant-Colonel A. H. Hewat, Royal Horse Artillery, Camp Commandant, Camp Palipahri," in *General Report of the Practice of the Royal Artillery, Bengal Command, 1900–1901* (Calcutta: Office of the Superintendent of Government Printing, India, 1901), 3, 39, 41.

7. Collier, *Leader of the Few*, 52–54, 58, 60–61, 64–65, 68. On the stereotype of the British army officer as a sporting, gentleman-amateur, see Simon Robbins, *British Generalship on the Western Front, 1914–18* (New York: Frank Cass, 2005), 5–7.

8. Henry Probert, *High Commanders of the Royal Air Force* (London: Her Majesty's Stationery Office, 1954), 108.

9. Collier, *Leader of the Few*, 52–66, 70–75; Robert Wright, *The Man Who Won the Battle of Britain* (New York: Charles Scribner's Sons, 1969), 23; Mayer, *The Persistence of the Old Regime*, 180.

10. Collier, *Leader of the Few*, 73–74.

11. Ibid, 65–69.

12. Cf., John James, *The Paladins: A Social History of the RAF Up to the Outbreak of World War II* (London: MacDonald, 1990), 33.

13. Collier, *Leader of the Few*, 79–80, 84–85.

14. Ibid., 81–83; Travers, *The Killing Ground*, 39–40.

15. Travers, *The Killing Ground*, 39, 44–46, 49; Gerard J. De Groot, *Douglas Haig* (London: Unwin Hyman, 1988), 94–112.

16. Travers, *The Killing Ground*, 48–49, 55, 62, 88–89, 95, 127.

17. Ibid., 48–49, 55, 88–89, 95, 62, 127; Collier, *Leader of the Few*, 81–83; J. E. G. Dixon, *Dowding and Churchill* (Barnsley, South Yorkshire, UK: Pen & Sword Military, 2008), 127.

18. Macolm Cooper, *The Birth of Independent Air Power* (London and Boston: George Allen & Unwin, 1986), 1–8; Alfred Gollin, *The Impact of Air Power on the British People and their Government, 1909–14* (Stanford, CA: Stanford University Press, 1989), 9–22. Also, idem., "The Mystery of Lord Haldane and Early British Military Aviation," in *Albion* 11, no. 1 (Spring 1979): 46–65. Cf. Maurice Dean, *The Royal Air Force and Two World Wars* (London: Cassell, 1979), 4–8, 14.

19. Collier, *Leader of the Few*, 82–83; Andrew Boyle, *Trenchard* (London: Collins, 1962), 95–110; Biddle, *Rhetoric and Reality*, 12–21.

20. Collier, *Leader of the Few*, 83–84; James, *The Paladins*, 40–41.

21. Collier, *Leader of the Few*, 83–84, 86–87, 111–15; Wright, *The Man Who Won the Battle of Britain*, 27–28; Boyle, *Trenchard*, 19, 30–58, 104. Also Biddle, *Rhetoric and Reality*, 27; John H. Morrow Jr., *The Great War in the Air* (Washington, DC: Smithsonian Institution Press, 1993), 41.

22. Boyle, *Trenchard*, 19, 30–58, 90–102; Geoffrey Norris, *The Royal Flying Corps: A History* (London: Frederick Muller, Ltd., 1965), 141–42; Biddle, *Rhetoric and Reality*, 27. Cf. Collier, *Leader of the Few*, 86–87.

23. Boyle, *Trenchard*, 19–32; Norris, *The Royal Flying Corps*, 143–44; James, *The Paladins*, 20–26, 41.

24. Collier, *Leader of the Few*, 50–52; James, *The Paladins*, 24–25, 40–42; Shelford Bidwell and Dominick Graham, *Fire-Power* (London and Boston: George Allen & Unwin, 1982), 34; Travers, *The Killing Ground*, 48–49, 55, 88–89, 95, 62, 127; Harold R. Winton, *To Change an Army: General Sir John Burnett-Stuart and British Armored Doctrine, 1927–1938* (Lawrence: University Press of Kansas, 1988), 9–13. Cf. Brian Bond, *British Military Policy between the Two World Wars* (Oxford: Clarendon Press, 1980), 2, 36, 51.

25. Wright, *The Man Who Won the Battle of Britain*, 28; see also, Orange, *Dowding*, 17–18.

26. Collier, *Leader of the Few*, 89; Marc Ferro, *The Great War 1914–1918* (Boston: Routledge & Kegan Paul, 1973), 39–49.

2 THE MAKING OF AN AIR OFFICER 1914–1918

1. Basil Collier, *Leader of the Few* (London: Jarrolds, 1957), 89–91; Robert Wright, *The Man Who Won the Battle of Britain* (New York: Charles Scribner's Sons, 1969), 30–31; Andrew Boyle, *Trenchard* (London: Collins, 1962), 115–17, 120–21, 123; Maurice Dean, *The Royal Air Force and Two World Wars* (London: Cassell, 1979), 9–10; John James, *The Paladins: A Social History of the RAF Up to the Outbreak of World War II* (London: MacDonald, 1990), 48–50.

2. Collier, *Leader of the Few*, 90–94.

3. Ibid.

4. Ibid., 97–98.

5. Collier, *Leader of the Few*, 95–96; Geoffrey Norris, *The Royal Flying Corps: A History* (London: Frederick Muller, Ltd., 1965), 114.

6. Collier, *Leader of the Few*, 100–104; Vincent Orange, *Dowding of Fighter Command: Victor of the Battle of Britain* (London: Grub Street, 2008), 24–25.

7. Collier, *Leader of the Few*, 105–9; Duncan Grinnell-Milne, *Wind in the Wires* (Garden City, NY: Doubleday & Company, 1969), 47–56, 77–84. Also, John H. Morrow Jr., *The Great War in the Air* (Washington, DC: Smithsonian Institution

Press, 1993), 75. On "personal magnetism" and British military leadership at this time, see Gerard J. De Groot, *Douglas Haig* (London: Unwin Hyman, 1988), 237.

8. Collier, *Leader of the Few*, 109–111. The performance of Dowding's squadron in air-to-air combat was not as weak as this statistic might make it appear. During, for example, August 1915, the entire RFC in France recorded only sixteen air-to-air engagements, with a 25 percent kill rate. See Malcolm Cooper, *The Birth of Independent Air Power* (London and Boston: George Allen & Unwin, 1986), 29.

9. Collier, *Leader of the Few*, 111–12.

10. Ibid.; Boyle, *Trenchard*, 145–146; J. E. G. Dixon, *Dowding and Churchill* (Barnsley, South Yorkshire, UK: Pen & Sword Military, 2008), 127. Cf. Eric Ash, *Sir Frederick Sykes and the Air Revolution* (London: Frank Cass, 1999), 193, and note 49.

11. Grinnell-Milne, *Wind in the Wires*, 38–131. Captain Grinnell-Milne's memoir was written in the 1920s and originally published well before Dowding's ascent to public prominence. Cf., David E. Fisher, *A Summer Bright and Terrible* (Washington, DC: Shoemaker & Hoard, 2005), 38–39; Collier, *Leader of the Few*, 111–12; Boyle, *Trenchard*, 145–46.

12. Grinnell-Milne, *Wind in the Wires*, 41–42, 102, 112, 127, 131.

13. Collier, *Leader of the Few*, 111.

14. Wright, *The Man Who Won the Battle of Britain*, 33–34; Collier, *Leader of the Few*, 112–14; De Groot, *Douglas Haig*, 224–26, 237–49.

15. The issue of the so-called Fokker menace and theater air superiority has provoked varying historical interpretations. Cf. Boyle, *Trenchard*, 152–56, 162–64; Norris, *The Royal Flying Corps*, 145–46; Cooper, *The Birth of Independent Air Power*, 29–31; and Robin Higham, *The Military Intellectuals in Britain: 1918–1939* (Westport, CT: Greenwood Press, 1981), 140.

16. Boyle, *Trenchard*, 165–71; De Groot, *Douglas Haig*, 237–50; John Keegan, *The Face of Battle* (New York: Penguin Books, 1978), 215–19; Shelford Bidwell and Dominick Graham, *Fire-Power* (London and Boston: George Allen & Unwin, 1982), 80–81. On Dowding's role, see Collier, *Leader of the* Few, 113–14; Wright, *The Man Who Won the Battle of Britain*, 34.

17. Cooper, *The Birth of Independent Air Power*, 30–33, 71, 73, 77; Morrow, *The Great War in the Air*, 166.

18. Keegan, *The Face of Battle*, 274–84; De Groot, *Douglas Haig*, 251–78.

19. Tim Travers, *The Killing Ground: The British Army, the Western Front and the Emergence of Modern Warfare, 1900–1918* (London: Allen & Unwin, 1978), 37–190. The term "doctrine" is used here in the general, rather than the specific, sense. See also, De Groot, *Douglas Haig*, 94–112, 174–278; Cooper, *The Birth of Independent Air Power*, 72–76.

20. Collier, *Leader of the Few*, 114–15; Wright, *The Man Who Won the Battle of*

Britain, 34–36; Cooper, *The Birth of Independent Air Power*, 74–78; Morrow, *The Great War in the Air*, 169–73.

21. Boyle, *Trenchard*, 128, 136, 178–79; Cooper, *The Birth of Independent Air Power*, 71–81; Norris, *The Royal Flying Corps*, 71–76; Phillip S. Meilinger, "Trenchard, Slessor, and Royal Air Force Doctrine before World War II," in *The Paths of Heaven: The Evolution of Airpower Theory*, ed. Phillip S. Meilinger, 44–52 (Maxwell AFB AL: Air University Press, 1997); Tami Davis Biddle, *Rhetoric and Reality in Air Warfare* (Princeton, NJ, and Oxford: Princeton University Press, 2002), 27–28; Fisher, *A Summer Bright and Terrible*, 38–39.

22. H. A. Jones, *The War in the Air* (Oxford: The Clarendon Press, 1935), 5:426–29; Ash, *Sir Frederick Sykes and the Air Revolution*, 105; John Laffin, *Swifter Than Eagles* (Edinburgh: W. Blackwood, 1964), 74–77, 81–82.

23. Collier, *Leader of the Few*, 119–20; Wright, *The Man Who Won the Battle of Britain*, 37–38.

24. Cooper, *The Birth of Independent Air Power*, 97; Dean, *The Royal Air Force and Two World Wars*, 19–20, 24–26; cf. David Zimmerman, *Britain's Shield: Radar and the Defeat of the Luftwaffe* (Stroud, Gloucestershire, UK: Sutton Publishing, Ltd., 2001), 1–2.

25. Boyle, *Trenchard*, 250–60, 271; Dean, *The Royal Air Force and Two World Wars*, 26–31. Cf., James, *The Paladins*, 73–77, for his usual, bracing challenge to the conventional narrative.

26. Collier, *Leader of the Few*, 120–21; Dowding, *Lychgate* (Guildford, UK: White Crow Books, 2013), p. 11.

27. Boyle, *Trenchard*, 328–332; Martin Gilbert, *Winston S. Churchill: The Stricken World, 1916–1922* (Boston: Houghton Mifflin Company, 1977), 199–200; Dean, *The Royal Air Force and Two World Wars*, 33–37.

28. Collier, *Leader of the Few*, 121–22; Wright, *The Man Who Won the Battle of Britain*, 42–43.

29. Ibid. Also, Higham, *The Military Intellectuals in Britain*, 143.

3 POSTWAR SENIOR LEADER 1919–1930

1. John James, *The Paladins: A Social History of the RAF Up to the Outbreak of World War II* (London: MacDonald, 1990), 103, 179; Basil Collier, *Leader of the Few* (London: Jarrolds, 1957), 138–39; "British Military Aviation in 1918," available online at www.rafmuseum.org.uk

2. Robert Wright, *The Man Who Won the Battle of Britain* (New York: Charles Scribner's Sons, 1969), 45–46; Cf. J. E. G. Dixon, *Dowding and Churchill* (Barnsley, South Yorkshire, UK: Pen & Sword Military, 2008), 25.

3. Collier, *Leader of the Few*, 123; Wright, *The Man Who Won the Battle of Britain*, 42–46; David E. Fisher, *A Summer Bright and Terrible* (Washington, DC: Shoemaker & Hoard, 2005), 44–45, 76, 81, 260; Len Deighton, *Fighter* (New York: Knopf, 1978), 39. See John Laffin, *Swifter Than Eagles* (Edinburgh: W. Blackwood, 1964), 82.

4. Malcolm Cooper, *The Birth of Independent Air Power* (London and Boston: George Allen & Unwin, 1986), 114; James, *The Paladins*, 140.

5. Andrew Boyle, *Trenchard* (London: Collins, 1962), 517–18; Douglas of Kirtleside, *Combat and Command: The Story of an Airman in Two World Wars* (New York: Simon and Schuster, 1963), 305; Anthony Furse, *Wilfrid Freeman* (Staplehurst, Kent, UK: Spellmount Ltd., 2000), 47–48. Also, Robert Ferris, "Fighter Defence before Fighter Command," *Journal of Military History* 63, no. 4 (October 1999): 845–84; and Richard Hough and Denis Richards, *The Battle of Britain* (New York and London: W. W. Norton, 1990), 20–21.

6. Collier, *Leader of the Few*, 123–24; Douglas, *Combat and Command*, 295–96, 305–6; Vincent Orange, *Tedder: Quietly in Command* (London: Frank Cass, 2004), 36, 42, 45, 63.

7. Collier, *Leader of the Few*, 129; Boyle, *Trenchard*, pp. 464–474; Vincent Orange, *Coningham: A Biography of Air Marshal Sir Arthur Coningham* (Washington, DC: Center for Air Force History, 1992), 34; Dixon, *Dowding and Churchill*, 127. See also, Jeffrey L. Hughes, "The Origins of World War II in Europe: British Deterrence Failure and German Expansionism," *Journal of Interdisciplinary History* 18, no. 4 (Spring 1988): 858. Cf. James, *The Paladins*, 151, for the view that, in the absence of a credible, potential enemy, the RAF failed to develop either "a strategic philosophy" or a strategic plan.

8. John Terraine, *The Right of the Line: The Royal Air Force in the European War 1939–1945* (Ware, Hertsfordshire, UK: Wordsworth Editions Limited, 1997), 10; Tami Davis Biddle, *Rhetoric and Reality in Air Warfare* (Princeton, NJ, and Oxford: Princeton University Press, 2002), 82.

9. Scot Robertson, *Development of RAF Strategic Bombing Doctrine, 1919–1939* (Westport, CT: Praeger, 1995), 43 and note 5; N. H. Gibbs, *Grand Strategy*, vol. 1, *Rearmament Policy*, in *History of the Second World War*, United Kingdom Military Series, ed. Sir James R. M. Butler (London: Her Majesty's Stationery Office, 1976), 46–47.

10. Gibbs, *Grand Strategy*, 48; Keith Middlemas and John Barnes, *Baldwin: A Biography* (London: The Macmillan Company, 1970), 186; Martin Gilbert, *Winston S. Churchill: The Prophet of Truth, 1922–1939* (Boston: Houghton Mifflin Company, 1977), 8.

11. Henry Probert, *High Commanders of the Royal Air Force* (London: Her Majesty's Stationery Office, 1954), 103–8; T. C. G. James, *The Growth of Fighter*

Command, ed. Sebastian Cox (London: Frank Cass, 2002), 3. See also, Boyle, *Trenchard*, 493–494; Sir Charles Webster and Noble Frankland, *The Strategic Air Offensive against Germany, 1939–1945*, vol. 1, *Preparation*, in *History of the Second World War*, United Kingdom Military Series, ed. Sir James Butler (London: Her Majesty's Stationery Office, 1961), 53–54; Gibbs, *Grand Strategy*, 48; Ferris, "Fighter Defence before Fighter Command," 848.

12. Ferris, "Fighter Defence before Fighter Command," 849.

13. Ibid., 847–53; cf. David Zimmerman, *Britain's Shield: Radar and the Defeat of the Luftwaffe* (Stroud, Gloucestershire, UK: Sutton Publishing, Ltd., 2001), 40.

14. David E. Omissi, *Air Power and Colonial Control* (Manchester: Manchester University Press, 1990), 6, 211; Maurice Dean, *The Royal Air Force and Two World Wars* (London: Cassell, 1979), 35–36.

15. Omissi, *Air Power and Colonial Control*, 5–6.

16. Martin Gilbert, *Winston S. Churchill: The Stricken World, 1916–1922* (Boston: Houghton Mifflin Company, 1977), 490; Omissi, *Air Power and Colonial Control,* 18–21.

17. Omissi, *Air Power and Colonial Control*, 18–19.

18. Gilbert, *Winston S. Churchill: The Stricken World*, 796.

19. Boyle, *Trenchard*, 450–457, 476–478; Laffin, *Swifter Than Eagles*, 162–197; cf. Hough and Richards, *The Battle of Britain*, 20.

20. Boyle, *Trenchard*, 511–512; Collier, *Leader of the Few*, 122–26; Wright, *The Man Who Won the Battle of Britain*, 47.

21. Collier, *Leader of the Few*, 124–25; Boyle, *Trenchard*, 510–11.

22. Collier, *Leader of the Few*, 125–26.

23. Middlemas and Barnes, *Baldwin*, 320; Gibbs, *Grand Strategy*, 48–49; Dean, *The Royal Air Force and Two World Wars*, 38–39.

24. Collier, *Leader of the Few*, 127–28; Hough and Richards, *The Battle of Britain*, 28; Ferris, "Fighter Defence before Fighter Command," 862–63; Vincent Orange, *Tedder: Quietly in Command* (London: Frank Cass, 2004), 68–69, 75. See also, Boyle, *Trenchard*, 543.

25. Ibid.

26. Collier, *Leader of the Few*, 129–34; Wright, *The Man Who Won the Battle of Britain*, 48–51; Sebastian Ritchie, *The RAF, Small Wars and Insurgencies in the Middle East, 1919–1939* (RAF Leadership Centre, 2011), 57–58.

27. Collier, *Leader of the Few*, 132–34; Wright, *The Man Who Won the Battle of Britain*, 48–51.

28. Ferris, "Fighter Defence before Fighter Command," 853–55, 859; Vincent Orange, *Park: The Biography of Air Chief Marshal Sir Keith Park* (London: Grub Street, 2001), 49–50, 53; cf. Zimmerman, *Britain's Shield*, 2–5.

29. Ferris, "Fighter Defence before Fighter Command," 859–63; Hugh, Lord

Dowding, "Personal Notes," appendix A, Dixon, *Dowding and Churchill*, 229–30; Vincent Orange, *Dowding of Fighter Command: Victor of the Battle of Britain* (London: Grub Street, 2008), 59–60.

4 THE AIR COUNCIL 1930–1933

1. Air Council nomenclature varied somewhat across the decades. This outline is somewhat simplified, in the interests of brevity and clarity. In January 1935, the Air Ministry redesignated Dowding's post "air member for research and development," or AMRD, retaining him in place for another fourteen months.

2. Maurice Dean, *The Royal Air Force and Two World Wars* (London: Cassell, 1979), 82–83.

3. E.g., historians Vincent Orange and David Omissi.

4. Henry Probert, *High Commanders of the Royal Air Force* (London: Her Majesty's Stationery Office, 1954), 103, 108; John Laffin, *Swifter Than Eagles* (Edinburgh: W. Blackwood, 1964), 197; Vincent Orange, *Churchill and His Airmen* (London: Grub Street, 2013), 140–41.

5. Laffin, *Swifter Than Eagles*, 212–13.

6. Basil Collier, *Leader of the Few* (London: Jarrolds, 1957), 135–40, 147; Richard Hough and Denis Richards, *Battle of Britain* (New York and London: W. W. Norton, 1990), 29; Vincent Orange, *Dowding of Fighter Command: Victor of the Battle of Britain* (London: Grub Street, 2008), 62.

7. *Report of the R. 101 Inquiry presented by the Secretary of State for Air to Parliament by Command of His Majesty*, March 1931. Digital copy available at http://lordkingsnorton.cranfield.ac.uk/archive. Also, see *New York Times*, November 7, 1930.

8. *Report of the R. 101 Inquiry.*

9. Sebastian Ritchie, *Industry and Air Power* (London: Frank Cass, 1997), 22–33; cf., Colin Sinnott, *The RAF and Aircraft Design, 1923–39* (London: Frank Cass, 2001), 18–19, 23–43, 76–84; and John James, *The Paladins: A Social History of the RAF Up to the Outbreak of World War II* (London: MacDonald, 1990), 114–15.

10. James, *The Paladins*, 117; Orange, *Dowding*, 11.

11. See, for example, Sinnott, *The RAF and Aircraft Design*, 83, 139, 149–51. Cf., Ritchie, *Industry and Air Power*, 7, 16–17, 23; and Harald Penrose, *British Aviation: Ominous Skies, 1935–1939* (London: Her Majesty's Stationery Office, 1980), 26.

12. For the historiographical controversy surrounding this specification, see Sinnott, *The RAF and Aircraft Design*, 81, 86–87, 94.

13. Collier, *Leader of the Few*, 141; Len Deighton, *Fighter* (New York: Knopf, 1978), 60–61, 64–67, 73–77; Sinnott, *The RAF and Aircraft Design*, 78–87, 94–102. Cf., Ritchie, *Industry and Air Power*, 16–17.

14. Sinnott, *The RAF and Aircraft Design*, 108; 118–19; James, *The Paladins*, 116–17.

15. Sinnott, *The RAF and Aircraft Design*, 61, 123.

16. John Terraine, *The Right of the Line: The Royal Air Force in the European War 1939–1945* (Ware, Hertfordshire, UK: Wordsworth Editions Limited, 1997), 15–17, 44–45; cf., James, *The Paladins*, 164, for the view that Ellington was "more subtle than they [the politicians] could imagine." Also, Anthony Furse, *Wilfrid Freeman* (Staplehurst, Kent, UK: Spellmount Ltd., 2000), 95; Dean, *The Royal Air Force and Two World Wars*, 87–88; Brian Bond, ed., *Chief of Staff: The Diaries of Lieutenant-General Sir Henry Pownall*, vol. 1, *1933–1940* (Hamden, CT: Archon Books, 1973), 16 (May 19, 1933).

17. Sinnott, *The RAF and Aircraft Design*, 119–20, 123–24, 128–29.

18. Terraine, *The Right of the Line*, 16–20; James, *The Paladins*, 116–17; cf. Robert Wright, *The Man Who Won the Battle of Britain* (New York: Charles Scribner's Sons, 1969), 53–54. Also, Hough and Richards, *The Battle of Britain*, 37.

19. Sinnott, *The RAF and Aircraft Design*, 32. See also, Collier, *Leader of the Few*, 141–42, 148–50; Hough and Richards, *The Battle of Britain*, 56; Michael Korda, *With Wings Like Eagles* (New York: Harper Collins, 2009), 34–39, 111.

20. Sinnott, *The RAF and Aircraft Design*, 12, 137.

21. Ibid., 60, 138–44. See also, Keith Hayward, *The British Aircraft Industry* (Manchester and New York: Manchester University Press, 1989), 15; Peter Lewis, *The British Bomber Since 1914: Sixty Years of Design and Development* (London: Putnam, 1974), 195; James, *The Paladins*, 114–15.

22. Sinnott, *The RAF and Aircraft Design*, 141. Also, Terraine, *The Right of the Line*, 17–20, 28–29, 78–79; Neville Jones, *Beginnings of Strategic Air Power: A History of the British Bomber Force 1923–1939* (London: Frank Cass, 1987), 70; W. J. Reader, *Architect of Air Power: The Life of the first Viscount Weir of Eastwood, 1877–1959* (London: Collins, 1968), 207–18. Arthur "Bomber" Harris attributed the Hampden's shortcomings to what he regarded as the institutional incompetence of Handley-Page: see Orange, *Dowding*, 88.

23. Sinnott, *The RAF and Aircraft Design*, 142–44.

24. Keith Middlemas and John Barnes, *Baldwin: A Biography* (London: The Macmillan Company, 1970), 735–36; Martin Gilbert, *Winston S. Churchill: The Prophet of Truth, 1922–1939* (Boston: Houghton Mifflin Company, 1977), 449–52.

25. Middlemas and Barnes, *Baldwin*, 722–36; G. C. Peden, *British Rearmament and the Treasury* (Edinburgh: Scottish Academic Press, 1979), 107–8.

26. N. H. Gibbs, *Grand Strategy*, vol. 1, *Rearmament Policy*, in *History of the Second World War*, United Kingdom Military Series, ed. Sir James R. M. Butler (London: Her Majesty's Stationery Office, 1976), 96–97.

27. Sinnott, *The RAF and Aircraft Design*, 96, 134–35, 142, 145; cf., Lewis, *The British Bomber*, 194. Also, Gilbert, *Winston S. Churchill: The Prophet of Truth*, 455.

28. Peden, *British Rearmament and the Treasury*, 109; Gaines Post, Jr., *Dilemmas of Appeasement: British Deterrence and Defense* (Ithaca, NY: Cornell University Press, 1993), 31–35; Furse, *Wilfrid Freeman*, 60, 77. See also, Defence Requirements Committee, 28 February 34, quoted in T. C. G. James, *The Growth of Fighter Command*, ed. Sebastian Cox (London: Frank Cass, 2002), 8–9; Gibbs, *Grand Strategy*, 565; Penrose, *Ominous Skies*, 12; 23; James, *The Paladins*, 156, 160–66.

5 THE AIR COUNCIL 1933–1936

1. Robert Self, *Neville Chamberlain* (Aldershot, Hampshire, UK: Ashgate Publishing Limited, 2006), 261–64, provides an excellent thumbnail sketch. Cf. the assessments of Chamberlain and Churchill as politicians by a fervent admirer of the latter in William Manchester, *The Last Lion: Winston Spencer Churchill Alone, 1932–1940* (Boston and London: Little, Brown and Company, 1988), 78, 104–5.

2. On the disjointed planning process, see Wesley K. Wark, *The Ultimate Enemy* (Ithaca, NY, and London: Cornell University Press, 1985), 188–89.

3. Sir Charles Webster and Noble Frankland, *The Strategic Air Offensive against Germany, 1939–1945*, vol. 1, *Preparation*, in *History of the Second World War*, United Kingdom Military Series, ed. Sir James Butler (London: Her Majesty's Stationery Office, 1961), 65–68; N. H. Gibbs, *Grand Strategy*, vol. 1, *Rearmament Policy*, in *History of the Second World War*, United Kingdom Military Series, ed. Sir James R. M. Butler (London: Her Majesty's Stationery Office, 1976), 97–98, 108–9; Martin Gilbert, *Winston S. Churchill: The Prophet of Truth, 1922–1939* (Boston: Houghton Mifflin Company, 1977), 504, 506, 508; Maurice Dean, *The Royal Air Force and Two World Wars* (London: Cassell, 1979), 37–40; Weinberg, *Hitler's Foreign Policy 1933–1939*, 182–83; Brain Bond, ed., *Chief of Staff: Diaries of Lieutenant-General Sir Henry Pownall*, 34 (January 23, 1934); Gaines Post, Jr., *Dilemmas of Appeasement: British Deterrence and Defense* (Ithaca, NY: Cornell University Press, 1993), 35.

4. Gilbert, *Prophet of Truth*, 506–8; Gibbs, *Grand Strategy*, 104.

5. The force structure in Scheme A is rather incoherently described in T. C. G. James, *The Growth of Fighter Command*, ed. Sebastian Cox (London: Frank Cass, 2002), 8–9, and more clearly outlined on p. 13, note 4. See also, Gibbs, *Grand Strategy*, 93, 97–98; Gilbert, *Winston S. Churchill: The Prophet of Truth*, 504, 506; Post, *Dilemmas of Appeasement*, 31–37; but cf. John James, *The Paladins: A Social History of the RAF Up to the Outbreak of World War II* (London: MacDonald, 1990), 164–66.

6. James, *The Paladins*.

7. Defence Requirements Committee, 28 February 1934, quoted in T. C. G. James, *The Growth of Fighter Command*, 8–9. Also, Gibbs, *Grand Strategy*, 108–9, 565;

Harald Penrose, *British Aviation: Ominous Skies, 1935–1939* (London: Her Majesty's Stationary Office, 1980), 12, 23; James, *The Paladins.*

8. Typically for the Air Ministry, it took two years to fully implement Ludlow-Hewitt's suggestion. See Colin Sinnott, *The RAF and Aircraft Design* (London: Frank Cass, 2001), 147.

9. Ibid. 141, 146–47.

10. Sebastian Ritchie, *Industry and Air Power* (London: Frank Cass, 1997), 32; Sinnott, *The RAF and Aircraft Design*, 147–50.

11. Peter Lewis, *The British Bomber Since 1914: Sixty Years of Design and Development* (London: Putnam, 1974), 240–41, 270, 272; Francis K. Mason, *The British Bomber Since 1914* (Annapolis, MD: Naval Institute Press, 1994), 288–91; Sinnott, *The RAF and Aircraft Design*, 151–52.

12. Mason, *The British Bomber since 1914*, 268–69; Sinnott, *The RAF and Aircraft Design*, 145–46. See also, John Terraine, *The Right of the Line: The Royal Air Force in the European War 1939–1945* (Ware, Hertfordshire, UK: Wordsworth Editions Limited, 1997), 66–67.

13. David Zimmerman, *Britain's Shield: Radar and the Defeat of the Luftwaffe* (Stroud, Gloucestershire, UK: Sutton Publishing, Ltd., 2001), 45, 47–48; see also, T. C. G. James, *The Growth of Fighter Command*, 26; Richard Hough and Denis Richards, *The Battle of Britain* (New York and London: W. W. Norton, 1990), 49.

14. Zimmerman, *Britain's Shield*, 33, 55–58. For an amusing discussion of reckoning the value of 1930s British pounds in early twenty-first-century dollar amounts, see Roy Jenkins, *Churchill* (New York: Random House Trade Paperbacks, 2001), 508.

15. Hough and Richards, *The Battle of Britain*, 50.

16. Zimmerman, *Britain's Shield*, 36–39, 44–45, 55–62, 64–70, 74–77, 136–41, 150–51. On the Dowding-Tizard relationship, see also Peter Flint, *Dowding and Headquarters Fighter Command* (Shrewsbury, UK: Airlife Publishing Ltd., 1997), 38.

17. Cf. Ritchie, *Industry and Air Power*, 50. In re: "bridging," see ibid., 69.

18. RAF website, www.rafweb.org/AirMin2.htm; Michael Korda, *With Wings Like Eagles* (New York: Harper Collins, 2009), 33–39, 111; cf. Ritchie, *Industry and Air Power*, 32–33 and note 111; see also, 75.

19. Quoted in Gilbert, *Prophet of Truth*, 555; Gibbs, *Grand Strategy*, 174–77; Gerhard Weinberg, *Hitler's Foreign Policy 1933–1939* (New York: Enigma Books, 2005), 208–10; Post, *Dilemmas of Appeasement*, 39–42; R. A. C. Parker, *Chamberlain and Appeasement* (New York: St. Martin's Press, 1993), 26. Regarding the political origins of these ostensibly Air Staff–originated proposals, cf. Gibbs, *Grand Strategy*, 176, 539, 565–66; and James, *The Paladins*, 153–67, 204–10, 223–24.

20. Ritchie, *Industry and Air Power*, 44–45, 49–50, 69; also, Penrose, *Ominous Skies*, 70–71.

21. T. C. G. James, *The Growth of Fighter Command*, 10; James, *The Paladins*, 179–81; Hough and Richards, *The Battle of Britain*, 27.

22. "The Reorganization of Home Command," Air Council Letter, May 4, 1936, published as appendix 4 in T. C. G. James, *The Growth of Fighter Command*; see also, idem., 22–23.

23. See ibid., 48–49.

24. Cf. Basil Collier, *Leader of the Few* (London: Jarrolds, 1957), 168–70; and Stephen Bungay, *The Most Dangerous Enemy* (London: Aurum, 2000), 128. On Newall's earlier career, see Vincent Orange, *Churchill and His Airmen* (London: Grub Street, 2013), 53–54.

25. Korda, *With Wings Like Eagles*, 33–34. For comments on Dowding's honors, see Korda, 298, and Vincent Orange, *Dowding of Fighter Command: Victor of the Battle of Britain* (London: Grub Street, 2008), 37, 46, 74, 100–102, 217, 252–53; on the royal aides-de-camp, cf. Laffin, *Swifter Than Eagles* (Edinburgh: W. Blackwood, 1964), 197–98. Also, Robin Higham, "The Royal Air Force and the Battle of Britain," in *Case Studies in the Achievement of Air Superiority*, ed. Benjamin Franklin Cooling (Washington, DC: Air Force History and Museums Program, 1994), 123.

26. Sinnott, *The RAF and Aircraft Design*, pp. 80, 89, 92, 95–98, 139.

6 FIGHTER COMMAND 1936–1939

1. T. C. G. James, *The Growth of Fighter Command*, ed. Sebastian Cox (London: Frank Cass, 2002), 11–17; John Terraine, *The Right of the Line: The Royal Air Force in the European War 1939–1945* (Ware, Hertfordshire, UK: Wordsworth Editions Limited, 1997), 61.

2. John James, *The Paladins: A Social History of the RAF Up to the Outbreak of World War II* (London: MacDonald, 1990), 164; cf. Stephen Bungay, *The Most Dangerous Enemy* (London: Aurum, 2000), 60.

3. Wesley K. Wark, *The Ultimate Enemy* (Ithaca, NY, and London: Cornell University Press, 1985), 55–57.

4. Ibid., 191–202; cf. N. H. Gibbs, *Grand Strategy*, vol. 1, *Rearmament Policy*, in *History of the Second World War*, United Kingdom Military Series, ed. Sir James R. M. Butler (London: Her Majesty's Stationery Office, 1976), 565–66.

5. T. C. G. James, *The Growth of Fighter Command*, p. 29.

6. Gibbs, *Grand Strategy*, 461–64.

7. David Fraser, *Alanbrooke* (New York: Atheneum, 1982), 110, 121–22, 128. On Dowding's management style, cf. Vincent Orange, *Dowding of Fighter Command: Victor of the Battle of Britain* (London: Grub Street, 2008), 118.

8. Gibbs, *Grand Strategy*, 461–64. Also, Richard Hough and Denis Richards, *The Battle of Britain* (New York and London: W. W. Norton, 1990), 56, 58, 60.

9. Sir Charles Webster and Noble Frankland, *Strategic Air Offensive against Germany, 1939–1945*, vol. 1, *Preparation*, in *History of the Second World War*, United Kingdom Military Series, ed. Sir James Butler (London: Her Majesty's Stationery Office, 1961), 73–74; cf. Robert Self, *Neville Chamberlain* (Aldershot, Hampshire, UK: Ashgate Publishing Limited, 2006), 254–55, 259–260; G. C. Peden, *Arms, Economics and British Strategy* (Cambridge: Cambridge University Press, 2007), 131–32, 154–55; James P. Levy, *Appeasement and Rearmament* (New York: Rowman & Littlefield, 2006), 94.

10. Webster and Frankland, *Strategic Air Offensive against Germany*, 74–76.

11. H. C. T. Dowding, "Employment of the Fighter Command in Home Defence," PRO Document AIR 16/260, reprinted in ACSC LW AY08 Course book, 8–18.

12. Webster and Frankland, *Strategic Air Offensive against Germany*, 78, note 3; Gibbs, *Grand Strategy*, 103; James R. M. Butler, *Grand Strategy*, vol. 2, *September 1939–June 1941*, in *History of the Second World War*, United Kingdom Military Series, ed. Sir James R. M. Butler (London: Her Majesty's Stationery Office, 1957), 71–80; Jeffrey L. Hughes, "The Origins of World War II in Europe: British Deterrence Failure and German Expansionism," *Journal of Interdisciplinary History* 18, no. 4 (Spring 1988): 863–66; Tami Davis Biddle, *Rhetoric and Reality in Air Warfare* (Princeton, NJ, and Oxford: Princeton University Press, 2002), 114–15; Terraine, *The Right of the Line*, pp. 49–72.

13. Ibid. Also, Williamson Murray and Allan R. Millett, *Calculations: Net Assessment and the Coming of World War II* (New York: The Free Press, 1992), 39

14. Webster and Frankland, *Strategic Air Offensive against Germany*, 73–74; T. C. G. James, *The Growth of Fighter Command*, 19, 25, 29, 31–35; *Terraine, The Right of the Line*, 47, 49–72; Martin Gilbert, *Winston S. Churchill: Prophet of Truth, 1922–1939* (Boston: Houghton Mifflin Company, 1977), 920, 925; Self, *Neville Chamberlain*, 301–2; Gibbs, *Grand Strategy*, 582–83.

15. Freeman was air member for development and production in 1938–40. Freeman's postings through the years curiously shadowed Dowding's, although his career failed to culminate in high command. See "Air of Authority," http://www.rafweb.org/.

16. Webster and Frankland, *Strategic Air Offensive against Germany*, 101–2; Vincent Orange, *Park: The Biography of Air Chief Marshal Sir Keith Park* (London: Grub Street, 2001), 69–70; Orange, *Dowding*, 102–4.

17. Orange, *Dowding*, 103–4; *cf.* Orange, *Park*, 69–70. See also, Colin Sinnott, *The RAF and Aircraft Design, 1923–39* (London: Frank Cass, 2001), 109–13; 120–24.

18. Ibid.

19. Orange, *Dowding*, 102–4. Cf., T. C. G. James, *The Battle of Britain*, ed. Sebas-

tian Cox, Air Historical Branch narrative (London: Frank Cass, 2000), 135; Webster and Frankland, *Strategic Air Offensive against Germany*, 96, 100–101, 114, 116–17.

20. Webster and Frankland, 96, 100–101, 114, 116–17. Also, Orange, *Dowding*, 93, 100, 112–14. Orange appears to favor sheer incompetence as the major factor contributing to Bomber Command's noncooperation.

21. Orange, *Park*, 68–70.

22. Webster and Frankland, *Strategic Air Offensive against Germany*, 80; Williamson Murray, *Change in the European Balance of Power, 1938–1939: The Path to Ruin* (Princeton, NJ: Princeton University Press, 1984), 245–53. For the political impact of rumors regarding the air-defense situation, see, for example, Harold Nicolson, *Diaries and Letters 1930–1939*, ed. Nigel Nicolson (New York: Atheneum, 1966), 332, 340, 343, 365.

23. T. C. G. James, *The Growth of Fighter Command*, 42–52. Also, Bungay, *The Most Dangerous Enemy*, 66; Orange, *Dowding*, 120. On the capabilities and limitations of the Luftwaffe in 1938, see Webster and Frankland, *Strategic Air Offensive against Germany*, 99; Murray, *Change in the European Balance of Power*, 245–53.

24. See especially Cabinet Meeting of April 27, 1938, at http://filestore.nationalarchives.gov.uk/pdfs/large/cab-23-93.pdf. Retrieved: 5/4/2016.

25. T. C. G. James, *The Growth of Fighter Command*, 37–38, 41; Basil Collier, *Leader of the Few* (London: Jarrolds, 1957), 182–87; Webster and Frankland, *Strategic Air Offensive against Germany*, 102; Hough and Richards, *The Battle of Britain*, 58, 60–61. See also, Anthony Furse, *Wilfrid Freeman* (Staplehurst, Kent, UK: Spellmount Ltd., 2000), 86.

26. Dowding, "Employment of the Fighter Command in Home Defence," ACSC AY08 LW Course book, 15; Terraine, *The Right of the Line*, 72–73; Robin Higham, "The Royal Air Force and the Battle of Britain," in *Case Studies in the Achievement of Air Superiority*, ed. Benjamin Franklin Cooling (Washington, DC: Air Force History and Museums Program, 1994), 131; Michael Korda, *With Wings Like Eagles*, 34–39, 111; Orange, *Park*, 52–53, 68–84; Orange, *Dowding*, 129.

27. Collier, *Leader of the Few*, 168–69; Robert Wright, *The Man Who Won the Battle of Britain* (New York: Charles Scribner's Sons, 1969), 60–63, 68–69, 72–76; cf., Bungay, *The Most Dangerous Enemy*, 129.

28. Ibid; Orange, *Dowding*, 101, 122–23.

29. Orange, *Dowding*, 86.

30. Ibid.

31. Bungay, *The Most Dangerous Enemy*, 263; Sinnott, *The RAF and Aircraft Design*, 42; Orange, *Dowding*, 96; 110–11, 115, 117, 122–23.

32. Dowding, *Twelve Legions of Angels* (London: Jarrolds, 1946), 48.

33. Louis Brown, *Radar History of World War II* (Bristol, UK, and Philadelphia, PA: Institute of Physics Publishing, 1999), 53–55, 58, 63–64.

34. Peter Wykeham, *Fighter Command* (London: Putnam, 1960), 51–52; cf. Collier, *Leader of the Few*, 166–68; Orange, *Dowding*, 105–7, 118–19.

35. E. G. Bowen, *Radar Days* (Bristol, UK: Adam Hilger, 1987), 69–72; 78.

36. Ibid., 69–75.

37. Ian White, *The History of Air Intercept (AI) Radar and the British Nightfighter, 1935–1959* (Barnsley, South Yorkshire, UK: Pen & Sword Aviation, 2007), 21–22, 30, 34–35.

38. Orange, *Dowding*, 111–12, 117–19. See also, Orange, *Park*, 74–75.

39. John Frayn Turner, *Douglas Bader* (Shrewsbury, UK: Airlife Publishing Ltd., 1995), 89. Cf., Furse, *Wilfrid Freeman*, 164–65. David Eisenhower, *Eisenhower at War 1943–1945* (New York: Vintage Books, 1978), 126, 152–56, 240–42, 277–78. Cf., W. A. Jacobs, "Operation OVERLORD," in *Case Studies in the Achievement of Air Superiority*, ed. Benjamin Franklin Cooling (Washington, DC: Air Force History and Museums Program, 1994), 271–314, makes the case for the merits of Leigh-Malloy's position, as against those of his fellow airmen; see especially 300, 302–4.

40. Orange, *Park*, 70–72; Orange, *Dowding*, 121.

41. Orange, *Park*, 71–72.

42. Orange, *Dowding*, 121.

7 COMMAND IN WAR 1939–1940

1. Peter Flint, *Dowding and Headquarters Fighter Command* (Shrewsbury, UK: Airlife Publishing Ltd., 1997), 38.

2. Churchill, *The Gathering Storm* (Boston: Houghton Mifflin Company, 1948), 408; Wykeham, *Fighter Command*, 81.

3. Cf., Wykeham, *Fighter Command*, 81; and Stephen Bungay, *The Most Dangerous Enemy* (London: Aurum, 2000), 67.

4. Vincent Orange, *Dowding of Fighter Command: Victor of the Battle of Britain* (London: Grub Street, 2008), 119, 128. For AM (later ACM) Joubert de la Ferté, see "Air of Authority," http://www.rafweb.org/. Also, Frederick Pile *Ack-Ack: Britain's Defence against Air Attack during the Second World War* (London: George G. Harrap & Co., 1949), 161–64.

5. Orange, *Dowding*, 143; J. R. Robinson, "60 Signals Group Fighter Command Royal Air Force," available online at www.rquirk.com/cdnradar/cor/chapter12.pdf.

6. John Terraine, *The Right of the Line: The Royal Air Force in the European War 1939–1945* (Ware, Hertfordshire, UK: Wordsworth Editions Limited, 1997), 73–77.

7. Orange, *Dowding*, 146–47.

8. Martin Gilbert, *Winston S. Churchill: Finest Hour, 1939–1941* (Boston: Houghton Mifflin Company, 1983), 82–88.

9. Orange, *Dowding*, 122–23. See also, Gilbert, *Finest Hour*, 174–203.

10. RAF website, www.rafweb.org/Biographies/Gossage.htm.

11. Ibid., www.rafweb.org/Biographies/Welsh.htm.

12. Ibid., www.rafweb.org/Biographies/Park.htm; Vincent Orange, *Park: The Biography of Air Chief Marshal Sir Keith Park* (London: Grub Street, 2001), 69–73.

13. Bungay, *The Most Dangerous Enemy*, 132–33.

14. Denis Richards, *Portal of Hungerford* (London: William Heinemann, Ltd., 1977), 148. Cf,. Chiefs of Staff Committee Minutes, May 15, 1940, in Martin Gilbert, ed., *Churchill War Papers*, 3 vols. (New York and London: W. W. Norton, 1993–2000), 2:37.

15. Dowding to Peirse, May 14, 1940 (HCTD/S.315); published as appendix 10 in T. C. G. James, *The Growth of Fighter Command*, ed. Sebastian Cox (London: Frank Cass, 2002). Also, Gilbert, *Finest Hour*, 342–43.

16. Ibid.

17. Terraine, *The Right of the Line*, 130; Chiefs of Staff Committee minutes, May 14, 1940, in *Churchill War Papers*, 2:30; War Cabinet minutes, May14, 1940, in *Churchill War Papers*, 2:31–32; Chiefs of Staff Committee minutes, May 15, 1940, in *Churchill War Papers*, 2:36.

18. Chiefs of Staff Committee minutes, May 15, 1940, in *Churchill War Papers*, 2:37–38; Group Captain William Elliott, quoted in Terraine, *The Right of the Line*, 140. Cf. Gilbert, *Finest Hour*, 340–41.

19. War Cabinet minutes: confidential annex, May 15, 1940, in *Churchill War Papers*, 2:41. Dowding to Park, May 15, 1940, quoted in Terraine, *The Right of the Line*, 140; AOC-in-C, Fighter Command, to the Under Secretary of State for Air, May 16, 1940, quoted in Basil Collier, *Leader of the Few* (London: Jarrolds, 1957), 193–94; see also, ibid., 197–98; Robert Wright, *The Man Who Won the Battle of Britain* (New York: Charles Scribner's Sons, 1969), 109–10; and Orange, *Park*, 84–85.

20. War Cabinet minutes: confidential annex, May 16, 1940, in *Churchill War Papers*, 2:52; Gilbert, *Finest Hour*, 346–47.

21. Churchill to Chamberlain, May 17, 1940, in *Churchill War Papers*, 2:68; Churchil to Ismay, May 19, 1940, in *Churchill War Papers*, 2:91; Notes of a Meeting, 10 Downing Street, June 5, 1940, in *Churchill War Papers*, 2:252; and War Cabinet minutes: confidential annex, June 7, 1940, in *Churchill War Papers*, 2:263–64. For the impact of the BEF's situation see Colville Diary, May 27, 28, 29, 30, 31, 1940, in Colville, *The Fringes of Power: 10 Downing Street Diaries 1939–1955* (New York and London: W. W. Norton and Company, 1985), 140–44.

22. Gilbert, *Finest Hour*, 416.

23. Collier, *Leader of the Few*, 198–99; Terraine, *The Right of the Line*, 156–57; Colville Diary, June 2, 1940, in *Fringes of Power*, 146; Gilbert, *Finest Hour*, 456–58.

24. Christopher V. Jones, *Visualization and Optimization* (New York: Springer Science & Business Media, 1996), 6–7.

25. Gilbert, *Finest Hour*, 470–71, 482–85; Colville Diary, June 4, 1940, in *Fringes of Power*, 147.

26. Gilbert, *Finest Hour*, 506–7.

27. Terraine, *The Right of the Line*, 152–70; Roy Jenkins, *Churchill* (New York: Random House Trade Paperbacks, 2001), 597–621. Churchill, House of Commons, June 18, 1940, in Robert Rhodes James, ed., *Winston S. Churchill: His Complete Speeches*, vol. 6, *1935–1942* (New York and London: Chelsea House Publishers in association with R. R. Bowker Company, 1974), 6225–31; Dowding to Churchill, June 17, 1940, *Churchill War Papers*, 2:360; Churchill, House of Commons, June 18, 1940, in *Complete Speeches*, 6232–36.

28. Churchill, House of Commons, June 18, 1940, *Complete Speeches*, 6238. From among the endless commentary on this speech, see e.g., Bungay, *The Most Dangerous Enemy*, 25–26.

29. T. C. G. James, *The Battle of Britain*, ed. Sebastian Cox, Air Historical Branch narrative (London: Frank Cass, 2000), 20–21.

30. Air Historical Branch, *The Rise and Fall of the German Air Force* (London: Crown Copyright, 1983), 79; James, *The Battle of Britain*, 12–13, 21, 41–42; Francis K. Mason, *Battle Over Britain* (Bourne End, Buckinghamshire, UK: Aston Publications Ltd., 1990), 91–92, 109; Derek Wood, with Derek Dempster, *The Narrow Margin: The Battle of Britain and the Rise of Air Power* (Washington, DC: Smithsonian Institution Press, 1990), 140; Richard Hough and Denis Richards, *The Battle of Britain* (New York and London: W. W. Norton, 1990), 122; Williamson Murray, *Strategy for Defeat: The Luftwaffe 1933–1945* (Maxwell AFB, AL: Air University Press, 1983), 45; Bungay, *The Most Dangerous Enemy*, 108.

31. Alfred Price, *Britain's Air Defences, 1939–45* (Oxford: Osprey, 2004), 14–16. Cf. Colville Diary, July 22, 1940, and August 5, 1940, in *Fringes of Power*, 199, 209. It should be noted that the surprise employment of this device at RAF Kenley on August 18 helped break up an attacking Luftwaffe formation. Aficionados still debate whether or not the weapon ever actually brought down a hostile aircraft.

32. See, inter alia, Andrew Roberts, *Eminent Churchillians* (New York: Simon & Schuster, 1994), 137–60.

33. Colville Diary, June 27 and November 5, 1940, in *Fringes of Power*, 48, 91, 93, 172. Also, Gilbert, *Finest Hour*, 605–6; cf. 582.

34. Michael Hart, review of *Liberal Crusader: The Life of Sir Archibald Sinclair* by Gerard J. De Groot, in *English Historical Review* 111, no. 441 (April 1996): 535–36. 2012. Martin Petter, Review of *Liberal Crusader: The Life of Sir Archibald Sinclair* by Gerard J. De Groot, in *Albion* 26, no. 2 (Summer 1994): 392–94.

35. Colville Diary, May 23, 1940, June 18 and 28, 1940, July 9, 1940, in *Fringes of Power*, 139, 165, 175–76; 187–88; Sebastian Ritchie, "A Political Intrigue against the Chief of Air Staff," in *War & Society* 16, no. 1 (May 1998): 83–104. Also, Anthony Furse, *Wilfrid Freeman* (Staplehurst, Kent, UK: Spellmount Ltd., 2000), 147; Peter Howlett, "New Light through Old Windows: A New Perspective on the British Economy in the Second World War," *Journal of Contemporary History* 28, no. 2 (April 1993): 369.

36. Newall's aeronautical rating was flight observer, not pilot.

37. Ritchie, "A Political Intrigue," cited above; Orange, *Dowding*, 164–66; J. E. G. Dixon, *Dowding and Churchill* (Barnsley, South Yorkshire, UK: Pen & Sword Military, 2008), 15–16, 63, 66–71.

38. Churchill Archives website. See also, E. G. Bowen, *Radar Days* (Bristol, UK: Adam Hilger, 1987), 72–75.

39. Also, Churchill memo to Sinclair regarding pilot training on June 27; Sinclair memo for War Cabinet on the same subject, July 1. Gilbert, *Finest Hour*, 458, 476 and note 1; 605 and note 3; 673. Memorandum by the secretary of state for air (Sinclair), July 1, 1940, W.P. (40) 238, UK National Archives Microfilm cab-66-9-18-0001, retrieved August 2, 2012 from www.nationalarchives.gov.uk/cabinetpapers/default.htm 8/2/2012. Wood with Dempster, *The Narrow Margin*, 150. Also, R. V. Jones, quoted in *Churchill War Papers*, 2:388–89; Churchill, *Their Finest Hour* (Boston: Houghton Mifflin Company, 1949), 342.

40. Ibid. Also, Gilbert, *Finest Hour*, 654–55, 657–58. Cf. Colville Diary, August 10 and 11, 1940, in *Fringes of Power*, 217–18, 220.

41. Gilbert, *Finest Hour*, 658, 661; also, 665, note 3, and 685, note 2; Colville Diary, July 11, 12, 13, 1940, in *Fringes of Power*, 189–91, 194–95; *cf.* Bungay, *The Most Dangerous Enemy*, 155; Churchill, "War of the Unknown Warriors," in James, ed., *Complete Speeches*, 6:6249.

42. Churchill to Sir Archibald Sinclair, "Private and Confidential," July 10, 1940, in *Churchill War Papers*, 2:498; Gilbert, *Finest Hour*, 657–58; Wright, *The Man Who Won the Battle of Britain*, 136–43. See also, e.g., Freeman to Trenchard, February 24, 1948; quoted in Furse, *Wilfrid Freeman*, 95, footnote; cf. H. Montgomery Hyde, *British Air Policy between the Wars* (London: Heinemann, 1978), and Furse, *Wilfrid Freeman*, 150, 152.

8 THE BATTLE OF BRITAIN JULY–AUGUST 1940

1. Air Historical Branch, *The Rise and Fall of the German Air Force* (London: Crown Copyright, 1983), 79; T. C. G. James, *The Battle of Britain*, ed. Sebastian Cox, Air Historical Branch narrative (London: Frank Cass, 2000), 17–18, 41–42;

Williamson Murray, *Strategy for Defeat: The Luftwaffe 1933–1945* (Maxwell AFB, AL: Air University Press, 1983), 45; Richard Hough and Denis Richards, *The Battle of Britain* (New York and London: W. W. Norton, 1990), 122; Martin Gilbert, *Winston S. Churchill: Finest Hour, 1939–1941* (Boston: Houghton Mifflin Company, 1983), 606–26; 657.

2. Gerhard Weinberg, citing Edward L. Homze, claims that the Ju-88, the Luftwaffe's best medium bomber, was designed "with Britain in mind," and implies that Hitler's order of August 31, 1939, doubling its production rate reflected his expectations regarding the course of a conflict with the UK. Göring supposedly told the army as early as September 6, 1939, that the Führer intended "the main effort against Britain" to be made in 1940 by 1,500 Ju-88s, to be followed by the "death blow" in 1941. See Weinberg, *Germany, Hitler and World War II* (Cambridge: Cambridge University Press, 1995), 92.

3. Research Institute for Military History, Freiburg, "Plans and Preparations for a Landing in England," in *Germany and the Second World War* (Oxford and New York: Clarendon Press, 1990), 2:367–68; ibid., "The Battle of Britain," 374, 378; Horst Boog, "The Luftwaffe and the Battle of Britain," in *The Battle Re-Thought: A Symposium on the Battle of Britain*, ed. Henry Probert and Sebastian Cox (Shrewsbury, UK: Airlife Publishing Ltd., 1991), 18–19; cf. Derek Wood with Derek Dempster, *The Narrow Margin: The Battle of Britain and the Rise of Air Power* (Washington, DC: Smithsonian Institution Press, 1990), 157, 161–62.

4. "The Battle of Britain," in Research Institute for Military History, Freiburg, *Germany and the Second World War*, 2:378; Boog, "The Luftwaffe and the Battle of Britain," in Probert and Cox, eds., *The Battle Re-Thought*, 19; Wood with Dempster, *The Narrow Margin*, 162; Stephen Bungay, *The Most Dangerous Enemy* (London: Aurum, 2000), 122.

5. T. C. G. James, *The Battle of Britain*, 133; Colville Diary, June 18 and 28, 1940, in Colville, *The Fringes of Power: 10 Downing Street Diaries 1939–1955* (New York and London: W. W. Norton and Company, 1985), 167, 178; Bungay, *The Most Dangerous Enemy*, 122; cf. Gilbert, *Finest Hour*, 687–88, and Wood with Dempster, *The Narrow Margin*, 140.

6. Colville Diary, June 20, 1940, in *Fringes of Power*, 168. Cf. ibid., entry for June 26, 1940, 171. Also, Bungay, *The Most Dangerous Enemy*, 147–57, 179–85.

7. T. C. G. James, *The Battle of Britain*, 21–22, 30–31, 133; Francis K. Mason, *Battle Over Britain* (Bourne End, Buckinghamshire, UK: Aston Publications Ltd., 1990), 111–12; Gilbert, *Finest Hour*, 657; Bungay, *The Most Dangerous Enemy*, 180; Wood with Dempster, *The Narrow Margin*, 152–53, 175, 184.

8. T. C. G. James, *The Battle of Britain*, 30, 39–40; Bungay, *The Most Dangerous Enemy*, 241–46.

9. Gilbert, *Finest Hour*, 658, 668–69, 713–14; Colville Diary, July 16, 1940, in *Fringes of Power*, 197; T. C. G. James, *The Battle of Britain*, 41–42.

10. Defence Committee Minutes, July 26, 1940, in Martin Gilbert, ed. *Churchill War Papers*, 3 vols. (New York and London: W. W. Norton, 1993–2000), 2:574–75 and 2:588–89; T. C. G. James, *The Battle of Britain*, 20, 44; Harold Nicolson, *Diaries and Letters, 1939–1945*, ed. Nigel Nicolson (New York: Atheneum, 1967), 101; Gilbert, *Finest Hour*, 668, 670; Mason, *Battle Over Britain*, 147; Bungay, *The Most Dangerous Enemy*, 157, 179–80.

11. See Bungay, *The Most Dangerous Enemy*, 179.

12. T. C. G. James, *The Battle of Britain*, 45, 124–25; Mason, *Battle Over Britain*, 152, 161; Wood with Dempster, *The Narrow Margin*, 196, 280.

13. "The Battle of Britain," in Research Institute for Military History, Freiburg, *Germany and the Second World War*, 2:379–80.

14. Defence Committee Minutes, July 26, 1940; Prime Minister to First Sea Lord (Pound), August 8, 1940; Dalton Diary, August 12, 1940, in *Churchill War Papers*, 2:575, 635, 656; Colville Diary, August 8 and 9, 1940; in *Fringes of Power*, 212–13; Gilbert, *Finest Hour*, 718; Mason, *Battle Over Britain*, 172; Bungay, *The Most Dangerous Enemy*, 181.

15. The Luftwaffe at this point was actually winning the fighter battles by about 1.6:1, but RAF fighters more than made up the difference by downing German bombers. German aircrew losses, killed and captured, were (for obvious reasons) far greater than Fighter Command's pilot losses. Published comparisons of RAF and Luftwaffe combat losses during this period almost invariably omit those of Bomber Command and Coastal Command.

16. Bungay, *The Most Dangerous Enemy*, 192–202. On the Luftwaffe's objectives during this phase of its operations, see, "The Battle of Britain," in Research Institute for Military History, Freiburg, *Germany and the Second World War*, 2:379.

17. Bungay, *The Most Dangerous Enemy*, 182–84. See, Colville Diary, August 11, 1940, in *Fringes of Power*, 218; Nicolson Diary, August 13 and 15, 1940, in *Diaries and Letters, 1939–1945*, 107. Churchill's unstinted admiration for RAF aircrew did not, however, entirely still the suspicion of official statistics that was the natural product of half a lifetime in government. Around this time he made a point of asking Dowding whether or not a form of operations analysis could be used to substantiate the claims. See *Churchill War Papers*, 2:680.

18. Bungay, *The Most Dangerous Enemy*, 216, 218.

19. Ibid., 137, 184–85; Mason, *Battle Over Britain*, 195. Also, Colville Diary, August 13, 1940, in *Fringes of Power*, 222.

20. Bungay, *The Most Dangerous Enemy*, 289.

21. Ibid., 137.

22. T. C. G. James, *The Battle of Britain*, 91, 125; Colville Diary, August 15, 1940, in *Fringes of Power*, 223; Bungay, *The Most Dangerous Enemy*, 137; but see Park's famous comment to the prime minister on the fifteenth of September, quoted in Churchill, *Finest Hour*, 336. Also, Gilbert, *Finest Hour*, 734–35.

23. David E. Fisher, *A Race on the Edge of Time* (New York: Paragon House, 1989), 208.

9 THE BATTLE OF BRITAIN AUGUST–SEPTEMBER 1940

1. Richard Hough and Denis Richards, *The Battle of Britain* (New York and London: W. W. Norton, 1990), 219–20; Stephen Bungay, *The Most Dangerous Enemy* (London: Aurum, 2000), 218–19.

2. Francis K. Mason, *Battle Over Britain* (Bourne End, Buckinghamshire, UK: Aston Publications Ltd., 1990), 210–18.

3. Hough and Richards, *The Battle of Britain,* 192–96; Bungay, *The Most Dangerous Enemy*, 223.

4. Bungay, *The Most Dangerous Enemy*, 224.

5. Mason, *Battle Over Britain*, 226–27.

6. Ibid., 227.

7. War Cabinet minutes, August 19, 1940, in Martin Gilbert, ed., *Churchill War Papers*, 3 vols. (New York and London: W. W. Norton, 1993–2000), 2:682; Colville Diary, August 16, 1940, in Colville, *The Fringes of Power: 10 Downing Street Diaries 1939–1955* (New York and London: W. W. Norton and Company, 1985), 224.

8. T. C. G. James, *The Battle of Britain*, ed. Sebastian Cox, Air Historical Branch narrative (London: Frank Cass, 2000), 126–28; Mason, *Battle Over Britain*, 199; Bungay, *The Most Dangerous Enemy*, 292–93; Hough and Richards, *The Battle of Britain*, 238.

9. T. C. G. James, *The Battle of Britain*, 126–27; Churchill to Ismay, August 2, 1940 ("Action this Day") in *Churchill War Papers*, 2:599; Defence Committee minutes, August 13, 1940; Churchill to Newall and Peirse, August 24, 1940; Churchill to Sinclair ("Private"), August 25, 1940, in *Churchill War Papers*, 2:658–59, 710, 721; Colville Diary, August 13 and 27, 1940, in *Fringes of Power*, 212, 231.

10. T. C. G. James, *The Battle of Britain*, 127–28; Dowding, "Dispatch," para. 164. See also, Adam Zamoyski, *The Forgotten Few: The Polish Air Force in the Second World War* (London: John Murray, 1995), 58, 66, 92–97.

11. Zamoyski, *The Forgotten Few*, 75–78, 92.

12. Among the innumerable published commentaries on this issue, see especially, Denis Richards, *The Fight at Odds* vol. 1, *The Royal Air Force 1939–1945* (London: Her Majesty's Stationery Office, 1953), 193–95; Mason, *Battle Over Britain*, 253; and John

Terraine, *The Right of the Line: The Royal Air Force in the European War 1939–1945* (Ware, Hertfordshire, UK: Wordsworth Editions Limited, 1997), 194–205; Vincent Orange, *Dowding of Fighter Command: Victor of the Battle of Britain* (London: Grub Street, 2008), 177.

13. No. 11 Group Instructions to Controllers No. 7, 27 August 1940; T. C. G. James, *The Battle of Britain*, Appendix 10, 356. See also Hough and Richards, *The Battle of Britain*, 316; Mason, *Battle Over Britain*, 248; Bungay, *The Most Dangerous Enemy*, 272.

14. Mason, *Battle Over Britain*, 248–49.

15. Martin Gilbert, *Winston S. Churchill: Finest Hour, 1939–1941* (Boston: Houghton Mifflin Company, 1983), 765–66; Colville Diary, August 28 and 31, September 1, 1940, in *Fringes of Power*, 231–32, 235–37. See also, T. C. G. James, *The Battle of Britain*, 201; Mason, *Battle Over Britain*, 248–49. Bungay, *The Most Dangerous Enemy*, 280–81, 291.

16. Colville Diary, August 31, 1940, in *Fringes of Power*, 235.

17. T. C. G. James, *The Battle of Britain*, 228; Derek Wood with Derek Dempster, *The Narrow Margin: The Battle of Britain and the Rise of Air Power* (Washington, DC: Smithsonian Institution Press, 1990), 184, 249–50; Mason, *Battle Over Britain*, 266–67; John James, *The Paladins: A Social History of the RAF Up to the Outbreak of World War II* (London: MacDonald, 1990), 177; Bungay, *The Most Dangerous Enemy*, 194.

18. The RAF carefully studied German pilots shot down over Britain. Throughout the campaign, the data continued to show that most had been trained before the outbreak of war in 1939. See Dowding lecture to US Air War College, February 7, 1951, AFHRA Microfilm 483224.

19. Bungay, *The Most Dangerous Enemy*, 298–301.

20. T. C. G. James, *The Battle of Britain*, 225–27; 240; Mason, *Battle Over Britain*, 285; Wood with Dempster, *The Narrow Margin*, 262–63.

21. James, *The Paladins*, 92–95, 100, 103–4, 151.

22. Bungay, *The Most Dangerous Enemy*, 292–296.

10 THE BATTLE OF BRITAIN SEPTEMBER–OCTOBER 1940

1. Derek Wood with Derek Dempster, *The Narrow Margin: The Battle of Britain and the Rise of Air Power* (Washington, DC: Smithsonian Institution Press, 1990), 71.

2. Francis K. Mason, *Battle Over Britain* (Bourne End, Buckinghamshire, UK: Aston Publications Ltd., 1990), 235–36; Colville Diary, August 26, 1940, in Colville, *The Fringes of Power: 10 Downing Street Diaries 1939–1955* (New York and London: W. W. Norton and Company, 1985), 229.

3. Cf., Prime Minister to AOC-in-C Bomber Command (Peirse) September 6,

1940, in Martin Gilbert, ed., *Churchill War Papers*, 3 vols. (New York and London: W. W. Norton, 1993–2000), 2:784.

4. Stephen Bungay, *The Most Dangerous Enemy* (London: Aurum, 2000), 305.

5. Wood with Dempster, *The Narrow Margin*, 227; Bungay, *The Most Dangerous Enemy*, 312.

6. James R. M. Butler, *Grand Strategy*, vol. 2, *September 1939–June 1941*, in *History of the Second World War*, United Kingdom Military Series, ed. Sir James R. M. Butler (London: Her Majesty's Stationery Office, 1957), 2:288; see also, Martin Gilbert, *Winston S. Churchill: Finest Hour, 1939–1941* (Boston: Houghton Mifflin Company, 1983), 769, 773.

7. Bungay, *The Most Dangerous Enemy*, 309–10.

8. Mason, *Battle Over Britain*, 298–306; Bungay, *The Most Dangerous Enemy*, 314.

9. Mason, *Battle Over Britain*, 310–11.

10. HQ 11 Group (Park) to HQ, Fighter Command (Dowding), September 12, 1940 (AIR 16/635/4A), digital image available at https://images.nationalarchives.gov.uk/assetbank-nationalarchives. See also, Gilbert, *Finest Hour*, 761; and Robin Prior, *When Britain Saved the West* (New Haven, CT: Yale University Press, 2015), 220–22 and 309, note 39.

11. Fighter Command (Dowding) to under secretary of state, Air Ministry, September 22, 1940 (AIR 16/635/12A), digital image available at https://images.nationalarchives.gov.uk/assetbank-nationalarchives.

12. Ibid.

13. Bungay, *The Most Dangerous Enemy*, 318–35.

14. Gilbert, *Finest Hour*, 783–86.

15. Meeting with the French high command in Paris on May 16, Churchill had asked Gamelin, "*Ou est la masse de manouvre?*" ("Where is the strategic reserve?") and received the reply, "*Aucune*" ("None"). Gamelin later claimed in *his* memoirs that he actually replied, "*Il n'aucun plus*," or in idiomatic English, "It no longer exists." Gilbert, *Finest Hour*, 350.

16. For example, Richard Hough and Denis Richards, *The Battle of Britain* (New York and London: W. W. Norton, 1990), 282; David Reynolds, *In Command of History* (New York: Random House, 2005), 166–67, 185–86.

17. The British loss numbers are from the *Daily Telegraph and Morning Post* of September 16, 1940, p. 1; reproduced in Hough and Richards, *The Battle of Britain,* 283.

18. HQ 11 Group (Park) to HQ, Fighter Command (Dowding), September 12, 1940 (AIR 16/635/4A) digital image available at https://images.nationalarchives.gov.uk/; Fighter Command (Dowding) to Under Secretary of State, Air Ministry, September 22, 1940 (AIR 16/635/12A) digital image available at https://images.nationalarchives.gov.uk/.

19. Vincent Orange, *Dowding of Fighter Command: Victor of the Battle of Britain*

(London: Grub Street, 2008), 200–201; Orange, *Park: The Biography of Air Chief Marshal Sir Keith Park* (London: Grub Street, 2001), 123.

20. Orange, *Park*, 111.

21. Ibid., 111–112; Wood with Dempster, *The Narrow Margin*, 276; Hough and Richards, *Battle of Britain*, 284–90.

22. Helen Jones, *British Civilians in the Front Line* (Manchester and New York: Manchester University Press, 2006), 32–40.

23. Ibid.

24. The Order of the Bath takes fourth place in precedence behind the Order of the Garter, the Order of the Thistle, and the Order of St. Patrick; honors usually confined to royalty and the higher ranks of the peerage. In such cases, as the 1st Duke of Wellington supposedly remarked about the Garter, "There is no damned nonsense about merit" connected with them. The Military Division of the Order of the Bath, in its turn, is confined to senior military officers. Dowding had been a Knight Commander of the Order since 1933.

11 THE BLITZ OCTOBER–NOVEMBER 1940

1. Martin Gilbert, *Winston S. Churchill: Finest Hour, 1939–1941* (Boston: Houghton Mifflin Company, 1983), 823–24.

2. Churchill, *Their Finest Hour* (Boston: Houghton Mifflin Company, 1949), 369–70.

3. Ibid.

4. Gilbert, *Finest Hour*, 823–24; Derek Wood with Derek Dempster, *The Narrow Margin: The Battle of Britain and the Rise of Air Power* (Washington, DC: Smithsonian Institution Press, 1990), 116.

5. Wood with Dempster, *The Narrow Margin*, 94–95.

6. Churchill Archives website. See also, E. G. Bowen, *Radar Days* (Bristol, UK: Adam Hilger, 1987), 72–75.

7. Ian White, *The History of Air Intercept (AI) Radar and the British Nightfighter, 1935–1959* (Barnsley, South Yorkshire, UK: Pen & Sword Aviation, 2007), 38.

8. Dowding to Air Ministry, July 10, 1939; quoted in White, *Air Intercept Radar*, 21 and 26, note 21; cf. also 30, 34. Also, Bowen, *Radar Days*, 81–82, 121–23,

9. See for example, Gilbert, *Finest Hour*, 553, note 2.

10. Gilbert, *Finest Hour*, 553, 713; White, *Air Intercept Radar*, 47–50.

11. Churchill to Neville Chamberlain, August 31, 1940, quoted in Gilbert, *Finest Hour*, 763, 767; Colville Diary, August 30, 1940, in Colville, *The Fringes of Power: 10 Downing Street Diaries 1939–1955* (New York and London: W. W. Norton and Company, 1985), 233; Colville Diary, September 1, 1940 in Martin Gilbert, ed., *Churchill*

War Papers, 3 vols. (New York and London: W. W. Norton, 1993–2000), 2:758–59. Also, White, *Air Intercept Radar*, 34–36, 45–46, 49–51, 60–62; Gilbert, *Finest Hour*, 553, note 2.

12. Nicolson Diary, especially September 17, 18, 19, 25, and October 15 and 19, 1940, in *Diaries and Letters, 1939–1945*, ed. Nigel Nicolson (New York: Atheneum, 1967), 105–22. An acute observer, as parliamentary secretary at the Ministry of Information and a member of the Civil Defence Committee operating under the War Cabinet, Nicolson was exceptionally well placed to assess the crosscurrents of opinion between the political elite and the mass public. Also, War Cabinet Minutes, August 19, 1940, October 15, 1940, in *Churchill War Papers*, 2:682, 1010–11; Colville Diary, August 16, 1940, in *Fringes of Power*, 224. Also, T. C. G. James, *The Battle of Britain*, ed. Sebastian Cox, Air Historical Branch narrative (London: Frank Cass, 2000), 208–9, 301–2; Richard Hough and Denis Richards, *The Battle of Britain* (New York and London: W. W. Norton, 1990), 219–20, 224; Stephen Bungay, *The Most Dangerous Enemy* (London: Aurum, 2000), 218–19; Vincent Orange, *Dowding of Fighter Command: Victor of the Battle of Britain* (London: Grub Street, 2008), 208.

13. Churchill broadcast, September 11, 1940, in *Churchill War Papers*, 2:801–801; Hough and Richards, *The Battle of Britain*, 290–91; Vincent Orange, *Park: The Biography of Air Chief Marshal Sir Keith Park* (London: Grub Street, 2001), 99. For Douglas's continuity of appointment, see "Air of Authority," RAF website, www.rafweb.org.

14. T. C. G. James, *The Battle of Britain*, 313; Orange, *Park*, 99; Bungay, *The Most Dangerous Enemy*, 195–96.

15. Orange, *Dowding*, 208.

16. J. E. G. Dixon, *Dowding and Churchill* (Barnsley, South Yorkshire, UK: Pen & Sword Military, 2008), 68.

17. See Salmond to Trenchard, September 25, 1940, quoted in Dixon, *Dowding and Churchill*, 68–69.

18. Dixon, *Dowding and Churchill*, 104–5.

19. Hough and Richards, *The Battle of Britain*, 290; Gilbert, *Finest Hour*, 801; Colville Diary, September 21 and 22, 1940, in *Fringes of Power*, 245–48.

20. *Churchill War Papers*, 2:905, note 2; Gilbert, *Finest Hour*, 826–27; cf. T. C. G. James, *The Battle of Britain*, 303; Dixon, *Dowding and Churchill*, 210.

21. Gilbert, *Finest Hour*, 828–30; Sir Frederick Pile, quoted in *Churchill War Papers*, 2:907–10. See also Pile, *Ack-Ack: Britain's Defence against Air Attack during the Second World War* (London: George G. Harrap & Co., 1949), 169–72.

22. Colville Diary, October 10, 1940; Brooke Diary, October 11, 1940, both quoted in *Churchill War Papers*, 2:931. Also, T. C. G. James, *The Battle of Britain*, 310; Wood with Dempster, *The Narrow Margin*, 304; Gilbert, *Finest Hour*, 838, 841–42; Dixon,

Dowding and Churchill, 211.

23. Gilbert, *Finest Hour*, 857 and note 6.

24. Night Air Defence Committee minutes, October 7, 1940, in *Churchill War Papers*, 2:905; Dixon, *Dowding and Churchill*, 107–8, 110, and note xi, 118–19. Also, ibid., 211–12; White, *Air Intercept Radar*, 72.

25. Dixon, *Dowding and Churchill*, 84–90; Orange, *Dowding*, 216.

26. Sebastian Ritchie, "A Political Intrigue against the Chief of Air Staff," *War & Society* 16, no. 1 (May 1998): 83–104. See also, Dixon, *Dowding and Churchill*, 56–60.

27. Dixon, *Dowding and Churchill*, 56–57, 60–61. Cf., Anthony Furse, *Wilfrid Freeman* (Staplehurst, Kent, UK: Spellmount Ltd., 2000), 147–49.

28. Ritchie, "A Political Intrigue"; Furse, *Wilfrid Freeman*, 149–50, 152–66, 170; see above, chapter 3; also Vincent Orange, *Slessor: Bomber Champion* (London: Grub Street, 2006), 72.

29. Denis Richards, *Portal of Hungerford* (London: William Heinemann, Ltd., 1977), 160–61.

30. Dixon, *Dowding and Churchill*, 67.

31. Colville Diary, September 25, 26, 30, and October 1, 2, 9, 1940; in *Fringes of Power*, 252–59. For the changing composition of the Air Council, see Royal Air Force, *Air Force List*, August, October, and December 1940, available online at National Library of Scotland, http://digital.nls.uk/british-military-lists.

32. *Air Force List*, August, October, and December 1940, available online at National Library of Scotland, http://digital.nls.uk/british-military-lists. Also, Furse, *Wilfrid Freeman*, 163.

33. Bungay, *The Most Dangerous Enemy*, 353–54.

34. Dixon, *Dowding and Churchill*, 77.

35. Cross, quoted in Garry Campion, *The Battle of Britain, 1945–1965: The Air Ministry and the Few* (New York: Palgrave MacMillan, 2015), 267, note 99. Cf., T. C. G. James, *The Battle of Britain*, 300, 322–23.

36. Dixon, *Dowding and Churchill*, 77. Cf. Denis Richards, *The Fight at Odds*, vol. 1, *The Royal Air Force 1939–1945* (London: Her Majesty's Stationery Office, 1953), 193.

37. Dixon, *Dowding and Churchill*, 84–90; Orange, *Dowding*, 216.

38. Quoted in Orange, *Dowding*, 216.

12 LAYING DOWN THE SWORD 1941–1942

1. Andrew Roberts, *Eminent Churchillians* (New York: Simon & Schuster, 1994), 137–202; David Reynolds, *In Command of History* (New York: Random House, 2005), 178–81.

2. *E.g.*, Progress of the War. HL Deb August 20, 1940, vol. 117 cc 272–318; War

Situation. HC Deb 8 October, 1940 vol. 365 cc 261–352. Regarding the political effect of the Dakar episode, see Roberts, *Eminent Churchillians*, 179–80; and Woolton Diary, November 13, 1940, quoted in Roberts, 192. See also Reynolds, *In Command of History*.

3. Roberts, *Eminent Churchillians*, 201–2.

4. Ibid. Also, John Cotesworth Slessor, *The Central Blue* (London: Cassell & Co., 1956), 317–20.

5. Anthony Cumming, *The Royal Navy and the Battle of Britain* (Annapolis, MD: Naval Institute Press, 2010), 123–49

6. *New York Times*, September 29, 1940, p. 9.

7. *New York Times*, November 18, 1940, p. 1; and December 15, 1940, p. 118.

8. Ibid.

9. Ibid.

10. Ibid.

11. *New York Times*, January 6, 1941, p. 3; and January 8, 1941, p. 7.

12. *New York Times*, 2 Feb 1941, p. E 3.

13. Defence Committee: Confidential Annex, October 31, 1940, in Martin Gilbert, ed., *Churchill War Papers*, 3 vols. (New York and London: W. W. Norton, 1993–2000), 2:1012.

14. *Chicago Tribune*, February 27, 1941, p. 1. Available online at archives.chicagotribune.com.

15. William H. Bartsch, *December 8, 1941* (College Station: Texas A & M University Press, 2003), 50–51.

16. E. G. Bowen, *Radar Days* (Bristol, UK: Adam Hilger, 1987), 185.

17. Cf. Vincent Orange, *Dowding of Fighter Command: Victor of the Battle of Britain* (London: Grub Street, 2008), 234–35.

18. Basil Collier, *Leader of the Few* (London: Jarrolds, 1957), 229.

19. The Air Ministry version was that Dowding not only departed from the RAF script that had been supplied to Scotty Reston before the air chief marshal even left London, but actually advocated giving priority in production to tanks over bombers. See Anthony Furse, *Wilfrid Freeman* (Staplehurst, Kent, UK: Spellmount Ltd., 2000), 164.

20. Prime Minister to Secretary of State for Air, "Private," April 12, 1941, in *Churchill War Papers*, 3:483.

21. Prime Minister to Secretary of State for Air, June 2, 1941; WSC "Private" to Sir Archibald Sinclair; in *Churchill War Papers*, 3:748–49.

22. Ibid. Also, Gilbert, *Finest Hour*, 1101, note 2. Cf., Furse, *Wilfrid Freeman*, 164, 175–79. WSC minute for General Ismay, October 22, 1941, in *Churchill War Papers*, 3:1363. Cf., Vincent Orange, *Tedder: Quietly in Command* (London: Frank Cass,

2004), 128–60; and Robert Wright, *The Man Who Won the Battle of Britain* (New York: Charles Scribner's Sons, 1969), 269.

23. Ibid.

24. Orange, *Dowding*, 238–39. Orange quotes an Air Council letter sent to Dowding at this time "expressing 'High appreciation of the valuable services you have rendered during your long and distinguished career.'"

25. Orange, *Dowding*, 241–46. Churchill's recurrent disputes with the service ministries and the Chiefs of Staff regarding the manpower consumed by support services is a recurring theme in Gilbert, *Finest Hour*.

26. Prime Minister to Secretary of State for Air and Chief of Air Staff, October 31, 1941; WSC to Air Chief Marshal Sir Hugh Dowding, November 5, 1941; in *Churchill War Papers*, 3:1394, 1415.

27. *Churchill War Papers*, 3:1451, note 2. Dowding, *Twelve Legions of Angels* (London: Jarrolds, 1946), 7–15; Collier, *Leader of the Few*, 235–36; Wright, *The Man Who Won the Battle of Britain*, 266–69.

28. Freeman's version of the episode was that "he did not waste time on those who simply refused to co-operate, such as Dowding . . . finally abandoned any residual hope of accommodating him, and accepted his resignation with relief." See Furse, *Wilfrid Freeman*, 164.

29. Supplement to the *Sunday Sun and Guardian*, July 26, 1942, p. 2, available online at http://trove.nla.gov.au/newspaper/article/; *The Cairns Post*, available online at http://trove.nla.gov.au/newspaper/article/. Also Wright, *The Man Who Won the Battle of Britain*, 263.

30. Orange, *Dowding*, 76–78; Cumming, *The Royal Navy and the Battle of Britain*, 106–7; idem, *The Battle for Britain* (Annapolis, MD: Naval Institute Press, 2015), 69.

31. Ibid.

32. HL Deb January 27, 1943 vol. 125 cc 794–829. Cumming, *The Royal Navy and the Battle of Britain, 106–7*.

33. Orange, *Dowding*, 241, 249–50, 256.

13 TAKING UP THE PEN 1942–1951

1. Lloyd Thomas, "Casual Comment," in *South Western Advertiser*, August 28, 1942, p. 2, available online at http://trove.nla.gov.au/newspaper/article/07-16-17.

2. Ibid. See Denis Richards, *The Fight at Odds*, vol. 1, *The Royal Air Force 1939–1945* (London: Her Majesty's Stationery Office, 1953), the photo is facing page 156.

3. A thought-provoking discussion of the problem of strategic narratives in war can be found in Emile Simpson, *War from the Ground Up* (Oxford: Oxford University Press, 2012).

4. Campion, *The Battle of Britain, 1945–1965: The Air Ministry and the Few* (New York: Palgrave MacMillan, 2015), 91–115. For Peck's assignment history, see "Air of Authority," RAF website, www.rafweb.org/. Also, John James, *The Paladins: A Social History of the RAF Up to the Outbreak of World War II* (London: MacDonald, 1990), 236.

5. Ibid.

6. James Molony Spaight, *The Battle of Britain 1940* (London: Geoffrey Bles, 1941), 42 and passim. For reviews of Austin, *Fighter Command*, see http://trove.nla.gov.au/newspaper/.

7. C. S. H. Vane-Tempest-Stewart Marquess of Londonderry, *Wings of Destiny* (London: MacMillan & Co., 1943), 230, 233.

8. Dowding, *Lychgate* (Guildford, UK: White Crow Books, 2013), 7–8.

9. Ibid., 1.

10. *New York Times*, September 1, 1943, p. 4. For reporting on Dowding's pubic activities during the second half of 1943, see e.g., "Weird Story by Air Chief," *Truth* (Sydney) June 13, 1943, available online at http://trove.nla.gov.au/newspaper/article/ and "The Other Life," *The Advocate,* December 9, 1943, p. 5, available online at http://trove.nla.gov.au/newspaper/article/. Also, Australian Associated Press, *The Advertiser* (Adelaide) available online at http://trove.nla.gov.au/newspaper/article/.

11. Dowding, *Many Mansions* (Guildford, UK: White Crow Books, 2013), 9. Vincent Orange, *Dowding of Fighter Command: Victor of the Battle of Britain* (London: Grub Street, 2008), 259–60.

12. Committee report quoted in Jenny Hazelgrove, *Spiritualism and British Society between the Wars* (Manchester and New York: Manchester University Press, 2000), 18.

13. Dowding, *Many Mansions*, 7–13; Hazelgrove, *Spiritualism and British Society between the Wars*, 18–19.

14. Dowding, *Many Mansions*, 2–13.

15. Hazelgrove, *Spiritualism and British Society between the Wars*, 5, 24–28, 194–95, 199; also, biographical entry for Oliver Lodge in *Encyclopædia Britannica*, 1947, 14:293. See F. X. Charet, *Spiritualism and the Foundations of C. G. Jung's Psychology* (Albany, NY: State University of New York Press, 1993), 3–4, for a critique of some mainstream, Christian responses to Spiritualism that is similar to Dowding's. Cf. Dowding, *Many Mansions*, 15–32.

16. Charet, *Spiritualism and the Foundations of C. G. Jung's Psychology*, 95, 97, 100, 114–15, 287. Cf. Dowding, *Many Mansions*, 25.

17. Charet, *Spiritualism and the Foundations of C. G. Jung's Psychology*, 291, 295–96.

18. "Spiritualist," in the *Sunday Mail*, December 26, 1943, p. 7, available online at http://trove.nla.gov.au/newspaper/article/; "Charges against Spiritualists," *Army News*, January 8, 1944, p. 4, available online at http://trove.nla.gov.au/newspaper

/article/. See also, Hazelgrove, *Spiritualism and British Society between the Wars*, 270–71, 275–76.

19. Dowding, *Many Mansions*, 9.

20. *The Advertiser* (Adelaide), December 14, 1943, p. 1, available online at http://trove.nla.gov.au/newspaper/article/. Also, Orange, *Dowding*, 267–68.

21. Dowding, *Lychgate*, 13.

22. Orange, *Dowding*, 251–52, 259. Dowding lecture to US Air War College, February 7, 1951, AFHRA Microfilm 483224. The views of General Frederick "Tim" Pile on the Dowding-Beaverbrook relationship are of interest. See Pile, *Ack-Ack: Britain's Defence against Air Attack during the Second World War* (London: George G. Harrap & Co., 1949), 109–10.

23. Basil Collier, *Leader of the Few* (London: Jarrolds, 1957), 233–34; Orange, *Dowding*, 238–39, 253.

24. Churchill, *The Gathering Storm* (Boston: Houghton Mifflin Company, 1948), 153–57.

25. Churchill, *Their Finest Hour* (Boston: Houghton Mifflin Company, 1949), 42. Cf., Collier, *Leader of the Few*, 188–94, and Robert Wright, *The Man Who Won the Battle of Britain* (New York: Charles Scribner's Sons, 1969), 102–7, 110–12, 118–21. See also, David Reynolds, *In Command of History* (New York: Random House, 2005), 167.

26. Churchill, *Their Finest Hour*, 146, 154, 319–80.

27. Reynolds, *In Command of History*, 188, 215–16. It might also be argued that Churchill was somewhat constrained by his inability to quote official documents other than this own records, which is one reason for the often-criticized one-sidedness of the books.

28. Pile, *Ack-Ack*, 109–10; 262.

29. Ibid.

30. Ibid.

14 HISTORY AND MYTH 1951–1970

1. Transcript of recorded lecture by ACM Lord Dowding to US Air War College, February 7, 1951; AFHRA, IRIS # 00483224.

2. Ibid.

3. Ibid.

4. Ibid.

5. ACM Lord Dowding, "Through Death to a New Life," *The Mail* (Adelaide), December 8, 1951, p. 4, available online at http://trove.nla.gov.au/newspaper/article/.

6. Criminal Justice Bill, HL Deb 28 April 1948 vol. 155 cc466–554.

7. Available online at http://trove.nla.gov.au/newspaper/article/.

8. HL Deb 03 May 1951 vol. 171 cc718–29.

9. *The Advertiser* (Adelaide), September 12, 1951, p. 12, available online at http://trove.nla.gov.au/newspaper/article/; "Obituary: Muriel Dowding," *The Independent*, December 2, 1993, available online at http://independent.co.uk/news/people/.

10. HL Deb 03 April 1952 vol. 175 cc1361–428.

11. HL Deb 17 February 1953 vol. 180 cc475–506.

12. Denis Richards, *The Fight at Odds*, vol. 1, *The Royal Air Force 1939–1945* (London: Her Majesty's Stationery Office, 1953), 63–69.

13. Ibid., 131–37.

14. Ibid., 193–95.

15. Ibid., 197.

16. Published in the United States as *The Man Who Won the Battle of Britain*.

17. E.g., *Kirkus Reviews*, April 1, 1970, available online at www.kirkusreviews.com.

CODA

1. Simpson, *History of the Battle of Britain Fighter Association*, 46, available online at books.google.com.

BIBLIOGRAPHY

DOCUMENTS AND COLLECTIONS

Dowding, H. C. T., 1st Baron. "The Battle of Britain." Dispatch submitted to the Secretary of State for Air on August 20, 1941. Supplement to the *London Gazette*, Tuesday, September 10, 1946.

———. "Employment of the Fighter Command in Home Defence." PRO Document AIR 16/260. Reproduced in Air Command and Staff College "Leadership and Command" course book, AY 2008.

Gilbert, Martin, ed. *The Churchill War Papers*. 3 vols. New York and London: W. W. Norton, 1993–2000.

James, Robert Rhodes, ed. *Winston S. Churchill: His Complete Speeches*. Vol. 6, *1935–1942*. New York and London: Chelsea House Publishers in association with R. R. Bowker Company, 1974.

Parliamentary Debates, Lords. Hansard 1803–2005.

Report of the R. 101 Inquiry Presented by the Secretary of State for Air to Parliament by Command of His Majesty, March 1931. Available online at lordkingsnorton.cranfield.ac.uk.

Robinson, J. R. *60 Signals Group Fighter Command Royal Air Force.* Available online at www.rquirk.com.

Royal Artillery, Bengal Command. *General Report of the Practice of the Royal Artillery, Bengal Command, 1900–1901.* Calcutta: Office of the Superintendent of Government Printing, India, 1901. Available online at books.google.com.

US Air Force Air War College. Transcript of recorded lecture by ACM Lord Dowding, February 7, 1951; AFHRA, IRIS # 00483224.

ARTICLES AND BOOKS

Air Historical Branch, Air Ministry, United Kingdom. *The Rise and Fall of the German Air Force.* London: Crown Copyright, 1983.

Ash, Eric. *Sir Frederick Sykes and the Air Revolution.* London: Frank Cass, 1999.

Bartsch, William H. *December 8, 1941.* College Station: Texas A & M University Press, 2003.

Biddle, Tami Davis. *Rhetoric and Reality in Air Warfare.* Princeton, NJ, and Oxford: Princeton University Press, 2002.

Bidwell, Shelford and Dominick Graham. *Fire-Power.* London and Boston: George Allen & Unwin, 1982.

Bond, Brian. *British Military Policy between the Two World Wars.* Oxford: Clarendon Press, 1980.

———. ed. *Chief of Staff: The Diaries of Lieutenant-General Sir Henry Powell.* Vol. 1: *1933–1940.* Hamden, CT: Archon Books, 1973.

Boog, Horst. *The Conduct of the Air War in the Second World War.* New York and Oxford: Berg Publishers Limited, 1992.

Bowen, E. G. *Radar Days.* Bristol, UK: Adam Hilger, 1987.

Boyle, Andrew. *Trenchard.* London: Collins, 1962.

Brown, Louis. *Radar History of World War II.* Bristol, UK, and Philadelphia, PA: Institute of Physics Publishing, 1999.

Bungay, Stephen. *The Most Dangerous Enemy.* London: Aurum, 2000.

Butler, James R. M. *Grand Strategy.* Vol. 2, *September 1939–June 1941.* In *History of the Second World War,* United Kingdom Military Series. Edited by Sir James R. M. Butler. London: Her Majesty's Stationery Office, 1957.

Campion, Garry. *The Battle of Britain, 1945–1965: The Air Ministry and the Few.* New York: Palgrave MacMillan, 2015.

Charet, F. X. *Spiritualism and the Foundations of C. G. Jung's Psychology.* Albany, NY: State University of New York Press, 1993.

Churchill, Winston S. *The Gathering Storm.* Boston: Houghton Mifflin Company, 1948.

———. *Their Finest Hour.* Boston: Houghton Mifflin Company, 1949.

Collier, Basil. *The Defence of the United Kingdom.* In *History of the Second World War*, United Kingdom Military Series. Edited by Sir James R. M. Butler. London: Her Majesty's Stationery Office, 1957.

———. *Leader of the Few*. London: Jarrolds, 1957.

Colville, John. *The Fringes of Power: 10 Downing Street Diaries 1939–1955*. New York and London: W. W. Norton and Company, 1985.

Cooper, Malcolm. *The Birth of Independent Air Power*. London and Boston: George Allen & Unwin, 1986.

Cumming, Anthony J. *The Battle for Britain*. Annapolis, MD: Naval Institute Press, 2015.

———. *The Royal Navy and the Battle of Britain*. Annapolis, MD: Naval Institute Press, 2010.

Davis, R. W. and R. J. Helmstadter, eds. *Religion and Irreligion in Victorian Society.* London and New York: Routledge, 1992.

Dean, Maurice. *The Royal Air Force and Two World Wars*. London: Cassell, 1979.

De Groot, Gerard J. *Douglas Haig*. London: Unwin Hyman, 1988.

Deighton, Len. *Fighter*. New York: Knopf, 1978.

Dixon, J. E. G. *Dowding and Churchill.* Barnsley, South Yorkshire, UK: Pen & Sword Military, 2008.

Douglas of Kirtleside, Sholto Douglas, 1st Baron. *Combat and Command: The Story of an Airman in Two World Wars.* New York: Simon and Schuster, 1963.

Dowding, H. C. T., 1st Baron. *Lychgate*. Guildford, UK: White Crow Books, 2013.

———. *Many Mansions*. Guildford, UK: White Crow Books, 2013.

———. *Twelve Legions of Angels*. London: Jarrolds, 1946.

Eisenhower, David. *Eisenhower at War 1943–1945*. New York: Vintage Books, 1978.

Ferris, Robert. "Fighter Defence before Fighter Command." *Journal of Military History* 63, no. 4 (October 1999): 845–84.

Ferro, Marc. *The Great War 1914–1918*. Boston: Routledge & Kegan Paul, 1973.

Fisher, David E. *A Race on the Edge of Time*. New York: Paragon House, 1989.

———. *A Summer Bright and Terrible*. Washington, DC: Shoemaker & Hoard, 2005.

Flint, Peter. *Dowding and Headquarters Fighter Command*. Shrewsbury, UK: Airlife Publishing Ltd., 1997.

Fraser, David. *Alanbrooke*. New York: Atheneum, 1982.

Furse, Anthony. *Wilfrid Freeman*. Staplehurst, Kent, UK: Spellmount Ltd., 2000.

Gibbs, N. H. *Grand Strategy*. Vol. 1, *Rearmament Policy*. In *History of the Second World War*, United Kingdom Military Series. Edited by Sir James R. M. Butler. London: Her Majesty's Stationery Office, 1976.

Gilbert, Martin. *Winston S. Churchill: The Stricken World, 1916–1922*. Boston: Houghton Mifflin Company, 1977.

———. *Winston S. Churchill: Prophet of Truth, 1922–1939*. Boston: Houghton Mifflin Company, 1977.

———. *Winston S. Churchill: Finest Hour, 1939–1941*. Boston: Houghton Mifflin Company, 1983.

Gollin, Alfred. *The Impact of Air Power on the British People and Their Government*. Stanford, CA: Stanford University Press, 1989.

———. "The Mystery of Lord Haldane and Early British Military Aviation." *Albion* 11, no. 1 (Spring 1979): 46–65.

Gray, Peter. *The Leadership, Direction and Legitimacy of the RAF Bomber Offensive from Inception to 1945*. War Studies Series. Birmingham, UK: University of Birmingham, 2012.

Gray, Peter W., and Sebastian Cox. *Air Power Leadership: Theory and Practice.* London: The Stationery Office, 2002.

Grey, C. G. *A History of the Air Ministry*. London: George Allen & Unwin, 1940.

Grinnell-Milne, Duncan *Wind in the Wires*. Garden City, NY: Doubleday & Company, 1969.

Hart, Michael. Review of *Liberal Crusader: The Life of Sir Archibald Sinclair* by Gerard J. De Groot. *English Historical Review* 111, no. 441 (April 1996): 535–36.

Haslam, E. B. "How Lord Dowding Came to Leave Fighter Command." *The Journal of Strategic Studies* 4, no. 2 (June 1981): 175–86.

Hayward, Keith *The British Aircraft Industry*. Manchester and New York: Manchester University Press, 1989.

Hazelgrove, Jenny. *Spiritualism and British Society between the Wars*. Manchester and New York: Manchester University Press, 2000.

Higham, Robin. *The Military Intellectuals in Britain: 1918–1939*. Westport, CT: Greenwood Press, 1966.

———. "The RAF and the Battle of Britain." In *Case Studies in the Achievement of Air Superiority*, edited by Benjamin Franklin Cooling. Washington, DC: Air Force History and Museums Program, 1994.

Holmes, Richard, ed. *The Oxford Companion to Military History*. Oxford and New York: Oxford University Press, 2001.

Hough, Richard and Denis Richards. *The Battle of Britain*. New York and London: W. W. Norton, 1990.

Howard, Michael. "Men against Fire: The Doctrine of the Offensive in 1914." In *Makers of Modern Strategy from Machiavelli to the Nuclear Age*, edited by Peter Paret, 515–21. Princeton, NJ: Princeton University Press, 1986.

Howlett, Peter. "New Light through Old Windows: A New Perspective on the

British Economy in the Second World War." *Journal of Contemporary History* 28, no. 2 (April 1993): 369.

Hughes, Jeffrey L. "The Origins of World War II in Europe: British Deterrence Failure and German Expansionism." *Journal of Interdisciplinary History* 18, no. 4 (Spring 1988): 851–91.

Hyde, H. Montgomery. *British Air Policy between the Wars*. London: Heinemann, 1978.

Jacobs, W. A. "Operation OVERLORD." In *Case Studies in the Achievement of Air Superiority* ed. Benjamin Franklin Cooling. Washington, DC: Air Force History and Museums Program, 1994.

James, John. *The Paladins: A Social History of the RAF Up to the Outbreak of World War II*. London: MacDonald, 1990.

James, T. C. G. *The Battle of Britain*. Edited by Sebastian Cox. Air Historical Branch narrative. London: Frank Cass, 2000.

———. *The Growth of Fighter Command*. Edited by Sebastian Cox. Air Historical Branch narrative. London: Frank Cass, 2002.

Jenkins, Roy. *Churchill*. New York: Random House Trade Paperbacks, 2001.

———. *Gladstone*. New York: Random House Trade Paperbacks, 2002.

Jones, Christopher V. *Visualization and Optimization*. New York: Springer Science & Business Media, 1996.

Jones, Helen. *British Civilians in the Front Line*. Manchester and New York: Manchester University Press, 2006.

Jones, H. A. [Henry Albert] *The War in the Air*. Vol. 5. Oxford: The Clarendon Press, 1935.

Jones, Neville. *The Beginnings of Strategic Air Power: A History of the British Bomber Force 1923–1939*. London: Frank Cass, 1987.

Keegan, John. *The Face of Battle*. New York: Penguin, 1976.

Kennedy, Paul. *The Rise and Fall of the Great Powers*. New York: Random House, 1987.

Korda, Michael. *With Wings Like Eagles*. New York: Harper Collins, 2009.

Laffin, John. *Swifter Than Eagles*. Edinburgh: W. Blackwood, 1964.

Levy, James P. *Appeasement and Rearmament*. New York: Rowman & Littlefield, 2006.

Lewis, Peter *The British Bomber Since 1914: Sixty Years of Design and Development*. London: Putnam, 1974.

Londonderry, C. S. H. Vane-Tempest-Stewart, 7th Marquess. *Wings of Destiny*. London: MacMillan & Co., 1943.

Magnusson, Magnus. *Cambridge Biographical Dictionary*. Cambridge: Cambridge University Press, 1990.

Manchester, William. *The Last Lion: Winston Spencer Churchill Alone, 1932–1940.* Boston and London: Little, Brown and Company, 1988.

Manchester, William, and Paul Reid. *The Last Lion: Winston Spencer Churchill Defender of the Realm, 1940–1965.* Boston and London: Little, Brown and Company, 2012.

Mason, Francis K. *Battle Over Britain.* Bourne End, Buckinghamshire, UK: Aston Publications Ltd., 1990.

———. *The British Bomber Since 1914.* Annapolis, MD: Naval Institute Press, 1994.

Mayer, Arno J. *The Persistence of the Old Regime.* New York: Pantheon Books, 1981.

Meilinger, Phillip S. "Trenchard, Slessor, and Royal Air Force Doctrine before World War II." In *The Paths of Heaven: The Evolution of Airpower Theory*, edited by Phillip S. Meilinger. Maxwell AFB AL: Air University Press, 1997.

Middlemas, Keith, and John Barnes. *Baldwin: A Biography.* London: The Macmillan Company, 1970.

Morrow, John H. Jr., *The Great War in the Air.* Washington, DC: Smithsonian Institution Press, 1993.

Murray, Williamson. *The Change in the European Balance of Power, 1938–1939: The Path to Ruin.* Princeton, NJ: Princeton University Press, 1984.

———. *Strategy for Defeat: The Luftwaffe 1933–1945.* Maxwell AFB, AL: Air University Press, 1983.

Murray, Williamson, and Allan R. Millett, eds. *Calculations: Net Assessment and the Coming of World War II.* New York: The Free Press, 1992.

Nicolson, Harold. *Diaries and Letters, 1930–1939.* Edited by Nigel Nicolson. New York: Atheneum, 1966.

———. *Diaries and Letters, 1939–1945.* Edited by Nigel Nicolson. New York: Atheneum, 1967.

Norris, Geoffrey. *The Royal Flying Corps: A History.* London: Frederick Muller, Ltd., 1965.

Omissi, David E. *Air Power and Colonial Control.* Manchester: Manchester University Press, 1990.

Orange, Vincent. *Churchill and His Airmen.* London: Grub Street, 2013.

———. *Coningham: A Biography of Air Marshal Sir Arthur Coningham.* Washington, DC: Center for Air Force History, 1992.

———. *Dowding of Fighter Command: Victor of the Battle of Britain.* London: Grub Street, 2008.

———. *Park: The Biography of Air Chief Marshal Sir Keith Park.* London: Grub Street, 2001.

———. *Slessor: Bomber Champion.* London: Grub Street, 2006.

———. *Tedder: Quietly in Command.* London: Frank Cass, 2004.

Overy, Richard. *The Battle of Britain: The Myth and the Reality*. New York and London: W. W. Norton, 2009.

Parker, R. A. C. *Chamberlain and Appeasement*. New York: St. Martin's Press, 1993.

Peden, G. C. *Arms, Economics, and British Strategy*. Cambridge: Cambridge University Press, 2007.

———. *British Rearmament and the Treasury*. Edinburgh: Scottish Academic Press, 1979.

Penrose, Harald *British Aviation: Ominous Skies, 1935–1939*. London: Her Majesty's Stationery Office, 1980.

Petter, Martin. Review of *Liberal Crusader: The Life of Sir Archibald Sinclair* by Gerard J. De Groot, in *Albion* 26, no. 2 (Summer 1994): 392–94.

Pile, Frederick. *Ack-Ack: Britain's Defence against Air Attack during the Second World War*. London: George G. Harrap & Co., 1949.

Post, Gaines, Jr. *Dilemmas of Appeasement: British Deterrence and Defense*. Ithaca, NY: Cornell University Press, 1993.

Price, Alfred. *Britain's Air Defences, 1939–1945*. Oxford: Osprey, 2004.

Prior, Robin. *When Britain Saved the West*. New Haven, CT: Yale University Press, 2015.

Probert, Henry. *High Commanders of the Royal Air Force*. London: Her Majesty's Stationery Office, 1954.

Probert, Henry, and Sebastian Cox, eds. *The Battle Re-Thought: A Symposium on the Battle of Britain*. Shrewsbury, UK: Airlife Publishing Ltd., 1991.

Reader, W. J. *Architect of Air Power: The Life of the first Viscount Weir of Eastwood, 1877–1959*. London: Collins, 1968.

Research Institute for Military History, Freiburg. *Germany and the Second World War*. Oxford and New York: Clarendon Press, 1990.

Reynolds, David. *In Command of History*. New York: Random House, 2005.

Richards, Denis. *Portal of Hungerford*. London: William Heinemann, Ltd., 1977.

———. *The Fight at Odds*. Vol. 1, *The Royal Air Force 1939–1945*. London: Her Majesty's Stationery Office, 1953.

Ritchie, Sebastian. *Industry and Air Power*. London: Frank Cass, 1997.

———. "A Political Intrigue against the Chief of Air Staff." *War & Society* 16, no. 1 (May 1998): 83–104.

———. *The RAF, Small Wars and Insurgencies in the Middle East, 1919–1939*. RAF Leadership Centre, 2011.

Robbins, Simon. *British Generalship on the Western Front, 1914–18*. New York: Frank Cass, 2005.

Robertson, Scot. *The Development of RAF Strategic Bombing Doctrine, 1919–1939*. Westport, CT: Praeger, 1995.

Roberts, Andrew. *Eminent Churchillians*. New York: Simon & Schuster, 1994.

Robinson, Derek. *Invasion, 1940*. New York: Carroll & Graf Publishers, 2005.

Royal Air Force. *AP 3003: A Brief History of the Royal Air Force*. London: Crown Copyright, 2004.

Schein, Edgar. *Organizational Culture and Leadership*. Fourth Edition . San Francisco, CA: Jossey-Bass, 2010.

Self, Robert. *Neville Chamberlain*. Aldershot, Hampshire, UK: Ashgate Publishing Ltd., 2006.

Simpson, Emile. *War from the Ground Up*. Oxford: Oxford University Press, 2012.

Simpson, Geoff. *History of the Battle of Britain Fighter Association*. Barnsley, South Yorkshire, UK: Pen & Sword Aviation, 2015. Available online at https://books.google.com/books.

Sinnott, Colin. *The RAF and Aircraft Design, 1923–39*. London: Frank Cass, 2001.

Slessor, John Cotesworth. *The Central Blue*. London: Cassell & Co., 1956.

Spaight, James Molony. *The Battle of Britain 1940*. London: Geoffrey Bles, 1941.

Strachan, Hew. *Politics of the British Army*.

Stone, Jay, and Erwin A. Schmidl. *The Boer War and Military Reforms*. New York: University Press of America, 1988.

Terraine, John. *The Right of the Line: The Royal Air Force in the European War 1939–1945*. Ware, Hertfordshire, UK: Wordsworth Editions Ltd., 1997.

Travers, Tim. *The Killing Ground: The British Army, the Western Front and the Emergence of Modern Warfare, 1900–1918*. London: Allen & Unwin, 1978.

Turner, John Frayn. *Douglas Bader*. Shrewsbury, UK: Airlife Publishing Ltd., 1995.

Vansittart, Lord [Robert Vansittart]. *Bones of Contention*. London: Hutchinson & Co., 1945.

Wark, Wesley K. *The Ultimate Enemy*. Ithaca, NY, and London: Cornell University Press, 1985.

Webster, Sir Charles, and Noble Frankland. *The Strategic Air Offensive against Germany, 1939–1945*. Vol. 1, *Preparation*. In *History of the Second World War*, United Kingdom Military Series. Edited by Sir James Butler. London: Her Majesty's Stationery Office, 1961.

Weinberg, Gerhard. *Germany, Hitler and World War II*. Cambridge: Cambridge University Press, 1995.

———. *Hitler's Foreign Policy 1933–1939*. New York: Enigma Books, 2005.

White, Ian. *The History of Air Intercept (AI) Radar and the British Night-Fighter 1935–1959*. Barnsley, South Yorkshire, UK: Pen & Sword Aviation, 2007.

Winter, J. M. "Spiritualism and the First World War." In *Religion and Irreligion in Victorian Society*, edited by R. W. Davis and R. J. Helmstadter. London and New York: Routledge, 1992.

Winton, Harold R. *To Change an Army: General Sir John Burnett-Stuart and British Armored Doctrine, 1927–1938*. Lawrence: University Press of Kansas, 1988.

Wood, Derek, with Derek Dempster. *The Narrow Margin: The Battle of Britain and the Rise of Air Power*. Washington, DC: Smithsonian Institution Press, 1990.

Wright, Robert. *The Man Who Won the Battle of Britain*. New York: Charles Scribner's Sons, 1969.

Wykeham, Peter. *Fighter Command*. London: Putnam, 1960.

Zamoyski, Adam. *The Forgotten Few: The Polish Air Force in the Second World War*. London: John Murray, 1995.

Zimmerman, David. *Britain's Shield: Radar and the Defeat of the Luftwaffe*. Stroud, Gloucestershire, UK: Sutton Publishing, Ltd., 2001.

INDEX